BASEBALL'S POWER SHIFT

BASEBALL'S POWER SHIFT

How the Players Union,
the Fans, and the Media Changed
American Sports Culture

KRISTER SWANSON

UNIVERSITY OF NEBRASKA PRESS
LINCOLN & LONDON

Library of Congress Cataloging-in-Publication Data

Names: Swanson, Krister, author.
Title: Baseball's power shift: how the players union, the fans,
and the media changed American sports culture / Krister Swanson.
Description: Lincoln: University of Nebraska Press, 2016.
Includes bibliographical references and index.
Identifiers: LCCN 2015034504
ISBN 9780803255234 (hardback: alk. paper)
ISBN 9780803288041 (epub)
ISBN 9780803288058 (mobi)
ISBN 9780803288065 (pdf)
Subjects: LCSH: Baseball players—Labor unions—United States—History. | Major League Baseball
Players Association—History. | Collective bargaining—Baseball—United States. | Baseball—
Economic aspects—United States. | Baseball—United States—History. | Baseball—Social
aspects—United States. | Mass media and sports—United States. | BISAC: SPORTS & RECREATION /
Baseball / History. | SPORTS & RECREATION / Business Aspects. | BUSINESS & ECONOMICS / Labor.
Classification: LCC GV880.2 .S83 2016 | DDC 796.357/640973—dc23
LC record available at http://lccn.loc.gov/2015034504

Set in Scala OT by M. Scheer.

CONTENTS

ACKNOWLEDGMENTS

It is simple, a total cliché, and absolutely true: this book was only possible because of the love and support of my family. My wife, Stacy, and sons, Dane, Erik, and Nate, made it possible for a full-time teacher and parent to be a full-time grad student as well. It is impossible to overstate how much they have meant to me throughout this process.

My mother, Jan Bowman, blazed the trail up to UC Santa Barbara, and my father, Gerry Swanson, helped her do it. Nobody was more excited about the publication of this book than my dad. My grandfather, Leroy Swanson, was the ultimate traditionalist fan. He took me to my first Major League game and nurtured my love for baseball throughout my childhood. Thanks also to my grandmother, Lois Swanson, who had all the best traits of both Marvin Miller and Branch Rickey.

I have tremendous gratitude as well for the support and help from my friends, colleagues, and the staff at the University of Nebraska Press. First and foremost in this group are Nelson Lichtenstein and Laura Kalman, who provided continued support, advice, and guidance throughout the course of this project. Many good friends in the teaching profession also played significant roles. Mark Kilmer and Brian Friefeld sounded out a wide variety of ideas, good and otherwise. My team-teaching partner, Tasha Beaudoin, was always a valuable sounding board, and Ron Kragthorpe, Heather Feigenbaum and Debbie Leibold provided a great deal of help in editing early versions of this project. Finally, I am deeply grateful for all of the invaluable help and support I received from the good people of the University of Nebraska Press, who embraced the spirit and purpose of this book and shepherded me through the publication process.

INTRODUCTION

While professional baseball remains very popular in the United States today, it is easy to forget that the game held an even more prominent place in our nation's everyday life from the late 1800s through the 1980s. It was truly our national pastime, and Americans from every ethnic background and walk of life shared a passion for the game. With its deep Yankee origins and traditions, the game introduced millions of new citizens to what it meant to be a true American. Baseball helped reinforce a shared sense of community in rapidly growing cities bursting at the seams with immigrants from all over Europe. It rode the wave of new media forms to even greater popularity, with radio stations like KMOX in St. Louis turning an entire region of the nation into Cardinals fans and publications like the *Sporting News* prospering almost exclusively on the public demand for the latest information about the game and the heroic men who played it.

Baseball's prominent place in American culture has led many historians to focus their work on the ways in which societal shifts brought about significant changes in the game. Over the course of the twentieth century, baseball's history was interwoven with major developments in race relations, life on the home front during World War II, and postwar expansion into the Sunbelt. These are all worthy topics, and many exceptional books explore them to the fullest. I share these historians' intellectual interest in the relationship between baseball and society, but instead of focusing on one particular historical moment or theme, I chose to look at a give-and-take relationship between the game and our society. I wanted to write not just about the ways in which society brought about change in the game but also the ways in which baseball, and specifically its players' union, reshaped American society and culture. The growth of the union movement provides an ideal opportunity for this type of study. The players' unionization efforts required public support in order for them to succeed. This forced the players, and their union leaders, to heed the shifting demands of public opinion in order to maintain this support. Over time the players' union members not only responded to public opinion, they actively worked to shape opinion in order to win the backing of the baseball public. As a result, the players' attempts to unionize had a major impact on the values and ideals of American sports fans, and ultimately on the entirety of American sports culture.

This story goes back nearly to the birth of the game. Baseball's beginnings date to the 1850s, and in short order it became a popular pastime among soldiers during the Civil War. Within a decade of the war's completion, there were professional baseball leagues throughout the northeastern United States. The highest level of competition, known as "Major League Baseball," was well established by the early 1880s. These early ballplayers enjoyed the same basic relationship with the capital class as workers of every stripe did during the Gilded Age. Team owners sought to exercise the same control over their players as factory owners enjoyed over their workers. The owners, often referred to as magnates, structured the standard player contract to limit the players' freedom of contract, bargaining power, and control over working conditions. Ballplayers, just like workers in other industries, sought to unionize in order to improve their conditions and found themselves dealing with the same frustrations as other nascent unions of the time.

Given the highly skilled nature of their work, it seemed the players might have better chances for success than the average coal miner or steelworker. That was not the case. For more than seventy years, player attempts at unionization failed. Several factors contributed to this ongoing failure. Until the 1930s, much of American society generally looked down upon unions, including the ownership class and many of the middle-class patrons that owners coveted. During the Great Depression, unions finally began to make headway. Through the advances of the Wagner Act and the formation of the AFL-CIO, many industries found themselves unionized by the start of World War II. Unions later helped bring many families into the middle class on the strength of the postwar industrial boom, but baseball players were unable to ride this wave of growth. The players consistently struggled to build public support for their attempts to unionize. Because baseball's customers, the fans, pay directly for the opportunity to watch the "workers" work, the game requires a much higher level of affinity between worker and customer than is usually the case. Consumers typically do not give a second thought to the auto or textile worker as long as the product he or she produces is of sufficient quality. Baseball players, on the other hand, badly need the support of their consumers—the fans and the media—in order to be successful.

There were other major obstacles beyond the need for public support. As with other industries that originated in an era friendly to pools and trusts, baseball owners used a variety of collusive tactics to keep a stranglehold on the supply of highly skilled baseball labor. As early as the 1880s, a portion of the standard player contract known as the reserve clause bound every player in the National League to his team. This clause gave the team exclusive rights to the player's services for the following season, rights that could be exercised solely at the team management's discretion. Even though player contracts were always written for one year, teams essentially owned a player for the length of his useful playing career because the reserve clause left the productive player with no other option than to re-sign with his existing team. Once a player's value diminished, his team could sell or trade him to another club, or simply release him.

In addition to the restrictions of the reserve clause, team owners had no qualms about openly blacklisting any player who protested the terms of his contract or tried to negotiate better terms with another club. Unfortunate timing heaped further misfortune on the players, because just as the Progressives started to usher in controls over monopolies and trusts in the rest of the economy, the business of baseball actually moved in the opposite direction. In 1922 the Supreme Court's ruling in *Federal Baseball Club v. National League* gave Major League Baseball a federal antitrust exemption, leaving most players all but powerless in their attempts to deal with a labor market designed solely for the benefit of club management.

A final barrier to unionization efforts was the game's place as a revered public institution, a status baseball magnates reinforced at every opportunity. The American League founder Ban Johnson was especially adept at making professional baseball appear to be something very different from a traditional large business enterprise. Johnson built and marketed his league around practices such as banning gambling and drinking at games, policies intended to foster a wholesome image and build public trust. This approach paid off quickly, as the American League arose to national prominence in short order and joined the National League as a true Major League in 1901. If the owners were the guardians of this public trust, then, who were the players to challenge the magnates' business practices, or their judgment in general? The baseball public of this time largely viewed players as men who should feel fortunate to be such an integral part of the national pastime, and any critique offered by players was seen as ungrateful selfishness.

Owner paternalism helped make this public view an even greater obstacle for the players. The magnates openly referred to the players as "their boys" and expertly cultivated player dependency. Owners catered to the more popular "superstar" players, such as Ty Cobb and Babe Ruth, who would bring fans to the park, and then used these star players as examples of the wonderful treatment afforded to all players. In exchange, the star players responded by criticizing their peers for any interest in collective action. In order to have any chance for success in forming a union, the players needed to help fans understand some of the fundamental flaws in the structure of their sacred institution; they also had to develop the solidarity necessary to overcome the divisiveness created by owner paternalism.

Developing player solidarity was no small feat. Fans and the media usually bought the notion that the owners were the noble guardians of this revered institution lock, stock, and barrel. Even as early as the 1920s, baseball fans were very traditional in their view of the game. These "traditionalists" subscribed enthusiastically to the widely held public view that the game remained pure and unchanged, even though owners constantly tinkered with the rules of the game in order to attract more fans and reduce escalating labor costs. The public ignored these changes, as it wanted to see the game as a timeless treasure. Different generations of fans used a variety of statistical measures to debate the merits of star players from various eras, even though rule changes made these numbers much less relevant and valuable than they first seemed. Fathers passed their love for the game down to their sons, and families developed deep affinities for their local teams and the ball-playing heroes who took the field on their behalf. Fans truly loved their star players and expected them to demonstrate appropriate gratitude and humility in exchange for the opportunity to make a living by playing a "boys' game," as well as the honor of representing the great tradition of the Cincinnati Reds, or New York Giants, or Chicago Cubs who preceded them. Fans counted on players, and especially their beloved stars, to relish the opportunity of having a long and prolific career in one city, which would, in turn, allow the fans an even greater chance to get to know and love their heroes. Given this view of the game, most fans had a difficult time recognizing that, ultimately, the average ballplayer was a workingman, just like them. In the public mind, a professional ballplayer could not possibly have legitimate grievances about his working conditions or the terms of his contract. This perspective became a significant obstacle to public support for unionization, especially when the drive for unionization challenged the practices, such as the reserve clause, that kept the players with one team and allowed fans to develop cherished, long-term relationships with "their boys."

I was born in the 1960s and learned the game from my grandfather, father, uncles, and older cousins, all dyed-in-the-wool traditionalists. My relatives held fairly progressive views on the social questions of their day, especially those tied to the civil rights movement, but to them baseball was a separate issue entirely and certainly not in need of any significant changes beyond the elimination of the color barrier. I came of age during the tumult created by the ongoing struggle between the players' first successful union, the Major League Baseball Players Association (MLBPA), and baseball's magnates. I loved the game and hated the strikes and lockouts that were a regular part of these protracted disputes. In the view of traditionalists like my relatives, there was no question which side was at fault. In their minds, ballplayers needed to embrace their good fortune and avoid the collective radicalism that tore at the fabric of so many of our social institutions in the 1960s and early 1970s. My mentors were especially fearful of free agency because it would surely disrupt the sacred continuity of team rosters and set a horrible example in terms of player greed.

In an effort to navigate its way around the traditionalist point of view, the MLBPA's early demands focused on the kind of "bread-and-butter" demands that resonated with fans of all types. It was a relatively easy first step for the players to convince traditionalist fans and sportswriters that ballplayers needed to secure a modest pension, similar to those of industrial workers across the nation in the postwar era. In a way, the pension became a bridge issue, as it garnered public support for the union without asking traditionalists to accept major changes in the structure of the game, like the elimination of the reserve clause. Once the pension was in place, players could move on to convince the baseball public to embrace complex freedom-of-contract issues whose resolution would reshape the entire game. This new stage presented an entirely different set of challenges. In order to win the public support they so badly required, the players and their union had to convince the game's tradition-bound public to rethink many of their core beliefs regarding the nature of the game. Players needed fans to see them as highly skilled workers who deserved both freedom of contract and a larger share of the ever-increasing revenue streams generated by their on-field work.

These became the critical questions the players faced as their union pushed beyond the pension and on to addressing the freedom-of-contract issues that had plagued baseball players since the 1880s: How could players help fans realize the need for and benefits of free agency, a practice that would allow players to sign multiyear contracts with the team willing to pay the most for their services? How could a union, the type of organization usually associated with set pay scales limiting high-end compensation, win these rights for its members, especially at a time when the union movement was beginning a sharp decline? The players needed to appeal to their public's sense of freedom, liberty, and capitalist impulses, all without threatening the romantic traditions of the game and the business of baseball. Ultimately the players accomplished their goals, and even though the National Football League has surpassed Major League Baseball in national popularity, baseball remains an important national pastime and institution, and a very profitable one at that. In the decades since the baseball labor revolution of the 1960s and 1970s, the Major Leagues have continued to expand, adding six new teams since 1977. Teams and taxpayers alike sponsored a stadium construction boom the likes of which no reasonable sports observer might have predicted in 1970, demonstrating a willingness to sink billions of dollars into a business that still helps us define community, more than 140 years after the Red Stockings began to do just that for the people of Cincinnati.

There has been a dramatic shift in our sports culture in the years since the MLBPA and baseball management resolved the free agency issue. Baseball fans led the way in adopting a new outlook on professional sports, one much more attuned to the business aspect of the game. Fans still appreciate loyalty and continuity in the teams they love, but they also have a growing appreciation for the significance of shrewd business and player personnel moves by team management. Information technology, first in the form of cable television and then the Internet, further fueled this shift by providing almost endless amounts of statistical information and commentary. With their new points of view firmly in place, fans are interested in much more than on-field play and maintaining team tradition; many have moved on to interacting with the game in a manner similar to that of a team's general manager. This trend is most evident in the way that fans embraced the rotisserie leagues that burst onto the scene in the early 1980s, right in the midst of the MLBPA's struggle to finalize the benefits of free agency. Today rotisserie leagues have morphed into the multibillion-dollar industry of fantasy sports. Today's younger fans, understandably, know little about a time when roster continuity and team tradition meant a great deal more than the strategic player personnel moves plotted by team management. These fans are completely a product of a new era, in which being a sports fan means not only following the game but debating the relative value of players in the lucrative free market of professional sports labor.

Finally, I would like to offer a few introductory words on sources. With the relationship between players and fans right at the center of this study, I put a premium on access to the right kinds of documentary sources. I started with the players' side of things and dove into the archives at the Giamatti Research Center at the Baseball Hall of Fame, which are the best collections of archived materials for all things baseball. MLBPA director Marvin Miller's papers in the Wagner Labor Archives at New York University were extraordinarily helpful in better understanding MLBPA strategy and its efforts to build public support. In an effort to understand the public dialogue around the players and their unions, I read thousands of articles, opinion pieces, and fan letters to editors from a variety of periodicals dedicated to the coverage of the game. I was helped in this by the fact that baseball is and was a newspaperman's dream. It generated compelling daily news items throughout the course of the season, as well as a fair amount of off-the-field action during the off-season. Many distinguished writers, men such as Red Smith, Shirley Povich, and Jim Murray, dedicated a good part of their careers to the coverage of baseball. These writers contributed to an expansive, well-considered discourse that helps us better understand evolving public sentiment regarding the players and their efforts to improve their lot through unionization. The ongoing conversation between these baseball writers and their readers provided valuable insight into the shifting nature of public sentiment and ultimately into the cultural shift that accompanied the start of free agency and the birth of a new era in professional sports.

Together these sources provided the necessary material to properly examine both sides of a relationship that forever changed our sports culture. Just as unions formed a collective workforce, they transformed a collective fan base. It is no longer enough to just root for your team, you must also follow the statistical achievements of the individual players on your fantasy team. Owners and players now compete independently for our interest and money on everything from merchandise-licensing agreements to luxury stadium seating to product placement during the annual Home Run Derby. As a result of the now-open nature of sports as a business, fans are far less patient with owners and players alike. While traditionalists would wait patiently through a two- or three-year rebuilding process in the hope of watching tomorrow's stars develop before their eyes, some modern-day fans can tolerate little more than one month of subpar performance before they call for drastic personnel moves. They are also far less patient with their aging, fallen heroes. A beloved perennial All-Star can quickly be seen as nothing more than a huge financial burden during the twilight of his career, and the fans who once adored him call stridently to get his guaranteed contract off the books. For better or worse, this is the sports culture we celebrate today, and this book is the story of how Major League Baseball players helped us get here.

BASEBALL'S POWER SHIFT

1

The Magnates, "Their Boys," and the Birth of a Pastime

Since its inception in the years after the Civil War, professional baseball has enjoyed a prominent position in the national consciousness. During the mid-nineteenth century, a rapidly growing nation developed a deep passion for the game. Many Americans, especially Yankee traditionalists and others of old immigrant stock, saw baseball as something uniquely American. Despite baseball's similarities to the British games of cricket and rounders, they believed baseball was born of the American spirit, a notion reinforced by the growth of the game's popularity with the Union army during the Civil War.

One aspect of the game that these traditionalists found particularly appealing was its emphasis on individual performance. Every play in baseball begins with individual confrontation, as pitcher and batter face one another in a contest of skill, strategy, and determination. Over the course of a game these confrontations add up to determine the success or failure of the greater team. The individual successes and failures of baseball players are much more apparent to the casual observer than they are in other popular team sports. No other major professional sport offers as many statistical measures for individual accomplishment as baseball. Over time, statistics such as batting average, runs batted in, earned run average, and the like have become the key determinants of a player's individual value.

This compartmentalization of individual contributions makes baseball players much more interchangeable than those in other team sports. If a professional basketball or football player leaves his team, he requires at least a few weeks of practice to get acclimated to the new team's system and become a valuable member of that team. In baseball the transition time is much shorter. Over the course of their careers, professional baseball players receive thousands of hours of standardized training for almost every possible game situation. As a result, each player knows exactly what is expected of him in any given situation. These standardized expectations allow a player to move relatively smoothly from one team to another and immediately become a contributing member of his new team.

This emphasis on individual contribution and interchangeability makes baseball players very liquid assets. They can be sold and traded between teams easily, a practice the owners of professional baseball clubs have eagerly participated in since the 1860s. The owners of professional baseball clubs always enjoyed this aspect of the game, exchanging players to improve areas of weakness, gain a quick infusion of cash, or cut salary costs at the end of a financially disappointing season. While these magnates enjoyed the freedom to buy, sell, and trade players, they were often frustrated by the players' willingness to use their interchangeability to their own advantage. Just as owners moved players, players often sought to change teams in search of the best possible contract. In order to maximize the financial value of their relatively short career, players were always ready to move on to a club willing to pay more for their services. The owners, citing the difficulties of running a team continually disrupted by unanticipated personnel changes, responded by seeking greater control over player movement. This conflict of interests over the players' freedom of contract set the stage for a baseball labor-management clash that lasted more than a century.

Baseball's public, its ardent fans and the members of the booming sports media of the late nineteenth century, were major players in this debate right from the start. Both owners and players understood the need to foster public support and nurture the relationship between baseball and its public. Toward that end, team management knew that roster continuity, especially their ability to hold on to key players, was critically important to building and maintaining fan interest. The magnates cultivated the notion that "their boys," as they often referred to the players, joyfully served the public interest as sporting representatives of their fine city. The owners enjoyed portraying themselves as the guardians of a game well on its way to becoming a national institution, in a clear effort to win public approval, increase interest, and boost the ticket sales that were their primary source of revenue.

The Players

The popularity of the professional game boomed in the years following the Civil War. By 1868 there were more than two hundred thousand paid admissions to professional baseball games in the northeastern United States alone, let alone fans that paid to see successful clubs in places like Chicago, St. Louis, and Cincinnati.[1]

As the professional game grew in popularity and stature it consistently drew the best players, regardless of class or background, to its player ranks. Largely, though, these men came from artisan, or working-class, backgrounds. Joining these players were a fair number of "college men." They generally had shorter careers than their working-class counterparts. College men were less willing to stay in the game by playing for a team outside of their hometown and were quicker to leave the game in order to take advantage of the wider variety of economic opportunities available to them. Working-class players' relative lack of opportunities outside of baseball kept many of them in the game for longer periods than their upper- and middle-class counterparts. In most cases, baseball was more lucrative than their other options for earning a living. These men were more than willing to do what it took, including playing wherever they were still wanted, to extend their playing careers to the fullest.[2]

The players' ethnic backgrounds contributed to the notion that baseball was, indeed, the most "American" of games. The vast majority of early baseball players were native-born Americans, not first-generation immigrants. This remained true throughout the first four decades of the game's history. Club owners intentionally maintained this type of ethnic makeup of their teams to reinforce the American character of the game for the steadily growing baseball public. The magnates did so with the full support of their players, who knew, just like workers in so many other industries, that welcoming players from all ethnic backgrounds would mean expanding the pool of potential workers. Players wanted to keep the labor pool small, because it limited competition for jobs and helped keep salaries up. Exclusivity, then, whether defined by playing skill, ethnicity, or socioeconomic background, played a major role in shaping baseball's early labor movement.

The Owners

Baseball owners in the 1870s were little different from the "business statesmen," or robber barons, in other booming industries of the Gilded Age. Like their peers, baseball magnates sought to limit the vagaries of the marketplace, especially as it related to control over their labor force. They were especially concerned with limiting player salaries, which were subject to wild inflation as clubs rushed to outbid each other for the services of talented "jumpers," or players who moved from club to club in search of higher pay. Signing a well-known, talented jumper could boost ticket sales dramatically the instant he joined your club and win you great favor in the court of public opinion. The magnates, in a sense, needed protection from their own impulses, as it was their own greed and competitive spirit that led to such bidding wars. They knew that the single most effective way to manage salaries was to limit the players' freedom of contract and restrict player movement.

In addition to their concerns regarding controlling labor costs and player movement, the owners had significant anxiety about the negative impact of gambling on the sport. Baseball provided a wide variety of things to wager on, from the outcome of the game, to the number of strikeouts a pitcher might record, to the outcome of a single at bat. Professional gamblers knew that a well-placed bribe was all that was needed to induce a key player, or two, to botch a critical play and change the outcome of a game. This practice, known as "hippodroming," was the scourge of magnates everywhere, especially those who sought to draw families of fans in search of an "honest entertainment." Ultimately, magnates believed they could make the game more attractive to a "more respectable" class of fan by freeing it from both the clutch of gamblers and immoral player behavior, such as excessive drinking and womanizing. Toward that end, men such as William Hulbert, a member of the Chicago Board of Trade, saw great potential for profit in baseball as long as they could exact the needed controls over player salaries, gambling, and questionable player behavior. Hulbert led a select group of magnates in the formation of the National League of Professional Baseball Clubs. The primary goal of Hulbert's organization was to wrest control of the game from the players and place it firmly in the hands of the team owners. The National League magnates quickly put up a strong, moral front. They portrayed themselves as the civic-minded men who brought baseball to the American people, even though they often suffered tremendous financial setbacks in the process. In reality, Hulbert and his fellow National League owners held a view of competition similar to that of railroad and steel magnates of the Gilded Age. These men crowed publicly about the merits of open, fair competition and then did what they could behind closed doors to establish monopolistic control over the professional game.

Each National League club enjoyed a monopoly on Major League professional baseball in its city. The league office served as a clearinghouse for recording player contracts, making it virtually impossible for a player who was already under contract to one club to "jump" to another club. Players who tried to jump risked being placed on the official league blacklist, which meant permanent expulsion from the game. In addition, any club that signed a blacklisted player was subject to banishment from the league. The clubs selected a five-member board to oversee the blacklist and run the league. True to the spirit of the age, the magnates believed this oligarchic system to be the most fair and efficient structure for operating the national game.[3]

The organization might have seemed democratic to the magnates, but it was extremely feudal in the way it defined the relationship between owner and player. The reality of the new National League was that players had little or no say in either their personal fate or the larger operation of the game. The owners believed their system included numerous practices designed to protect player interests. The best way to accomplish this was to protect the players from their less-than-virtuous selves, since in the owners' view most players were overgrown boys easily tempted by greed and vice. As a result, owner paternalism grew deep roots in the game, remaining prevalent well into the late twentieth century. The National League moved swiftly to build public trust. It dealt sternly with gamblers, quickly expelling all suspected "hippodromers" and any others who openly consorted with bettors and bookmakers. Additionally, in 1879 the National League banned the sale of liquor at games and the playing of any games on Sunday.

The mind-set of these National League owners is clearly illustrated in the story of Albert Goodwill Spalding, a star player of the era who went on to become a leading magnate. Spalding played a critical role in the National League's beginnings. Immediately after plans for the new league were announced, Spalding and four other key stars "jumped" to the Chicago White Stockings. This move helped assure Chicago's preeminence in the new league and accelerated the decline of the player-controlled National Association. Spalding used his public popularity to found a successful sporting goods empire and became one of the first of many players-turned-magnates when he took control of the White Stockings in the mid-1880s. Spalding relished his role as one of the game's formative figures. "The game [in 1876]," he held, "had sunk so low in the estimation of the general public that it was with the greatest effort that the public could be made to believe that the efforts of the League were honest. The first two years resulted in a financial loss to nearly every club connected with the League."[4] Spalding, writing in 1890, emphasized themes such as integrity and the willingness to withstand financial sacrifice for the good of the game, an approach that other owners followed over the next century as they promoted their contributions to the national pastime's health and prosperity.

The magnates, then, were very much men of their times. Socially and politically they saw themselves as among the national elite. They spoke openly of economic competition while seeking to limit it in a way that would best leverage their position in the burgeoning entertainment economy of the day. Morally, they believed it was their duty to save this uniquely American pastime from the evils lurking around every corner. They desired to keep baseball "American" in the face of corrupting influences such as gambling, liquor, and an unstable workforce. Their ability to guide the game through this tumultuous period fueled their claim that they were the men who "saved the game for the people," a claim they continued to put forward well into the twentieth century.

The Reserve Clause

The players almost immediately resented the magnates' success in creating a monopoly over the game by "protecting it from the players." This situation was not unique to baseball. Business owners all over the United States sought minimal competition and maximum control of their industry and workforce. By 1879 the National League magnates' primary concern was gaining a tighter grip on player salaries. National League owners found it maddening that some players made as much as twelve dollars a game, when the same men would be lucky to make ten dollars a week in the world of industry. Management viewed players in the same light as common laborers, not as an elite group with a rare and valuable skill set. The magnates knew that if they limited players' freedom of movement, open bidding would cease and salaries would be greatly reduced.

The magnates' solution to this problem, developed in a secret meeting during the fall of 1879, came to be known as the reserve clause. This section of the uniform player's contract provided the primary battleground for owners and players for the century to come: "It is further understood and agreed upon that the party of the first part (the club) shall have the right to 'reserve' the said party of the second part (the player) for the season next."[5] This policy, in effect, bound each player to the National League club he initially signed with for the entire length of his Major League career.

The reserve clause originated with the idea that each club could reserve five active players from its current roster for the following season. Other clubs could not sign a player once his existing club had reserved him. The number of reserved players quickly grew from five men per club to eleven, and eventually to fourteen by the 1887 season. In those days clubs rarely carried more than fourteen or fifteen players. Thanks to this reserve system, each club held exclusive contract rights over all of its players for as long as it liked. Inactive players, regardless of circumstance, could be reserved as well. This eliminated the possibility of a player choosing not to play during his "reserve season," in the hope of being freed from his contract and negotiating a better salary from another club. The clause placed each player in a one-bidder system when it came time to negotiate his salary for the upcoming season. The only factor that prevented a club from paying a player more than mere subsistence wages was the desire to keep the player relatively happy. The salary of a star player no longer had any connection to the free market, and player salaries dropped 10 percent with the clause's implementation.[6]

One factor that made the reserve system particularly effective was that by 1879 the National League had established itself as the premier circuit. Team owners had little or no fear of their players turning to a rival league for an equal or higher salary. When a rival league, the American Association, did emerge, the National League magnates persuaded their new competitors to enter into a National Agreement. Under the terms of this agreement, clubs from both leagues agreed to utilize and honor the reserve clause, primarily as a measure to prevent interleague "jumping." As the magnates further formalized the reserve rule and refined its practice, they came to enjoy what amounted to ownership of their labor force. This was precisely how they treated player contracts, as clubs actively bought, sold, and traded these contracts with other clubs.

From its inception, the magnates defended the reserve clause by arguing it was in the best interests of the game. To support this claim, they pointed to the tumultuous nature of the business of baseball in the decade immediately following the Civil War. This period was marked by one bankruptcy and scandal after another, as clubs sought out the best talent in an effort to boost ticket sales. This instability, the magnates argued, made the reserve clause necessary to "place the business of base-ball on a permanent basis and thus offers security to the investment of capital."[7] The clause also guaranteed reasonable player salaries that were, in the owners' view, also in the players' best interest because they protected jobs by reducing bankruptcies.

The owners believed the public should be grateful for the reserve system. They argued that the clause assured competitive balance by keeping the wealthiest clubs from signing and stockpiling all of the most talented players. The reserve system allowed teams to build unity and continuity, factors that improved play and made the teams more marketable in their communities as fans developed long-term relationships with their favorite players. The final reason magnates believed the clause would generate public support was that it assured fair play by guaranteeing fans that no player might intentionally play poorly in the hope of securing a larger contract the following season from an opposing team that benefited from his subpar efforts. These arguments were so successful that, whenever the reserve system came under fire, the magnates simply rolled out these same positions, time and again, throughout the following century. In time many influential individuals, from sportswriters to Supreme Court justices, accepted the idea that baseball was unique among sports, as well as the absolute necessity of the reserve clause for the preservation of the national game. In winning the early battle of public opinion on the reserve clause, the owners placed a monumental obstacle in the players' path as they sought to win greater freedom of contract and more equitable compensation for their services.

An 1884 trade war with the newly formed Union Association allowed the club owners to further tighten their control. When the Union Association collapsed, the surviving National League and American Association needed a way to deal with the reassignment of Union Association players, the terms of which were laid out in a new National Agreement.[8] The new agreement reflected the magnates' appetite for order and control. It established a maximum individual player salary of $2,000 per season. It prohibited players from jumping from one league to another, in effect blacklisting any player who attempted to use one league against the other in order to raise his market value. As harsh as they may seem, salary limits and blacklists were not the most significant aspects of the new agreement. The most severe component was the newly strengthened reserve clause, which gave each club the right to unilaterally renew the rights to the services of each of its players for the following season. As long as a team wanted to retain a particular player, the player had no choice in the matter; he was essentially bound to the team for the following season, and ultimately for the length of his usefulness as a Major League Baseball player.

This was the final addition to the original reserve clause, and it effectively gave each owner complete control over his labor pool. He could keep players under contract as long as they remained productive and then quickly sell, trade, or release them as soon as their playing skills diminished. Players were left with very little control over their working conditions, compensation, and career path. In order to change teams a player would have to be either traded or sold. Both situations benefited the clubs involved in the transaction, without providing any benefit to the individual players involved. A player might be bound to a team for several

THE BIRTH OF A PASTIME

seasons, then sold by a discontented owner when he decided the player's presence no longer helped boost gate receipts. To assure a final measure of owner control, the agreement sealed the fate of any player willing to sit out a year in order to void the reserve clause and then reenter the league as a "free agent" by banning this practice altogether.[9]

Baseball Unionism

In response to these measures of owner control, it is no surprise that baseball players began discussing the organization of a players' union in the late 1880s. They were not a group well suited for industrial-style unionism. Their relatively small numbers and highly specialized skill set made them better candidates for craft unionism, the type of organization best suited for workers sharing a unique set of skills or knowledge. Beyond the question of organizational structure, there were many barriers to successful unionism in baseball. By its very nature, the industry put players in constant competition with one another. Players on the same team constantly compete for playing time with one another. Playing time is a critical factor for each player as he tries to demonstrate his individual value and increase his compensation. Beyond this competition between individuals, teams compete against each other many times each season, building rivalry and division between various groups of players and making it more difficult for these fierce rivals to bond in the kind of brotherhood required by a craft guild. Unlike workers in industries with standardized wage scales, baseball players command a wide variety of salaries. Throughout the history of the game, it has not been uncommon for a star player to make as much as ten times, and sometimes as much as one hundred times, the salary of lesser-paid teammates. Such disparity in pay breeds jealousy and also makes it difficult to establish common cause. A star player had little incentive to risk his "golden goose" for the benefit of his poorly compensated teammate. Baseball magnates skillfully used these competitive divisions in the players' ranks to their own advantage. The owners quickly became expert in preventing players from uniting behind any kind of organization set on improving their collective lot.

Even more so than in other industries, the interest of fans and the media meant that baseball's labor-management battles played out openly in the court of public opinion. Both players and owners understood the importance of gaining the confidence and support of the baseball public; a group composed of both fans and the sports print media. Teams need the support of the media to build public interest and support for the local club, so that the fans, in turn, will buy tickets and come out to the games. Baseball magnates' need to promote a positive public image for their enterprise cannot be overstated. Players needed public support as well, both to increase the popularity and profitability of the game and because an unpopular player is much easier to replace than a popular one. With so many talented younger players coveting a spot on a Major League roster, players considering labor action needed to take a prudent approach or risk serious backlash from the baseball public.

Baseball is one of the very few industries that require the public popularity of their laborers, the players, in order to be profitable. Owners, especially those who strive to be seen as civic boosters, go to great lengths to connect the public with the men wearing the uniform of the local club. Baseball fans go to watch the game because it is intricate, involved, and exciting, but they are equally drawn by their need to support the people involved in the game, men often viewed by fans as the sporting heroes of their day, if not something just short of immortal. With a great deal of help from the sports media, the players become heroes, role models, nearly godlike figures in the eyes of their public. As with other forms of art, fans marvel at the players' ability to perform a task they've tried themselves, but at a skill level they cannot begin to comprehend. This puts baseball players in quite a different position than, say, a railroad worker involved in a labor dispute. The railroad worker is anonymous to the public and knows that he does not need average American consumers to admire him in order to keep them riding his train. Baseball players, from their

first attempts to form a union in the late 1880s, clearly understood the distinctively critical nature of fan and media support.
These men knew public backing was important, not just for the
success of their union but also for the success of their entire industry. The sporting press, in the midst of its own rapid growth in
the late nineteenth century, paid close attention to the struggle
mounting between the players and owners. The articles and columns they wrote about baseball's labor struggles both reflected
and helped shape public opinion on the key issues dividing players and management. Recognizing this, both players and owners
actively tried to sway the press, through interviews, letters, and
columns of their own making. No examination of baseball's
labor struggles is complete, therefore, without close attention
to the attitudes and workings of baseball's public.

As would be the case repeatedly in baseball, the initial labor
conflict came on the heels of the trade war, this one precipitated
by a Union Association assault on National League dominance in
the mid-1880s. This first labor clash between players and owners set the stage for player-management relations in professional
baseball for a century to come. The key issues under contention
included a player's right to sign with the team of his choosing
(later called free agency), guaranteed contracts, overall limits
on player salaries, and a pension plan to provide players greater
long-term financial security. These same issues remained at
the center of labor relations in Major League Baseball for most
of the next century.

A Brotherhood for Change

When the owners tightened and refined the reserve clause in
the late 1880s, they created a sense of powerlessness among
the players that drove them toward collective action. The players found their leader in John Montgomery Ward, a well-known
pitcher for the National League's Providence club and later a
star shortstop for the New York Giants. It was Ward and a few
other elite players who formed baseball's first union, the Brotherhood of Professional Baseball Players, in 1885. Ward was, in

many respects, the owners' definition of an ideal player. He was a well-educated Yankee, moderate in his habits, and a top-level performer on the field.

To the owners' dismay, Ward was more than happy to put his intellect and education to work for the Brotherhood's cause. He began his efforts to build public support with a series of editorials detailing the evils of the reserve clause. The shortstop pulled no punches, often comparing baseball's contractual restrictions with those that had allowed slavery and indentured servitude in earlier times.[10] Ward believed the magnates would further tighten their control unless the players organized some kind of resistance. "Encouraged by the apparent inactivity of the players," he wrote, "the clubs have gone on from one usurpation to another until, in the eye of the baseball 'magnate', the player has become a mere chattel."[11] Ward may have been the first baseball player to publicly compare his working conditions with those of slavery, but he would not be the last. Baseball players often used the image of slavery as a way of expressing frustration over being held and treated like the property of their clubs. Ward expressed specific concern over the owners' use of the reserve clause as a tool for illegally reducing the pay of underperforming players. An owner could easily reduce the pay of such a player by cutting him from the active roster for a few weeks, only to bring him back on the roster at a lower rate of pay. The player had no alternative. He may have been cut at the club's prerogative, but the club maintained the exclusive right to his playing services. This was a huge advantage, as the club owners knew they were the player's only hope for continuing to play professional baseball.

Ward's rhetoric resonated with his fellow players, and the ranks of the Brotherhood quickly swelled, much to the dismay of the National League club owners, who abhorred the idea of any kind of players' association or union. Their first response was an effort to ignore the union and wait it out in the hope that the Brotherhood might just fade away. The owners' hopes were dashed when Brotherhood members refused to sign contracts with any club for the 1888 season. These players said they would only sign when the "capitalists" officially recognized their organization's right to exist and agreed to meet with a delegation of Brotherhood officials.

For his part, Ward was not overly concerned with the possibility that management might refuse to negotiate with the Brotherhood. He was confident the players had other options at their disposal, should the magnates decide not to negotiate with Brotherhood members. Ward, in fact, believed the players' best option was to regain control over the industry by creating a league of their own: "There is plenty of money at our disposal to organize any association or league. We know of any amount of capitalists who want to invest their money in baseball. I will go further and say that we will be recognized as an organization, and we will all play next year whether the [National] League people like it or not."[12] Ward understood that the players' popularity played a large role in the success of the game. He sensed that the timing might be right for a new Major League, especially one built around the talent of the game's very best players. The business of Major League Baseball was in its relative infancy, and Ward believed public interest would follow the most talented players, regardless of the league in which they played.

The Brotherhood leader eagerly took his conflict with the National League owners into the court of public opinion. In September 1887 Ward and representatives of the Brotherhood pressed league administrators for a meeting to discuss the buying and selling of players, a relatively new practice at the time. The league flatly refused. When National League president Young decided not to respond to any of Ward's correspondence, Ward got an open letter to Young published in the *New York Times*. The Brotherhood leader asserted that magnates must meet with the Brotherhood, as "the Brotherhood is practically the players." Ward warned National League leaders not to take the Brotherhood lightly. He asked, "Is their opinion of their players such as to lead them to believe that a mere refusal to recognize their Brotherhood will choke it out of existence? If so, they make a most grievous mistake. . . . Since we cannot go forward with you we will be forced to go it alone."[13] Despite the obvious specialization and skill so important in baseball, Ward often described the players as members of the producing class. He utilized much of the same language as the Knights of Labor and other organizations seeking workplace democracy, in the face of the decidedly undemocratic conditions created by the reserve clause. Ward clearly saw these appeals to democracy as a critical step toward gaining greater public support for the players, should they need to set out on their own.

National League magnates continued to wait out the Brotherhood, while Ward and other Brotherhood leaders remained frustrated by the league's denial of recognition. One month later, the players sent an ultimatum to league president Young, demanding official recognition of the Brotherhood by November 15. After this date, the 125 members of the Brotherhood would "consider themselves absolved from all allegiance to the league."[14] The club presidents rejected the players' demands, accusing Ward of failing to act in good faith. Their charges were all part of the owners' attempts to counter Ward's populist appeals by branding him a labor maverick. Ward was, in the magnates' view, the kind of man determined to stir up unrest akin to the previous year's Haymarket Square uprising. While Ward hoped the baseball public might rally around workers' rights, the owners clearly felt that the responsible, sensible baseball public could be scared away from a group of labor radicals. Unsurprisingly, some magnates chose to summon the specter of labor radicalism in the face of player activism throughout the century to come. After all, they reasoned, if baseball was the most American of pursuits, how better to turn public support against the players than by painting them as un-American collectivists?

Despite their public posturing to the contrary, league officials recognized the Brotherhood two weeks later and agreed to meet with their representatives on November 17 in an attempt to ascertain the players' grievances. At this meeting Ward continued to cast the Brotherhood in terms similar to the Knights of Labor: "The objects [of the Brotherhood] are to protect a needy brother, visit a sick brother, bury a dead brother, promote harmony in our ranks, and do our utmost to promote the interests of the game."[15] Ward believed he was leading his brethren, a respectable group of old immigrant stock, on a quest for what the social, economic, and baseball labor historian Robert Burk calls "the restoration of each individual's economic rights and functional control over his work life and geographic mobility."[16] Essentially, Ward sought to increase player control over working conditions and specifically denied that the Brotherhood sought to "boom salaries, interfere with the reserve rule, or prevent the imposition of fines on players."[17] Ward wanted to avoid casting the Brotherhood's membership as greedy, set on destroying the league's competitive balance, or out for personal gain. He certainly sought ownership approval, but he also badly wanted the respect of the baseball public. The Brotherhood leader felt that these reasonable goals would resonate with middle- and working-class fans and also would steer clear of any demands that might reinforce the magnates' efforts to brand the Brotherhood as a radical labor organization.

The owners appeared satisfied with Ward's answers. They recognized the Brotherhood, and a short period of relative peace ensued. For a time, the reserve clause remained a storm cloud on the horizon. The cease-fire between players and magnates lasted only one season. With the Brotherhood's leadership on a barnstorming tour of Europe and safely out of touch with what was taking place stateside, A. G. Spalding and the owners unveiled their plans for a new salary classification system in 1888. This system set specific guidelines for separating players into five categories, based on productivity and years of service. Each category had its own maximum salary, the highest of which was $2,500. The magnates' classification plan also set an overall cap on total team spending. The plan amounted to a salary cap, or a fixed limit on the total amount of money a team could spend on player salaries.

This was a controversial move. One of Spalding's closest associates, former National League president Abraham G. Mills, sternly warned him against the adoption of such a plan. "A graded salary scheme is wrong in principle," Mills argued, "and when you come to superadd it to the reserve rule, which, in a technical view, is itself illegal, you are overloading the business end of the game.... I can't help but thinking that a manager that can't handle the salary question with a powerful reserve rule at his command ought to have a wetnurse!"[18] Spalding seemed determined to go ahead with his plan despite such warnings. This plan was precisely the kind of action the Brotherhood's leadership feared most. Ward and his peers were all veterans, the kind of star players who would be hurt most by a limit on maximum compensation. The prospect of the classification plan's salary limits, in combination with a reserve clause locking players into one team for life, pushed the players into action.

The Players League

Faced with this unexpected crisis, the Brotherhood developed three clear demands during the summer of 1889: rejection of the classification system, nullification of the reserve clause in cases where a club imposed a salary reduction on a player for his "reserved," or upcoming, season, and an end to the practice of selling players for cash.[19] The owners' new contract made it obvious to the players that they would continue to be treated as employees, and certainly not as partners, in National League operations. The Brotherhood's leadership saw this as a further assault on the players' rights and believed the only solution was a new league based on a partnership between owners and players. Filled with this revolutionary spirit, the Brotherhood's leaders met on Bastille Day 1889 and announced their plans for the new Players League. Ward encouraged Brotherhood members in each city to go forth and seek capital backing for Players League clubs.

The Brotherhood's specific plans for the new league reflect both the specific issues that were creating tension with the owners and a certain amount of foresight regarding the future of the professional sports business. The plans indicate a nascent understanding among the players of the equal importance of competitive balance and financial survival. Each Players League capitalist was responsible for securing playing grounds in the club's home city and providing $25,000 in start-up capital. Brotherhood officials helped provide labor-cost certainty for these new club owners by locking player salaries at their 1889 levels. Each player in the Players League would receive the same salary in the Players League as he had in the National League or American Association during the 1889 season. All expenses and revenues for the entire league were to be pooled. The Players League established a revenue sharing plan to see to the disbursement of these funds. The plan rewarded the top teams first ($10,000 in prize money), the teams' financial backers second ($80,000, or $10,000 for each team), and the players third ($80,000). All profits beyond the first $170,000 would be split evenly between players and financial backers. The plan to divide the profits in such a manner marked a major break from the existing structure of the game and foreshadowed the revenue sharing plans implemented in the 1980s.

The Brotherhood's membership contained nearly all of the established stars from both the National League and the American Association. This fact alone made the Brotherhood confident that the fans would turn out to support the new league in droves. This belief was based on a fan-player relationship that was much less formal than it is today. In many cases, playing grounds had a grandstand seating four to five thousand spectators. In addition, each ballpark had a loosely defined overflow "standing room" area for more popular contests. The physical barriers dividing player and fan were minimal at best. Greater opportunities existed for interaction between player and fan, increasing the fans' connection to their hometown players. In the view of the Brotherhood, the players' performance on the field was the principal product baseball fans consumed. The capitalist's role was limited to providing the organizational framework and venue for the staging the game. As a result, Brotherhood members believed they should be counted as full partners with the magnates, not merely as commodities or resources used by the magnates to produce their product.

Continuing in this vein, the Players League's financial structure went far beyond the kind of incentive bonuses so prevalent in modern-day professional sports. The plan promised not only to share revenues between franchises in order to maintain financial stability but also to reward players and owners equally for the overall financial success of the new venture. This was de facto recognition of the codependent relationship between players and team owners. Players stood to gain from both the success of their team on the field—each member of the league championship squad would receive individual bonuses—and the success of the league as a whole. The Brotherhood's leaders expressed great faith that combining revenues and expenses was the best way to pool the interests within their new league. These common interests ensured that each of the players would ultimately do his utmost to promote the welfare of the new league.[20] The Brotherhood's leadership believed strongly in the power of reform unionism and cooperation between management and workers. Brotherhood members, all of them veteran, star players, sensed that assuring players a financial stake in the league's revenues was the clearest path to success for the Players League. These plans included a combination of factors sure to resonate with many Americans in the late nineteenth century. They offered each worker a more equitable share of the wealth created by his labor, while at the same time delivering the greatest rewards to the most talented and industrious. Brotherhood leadership was confident these themes would resonate with the increasingly progressive economic views of the day.

In late October the players' chief nemesis, Chicago White Sox owner A. G. Spalding, attempted to dim Brotherhood optimism with a series of legal threats. Spalding promised that National League owners were prepared to bring legal action against any reserved players that "jumped" from the National League to the Players League. Spalding claimed that "not a single one of them will play ball in Chicago once I serve them with an injunction, and you can bet your last dollar that I will preserve my right."[21] The Brotherhood's leaders responded to these threats with a continued emphasis on rights and liberty when discussing the standard player's contract for their new league. "When the term of his contract has expired the brotherhood player is at perfect liberty again to go where he will," they explained, "and nothing in the constitution of the new league or in his contract deprives him of that right." Of the effects of the reserve clause and the classification plan the Brotherhood said, "We have no 'reserve rule,' no 'arbitrary $2,000 limit rule,' only one contract and the full salary written in it; nothing which encroaches on the player's natural rights, and when he goes from one club to another his 'consent' is not forced and no price is passed."[22] Despite the magnates' legal maneuvering and the continued threat of an injunction, Ward and the Brotherhood moved steadily forward with their plans for a new league, buoyed by faith in recent court decisions that were likely to swing the legal tide in their favor.[23]

Spalding responded by referring to the Brotherhood as a "secret organization," continuing to cast the players in a sinister light. Such remarks marked a clear effort to scare off the growing numbers of respectable middle-class fans that baseball clubs relied on as a steady source of ticket revenue. Spalding summoned all the antilabor demons of the era: "The [National] league has existed for fifteen years. It wiped out the gambling element in baseball and cleared it of crooked playing. Now that the game is clean . . . 'long chance' capitalists are ready to step in and assume the possible profits through the game. Supposing the games are as pure and clean as those played under the National League's reign, will the public have any belief in its purity under the pooling system and auspices of an oathbound, secret organization of strikers which has plotted against the life of the league through the care of which it became a possibility?"[24] Spalding reminded fans that it was the National League magnates, the very men under egregious assault from this secret society of players, who had rescued the national game from the players in the first place.

The assault on the Brotherhood's image continued with owner

charges that players were "overpaid and greedy," traits that could only lead to financial ruin for the players' new enterprise. National League leaders happily circulated rumors that called into question the new league's viability.[25] Henry Chadwick, the editor of *Spalding's Guide*, called the Brotherhood's manifesto a "revolutionary pronunciamento" by a small group looking to drag along the rest of the membership through the use of terrorist tactics.[26] The magnates of the American Association, who as recently as three years earlier had posed a great threat to the National League, were now brothers in arms with their former rivals. Chris Von der Ahe, the owner of the St. Louis club and president of the American Association, questioned the supposed irreplaceable nature of the former National League stars now jumping to the Players League: "If the Brotherhood players think their places can't be filled and they can consequently dictate terms to their employers they'll find themselves mightily mistaken. The woods are full of good ball-players, and all that is necessary to bring them out is for the brotherhood to create a demand for them by refusing to sign for next season."[27] All of these themes, from the ultimate interchangeability of labor to the ingratitude of the working class, were typical of the conservative response to labor during the Gilded Age. In this way, both sides competed to win the sympathies of the middle-class fan base, the owners through conservatism, the Brotherhood members by casting themselves as members of the producing class exercising their economic liberty.

Despite their public posture questioning the Players League's viability, the National League and American Association were clearly preparing for a trade war by early November 1889. The two leagues formed an alliance designed to combat the emerging Players League. Alliance plans called for the establishment of funds to guarantee the survival of clubs that suffered financial losses due to competition from the Players League. Rumors also spread of a "war chest," funds designated for luring the best players out of the Brotherhood and away from the Players League.[28] By early January, National League owners had these funds hard

at work in a series of all-out raids on the Players League's rosters. These incursions ended any hopes for a last-ditch peace
effort, and the Brotherhood turned its efforts to the final organizational details of securing capital and playing grounds for
its inaugural season.

Brotherhood Ideology

In addition to their financial efforts to lure players back to the
National League, the owners were readying to fight the Players
League in the courts. The magnates began legal proceedings
designed to reassert their rights under the reserve clause, seeking an injunction to force Brotherhood members back into the
National League fold. Ward responded to this campaign by
redoubling his public opinion campaign against the clause. He
reiterated charges that the reserve clause was simply the magnates' favorite tool for monopolizing the baseball labor market.
He believed that National League owners unfairly used the clause
as a tool for lowering player salaries from one year to the next,
even though such a practice stood in direct violation of contract
language. Ward expressed great confidence in the prospects for
the success of the Players League, as long as solidarity within
the ranks remained strong and the top-level players kept their
commitment to the Brotherhood's cause.[29] He appealed to what
he believed was a fair-minded baseball public, in the hopes that
fans would ultimately "vote" for the Players League with their
ticket dollars the following spring.

In addition to trying to build public support in their clash
over working conditions, the players also appealed directly to the
fans' desire for a quality product on the field of play. They decried
the way in which the National League owners had changed the
nature of the game: "There was a time when the National League
stood for integrity and fair dealing. Once it looked to the eleva-
tion of the game and an honest exhibition of the sport; to-day its
eyes are upon the turnstile." Players argued that most National
League magnates came into the baseball business solely to exploit
the game's profitability for every dollar in sight. Measures orig-

inally intended for the good of the game, such as the use of the reserve clause for competitive balance, were now being used in the "most arbitrary and mercenary way."[30]

Men like New York Giants owner John Day led the owners' response to Ward's campaign. Day emphasized themes established by magnates like Spalding and Von der Ahe by working hard to cast doubt on the Players League's long-term viability. He argued that Ward and the Brotherhood's leadership were essentially renegades who lacked the strong support of their 130 rank-and-file members. He painted the Brotherhood as a sinister secret labor society in the process of leading its naïve membership down the path to ruin.[31] Day's sentiments provide further evidence of the emerging paternalistic view that many magnates had of their players, as well as the owners' desire to keep "respectable" middle-class fans on their side of the fence. In the view of magnates like Day, he and his fellow capitalists were great men, the only men worthy of upholding the public trust to capably navigate the troubled waters of professional baseball.

The gathering storm between labor and management captured the attention of many, and some national labor leaders saw the Players League as a chance to use baseball's rising popularity toward their own ends. One organizer from the American Federation of Labor (AFL), called for the Brotherhood to officially align itself with either the AFL or the Knights of Labor, whichever organization best suited its needs. The organizer argued that this move would serve two very important purposes. It would inspire all workingmen across the nation who currently struggled against capital as well as draw a larger working-class contingent to the ballpark for Players League games. The players' response to overtures such as these speaks to their cautious approach to organization and their nascent labor consciousness. Most players actively supported the Brotherhood's aims as they related to improving the lot of the professional baseball player. However, most players lacked faith in the ability of a strong craft union to effectively secure their position in a struggle with the magnates. At this point in the game's history, baseball players were more comfortable with the idea of recruiting new, player-friendly capital than they were with embracing a more straightforward craft union approach. As much as they might have embraced a republican, producerist ideology and seen the need for forming a craft-style association, the players were not ready to accept a role limited to that of laborers performing at the whim of the magnates.

Ultimately, the players ignored the overtures of labor organizers and followed an independent path. While the Brotherhood borrowed heavily from the reform union ideals of the Knights of Labor and certainly met the AFL's criteria as a smaller craft union, there were significant differences. The Brotherhood stopped short of calling for the greater equality and workplace democracy the Knights pursued. The players also wanted much more than the economic concessions and greater share of shop floor control the AFL demanded. By launching the Players League, the Brotherhood's members made it clear that they saw themselves as highly skilled members of the producing class who deserved a full share of the wealth generated by their labor. Moreover, it is likely that the players understood they could not afford to offend middle-class sensibilities of their fan base by aligning themselves with a larger labor organization. In the wake of the Great Pacific Railroad Strike and the Haymarket Square Riot, many Americans equated organized labor with turmoil and upheaval. By deciding to forgo a formal relationship with a larger labor organization, the players showed the importance they placed on maintaining a positive relationship with the baseball public, right from the very beginning.

The players kept up their public relations effort through November and December, publishing in the *New York Times* a letter from the popular New York second baseman Danny Richardson designed to cast their historical spin on the founding of the Brotherhood. Richardson, an attractive spokesperson because he was outside the "sinister" leadership group, laid out several key reasons for the establishment of the Brotherhood. First he cited a straightforward desire by the players to move beyond the

$2,000 salary limit arbitrarily imposed by the owners.[32] Richardson argued that the players were simply following the course of good free-labor republicans: "We claim to have the same right to engage in business as clerks in a store, who, being competent men and having mastered their employer's business, decide to open an establishment of their own. It will be conceded that a man has the right at any time to cease working for others and engage in business on his own account." Richardson argued that National League management would be better served searching for replacements for the 130 Brotherhood members slated to leave the National League than by trying to hold Brotherhood members to their old contracts.[33]

Despite the members' best efforts, the Brotherhood suffered some serious setbacks in the court of public opinion on the eve of the 1890 season. The *Chicago Daily Tribune*, whose sports editor, Louis Meachem, was a longtime ally of Hulbert and Spalding, was a regular critic. More significant was criticism from the much more player friendly *New York Times*. On December 13 the *Times* ran an editorial casting serious doubt on the players' ability to serve as "Capital, Enterprise and Labor": "The downtrodden baseball player is about the queerest example extant of Labor crushed under the iron heel of Capital. It is quite true that a good deal of money has been made out of him, but it is also true that he has absorbed a very large proportion of it himself, and his present yearning is for all of it. This is what the opposition of the Brotherhood to the League seems really to mean, and, judging from analogy, it will not succeed in its modest object."[34] The *Times* assured its readers that the experienced capitalists of the National League would certainly find some way to short-circuit the new league. It further argued that, as the experienced stars of the Players League grew older, the National League would be able to replace them with fresh-faced younger stars, making the public forget all about the former greatness of the Brotherhood members. The Brotherhood's focus on the interests of veteran players led many to believe that it would not be an attractive employment alternative for the young, talented players needed to keep the league fresh to fans and investors alike. The critic's message was clear: the Players League's long-term prospects for public support were bleak.

As 1889 drew to a close, the National League owners, again under the leadership of A. G. Spalding, began to use their war chest to bring key Brotherhood members back to the National League fold. In some cases these players received unprecedented raises of nearly 50 percent over their 1889 salaries. This tactic worked especially well because the financial structure of the Players League kept it from entering into a bidding war with the National League magnates. By locking in player salaries at 1889 levels, the Players League guaranteed its own labor costs; however, this condition left it unable to increase player salaries in response to the aggressive wage increases offered by the National League. The Brotherhood counted on its members to stand strong against the temptation of a much larger payday. It had little actual leverage over its members and often had no choice but to publicly expel these "jumpers" from Brotherhood membership. The Brotherhood claimed it "must make examples of the traitors who sold themselves for the league gold," but these tactics often just made the deserters appear to be rats leaving a sinking ship.[35] Brotherhood leadership was especially disappointed in defectors such as Jerry Denny and Jack Glasscock, formerly underpaid stars for small-market teams, who saw the bidding war as an opportunity to finally get paid what they felt they deserved.[36] The magnates, for their part, held up Denny and Glasscock as the only decent men among the Brotherhood. They were not "deserters" but honorable men who "confirmed their agreement to discharge their valid contract obligation to National League clubs."[37]

Throughout this bidding war, maintaining solidarity within the ranks proved to be an ongoing challenge for the Brotherhood. Many players showed a shrewd understanding of the new labor market and the rare opportunity it offered to sell their services to the highest bidder. These players essentially made themselves free agents and set out in search of the highest possible salary.

The case of New York Giants right fielder Mike Tiernan provided a clear example of the new realities of the salary war. Tiernan claimed he was a "dyed in the wool brotherhood man" but held out for a $1,000 raise to his $2,500 salary because he felt it was only fair that he receive the same compensation as Jim O'Rourke, a player Tiernan felt he was at least the equal of, if not the better. Players such as Tiernan understood the fleeting nature of a professional ballplayer's window of economic opportunity. Such men were willing to risk ostracism from their peers in order to seize this unique opportunity for maximum compensation. This set of circumstances proved challenging to player solidarity time and again over the next ninety years, as players' unions attempted to keep men like Tiernan on board in the face of a lucrative contract offer from a magnate bent on breaking down player unity.

The Reserve Clause's First Day in Court

The second major challenge facing the Players League, in January 1890, was the National League's pursuit of a court injunction barring Brotherhood members "under reserve" from playing in the Players League. National League officials had great faith in the binding legality of the reserve clause. They used their campaign for an injunction to continue their portrayal of the Brotherhood's leadership as a small group bent on terrorizing and bullying its larger membership. The National League magnates freely used their players, who were not Brotherhood members, to reinforce this portrayal in the press. These men told tales of rampant fears among Brotherhood members who wanted to return to the National League but were nearly paralyzed with fear at the prospect of being labeled deserters. New York Giants first baseman Roger Connor claimed that many Brotherhood members eagerly awaited the court's enforcement of the reserve clause, as such enforcement would provide the players with an excuse to desert the Brotherhood. These players could then return to their National League clubs without any fear of retribution or of being seen as traitors in the public eye.[38]

Connor's comments were part of a greater public discussion on the legality of the reserve clause. Interest in the issue peaked in the days just prior to the Giants' breach-of-contract case against John Montgomery Ward. The club sought an injunction that would uphold the reserve clause and prevent Ward from playing for any baseball club other than the Giants during the 1890 season. This was a pivotal moment in the history of the young Players League. Many potential Players League capitalists held back their financial support, waiting until Ward's case was decided. These men knew their new venture was doomed if the courts upheld the reserve clause. Lawyers for the National League attempted to use the Players League capitalists' uncertainty to the National League's advantage by implementing a variety of legal strategies designed to delay the proceedings as long as possible and keep the Brotherhood effectively separated from its start-up capital. As is the case in most industries, financial capital was critical to many aspects of starting a new Major League Baseball club. Initial funding was required for everything from securing playing grounds to printing and selling tickets. National League owners knew that without funding the Players League could not move forward with its plans for the new season.

Beyond its implications for the potential success of the Players League, Ward's legal case offered significant insight into Major League Baseball's rationale as to why its operations deserved an exemption from antitrust legislation. During Ward's hearing, National League lawyers acknowledged that baseball was an entertainment industry but argued that the game was wholly different from enterprises such as vaudeville shows or circuses. These attorneys asserted that the key difference lay in the fact that baseball required not one, but two, quality acts on the stage, or field, at one time. This argument, in turn, established competitive balance as necessary for providing entertainment value to baseball's customers. The attorneys held that the primary purpose of the reserve rule was to preserve this competitive balance by preventing the best players from jumping from team to team in search of the highest salary. They maintained, therefore, that baseball players could not be turned loose to sell their services on the free market. Unrestrained bidding for player talent would enable two or three of the wealthiest teams to attract all of the most talented players and effectively destroy any semblance of competitive balance. This scenario, in the minds of the magnates, would surely ruin the professional game. The necessity of the reserve clause to maintaining competitive balance became the owners' primary argument for baseball's exceptionalism and would later lay the groundwork for Major League Baseball's antitrust exemption in 1922.[39]

The Brotherhood's prospects brightened a little more than two weeks later. Judge O'Brien denied the New York Giants' request for an injunction preventing Ward from playing in the Players League. This was good news for the Players League, but the legal victory was far from decisive. While the decision allowed the Brotherhood and the Players League to move forward, Judge O'Brien acknowledged that his decision was based more on issues of timing than on specific contract language. O'Brien cited the lack of time for sorting out the reserve rule's more complex legal issues before the start of the 1890 season. The judge clearly struggled with ascertaining a clear definition of "reserve":

> One of the principal questions discussed on the argument was as to the meaning of this word "reserve" as used in the contract. On the part of the plaintiff [the Giants] it is claimed that the meaning of this word is clear and unambiguous, requiring no explanation, being used in its ordinary sense of "to hold, to keep for future use." The defendant [Ward], on the other hand, claims that this word, which was not a new one to the parties, has a history. That it has always been used in a particular sense, . . . when the defendant accorded the right to reserve his services that it was not thereby meant that he was absolutely bound or pledged to plaintiff, but that his services were reserved to the exclusion of any other member of the league of baseball clubs.[40]

This question of whether the clause applied specifically to the National League or to professional baseball as a whole hit right at the heart of the Players League's challenge to the National League ownership. Judge O'Brien ruled that the language in Ward's contract with the Giants did establish the right to reserve Ward's services, but the language was otherwise weak, because it set no other terms regarding pay or length of service. While the decision was not a clear-cut victory for either side, the judge's decision paved the way for the Players League to move forward. Much to the relief of the Brotherhood, its financial backers immediately responded to the good news with the necessary funding.

Of course, Brotherhood president Ward was not one to miss the chance for a public relations victory, stating,

> I don't know what course our enemies will pursue, but it is safe to predict that the Brotherhood will come out on top. The temporary injunction the League called for was simply a bluff. The League men knew that the players knew little or nothing about law and that they could coerce our players. In some cases they have been successful, but the men who have been brave enough to hold out in spite of the inducements offered in the shape of league gold will reap their reward and they deserve it. As to the deserters in our ranks, I don't know what they will do.

Ward reveled in this opportunity to have his leadership of the Brotherhood vindicated by a third party, especially in light of the ongoing criticism from National League owners, as well as from Brotherhood defectors like Welch and Tiernan. National League owners attempted to spin O'Brien's decision in their favor, arguing that the judge decided against an injunction because he felt there was ample time for a full trial.[41] The owners maintained they could still use O'Brien's decision to keep Brotherhood men tied to their National League contracts across the country.[42]

Two weeks later, National League owners again raised the stakes in the bidding war for Brotherhood talent. The New York Giants launched a major campaign to break the highly regarded second baseman Danny Richardson free from his Brotherhood contract. The terms were extremely generous. The Giants offered Richardson the unheard-of amount of $15,000, guaranteed for the next three seasons. One Giants official acknowledged, "The [National] League proposed to dispose of the Brotherhood before the season opens, as it will be better to get rid of them in that way rather than compete for their patronage." The official went on to say, "Richardson was the key to the situation and they are determined to get him, no matter what it costs."[43] The owners obviously felt that their best course of action toward discrediting the Brotherhood was to land themselves a "jumper" of the highest possible profile. Richardson, a close friend of Ward's and an outspoken National League critic, seemed the ideal target. His defection would deal a major blow to public faith in the Players League. Operating without the expected assistance from the courts, the National League owners appeared ready to stake their future on the idea that every man has his price. Richardson ultimately stayed put, but the episode demonstrated the lengths to which National League magnates were willing to go to undermine the Players League.

Two weeks later, although they had suffered roughly a dozen defections by the likes of Tiernan and Welch, the Brotherhood's members believed they had withstood the National League's greatest assault. Brotherhood secretary F. H. Brunell declared, "The Players League is now ready to begin the season with the strongest group of eight clubs ever gathered in one baseball organization. Its men have withstood National League bombs, beaten the 'old masters' in the court, rejected huge bribes, and defeated National league plots. . . . Our men have proved the falsity of the old League's declaration that every player has his price." The secretary cast the struggle in ideological terms. He argued that the new season would be the best ever in the history of baseball, largely because "thousands of people who in the past have taken little or no interest in baseball have been attracted to it by our clean and consistent struggle for liberty and by the un-american [sic] tactics of the old masters. The American people have no sympathy for bluff, bribery, or boycotting." Finally, Brunell blasted the "slavish contracts" of the National League. His use of terms like slavery and liberty and charges of un-American behavior were, again, a clear attempt to paint the struggle between the Brotherhood and the National League in terms that would endear the Brotherhood to the hearts of its baseball fan base. These terms would resonate with working-class fans, who were wary of the increasing power of the capital class, as well as with the values of middle-class fans, concerned with fairness and liberty. The secretary emphasized these themes even further when he pointed out the hypocrisy of owners who declared loyal Brotherhood men traitors for breaking their National League contracts yet turned around and offered outrageous "bribes" in an attempt to bring players who were under Brotherhood contracts back to the National League.[44]

The tactical maneuvering and public relations battle continued throughout the month of March. Preparing for direct confrontation, the National League decided to drop two teams and rearranged its schedule to create the greatest amount of head-to-head competition with Players League clubs. This new schedule was arranged in such a way that there would be a National League contest occurring in the same city on the same day as a Players League game whenever possible. The National League obviously felt it would win the brand-recognition battle with fans, counting on already established ties between club and community to win the day, and the ticket revenue. Players League secretary Brunell said this was fine with him, so long as "the National League goes on record as the party forcing the conflict. Each [Players League team] has its old public favorites and public opinion with it and will, I believe, draw an average of two people to one attending National League games."[45] The Brotherhood believed, at this relatively early stage in the game's development, that star players had more drawing power than established team loyalties.

Brunell was eager to reinforce the notion that not only was the Players League much more "above board" than the National League but the superior collection of Players League talent offered a better product on the field. The Brotherhood's public relations message was clear: Players League baseball was superior to National League baseball, in large part because it was created under a more fair and honest relationship between capital and labor. As Ward explained, "The conduct of the Men [in the Brotherhood] has thoroughly refuted the National League's declaration that the base ball player was not able to do business for himself. . . . They show how undismayed by opposition, undaunted by desertions, unmoved by all the bluff and bluster a powerful enemy could devise, in the face of obstacles which might have crushed a less or weaker cause . . . today the Players National League stands brightly forth as the strongest group of eight clubs in playing talent and general personnel ever gathered together."[46] Ward, Brunell, and the Brotherhood's leadership believed these themes would resonate with the baseball public, even as National League magnates sought to wage a war of attrition through the intentional pursuit of head-to-head competition for the hearts, minds, and ticket revenue of the American baseball public.

The Players' Dream Becomes Reality, and Then a Nightmare

The financial viability of both leagues was in question right from the start of the 1890 season. By mid-July it was clear to many of the Players League capitalists that, although their clubs were selling more tickets than the National League clubs, they were well on their way to losing large sums of money. Things did not look much better for the National League magnates on the other side of the conflict. Ultimately, the decisive difference between the two sets of capitalists was the National League's taste for battle and willingness to see the fight through to the bloody end.[47]

As the season dragged on, many baseball insiders feared the war would bring about an end to a beloved national institution. An editorialist in the *New York Times* opined that without a successful amalgamation of the two leagues the "baseball public will virtually have disappeared altogether in 1891. . . . The survivor of this contest will not inherit what the contest has dissipated, for it no longer exists."[48] The writer believed that the team owners were so set on defeating each other they failed to recognize they were on their way to total ruin. The players, meanwhile, were so focused on personal gain they could not see that they were likely to wind up working for $2 a day, not playing baseball for $3,000 per season. All of this would surely happen, the argument went, as fans became so disenchanted with the business of the game that their interest in baseball ceased altogether. This kind of apocalyptic thinking foreshadowed public reaction to baseball's great labor showdowns of the next century and proved extremely difficult for players to overcome in their pursuit of meaningful union representation.

At the season's close, John Ward publicly admitted that it was time for an end to the "baseball war," acknowledging that the Brotherhood sought to be a part of negotiations designed to bring all of professional baseball back under "one tent." Ward's search for compromise was a clear admission of defeat in his attempts to bring players a greater share of baseball's capital stakes.[49]

The attitude of the press as to which party was chiefly to blame for baseball's troubles underwent a clear shift as writers began to discuss the possible consolidation of the three existing leagues. The previous winter, the press had portrayed owners as greedy men exploiting the players' labor through the use of the reserve rule. A year later, the magnates were wise men who understood that a continued "baseball war" would only serve to bring about the end of the game. The players, on the other hand, were seen as the only group that benefited from the war. The press was eager to point out that the Players League's emergence had led to a nearly 50 percent increase in the size of the player workforce and an overall increase in player salaries. The press pointed out that these conditions especially benefited the most coveted players, all of whom belonged to the Brotherhood.[50]

A Brotherhood faction, opposed to consolidation on the grounds that it would result in a huge reduction in player salaries, only further reinforced this image of the self-serving player. This group, led by New York outfielder George Gore, questioned the ability of Ward and other Brotherhood leaders to act on behalf of the entire membership. Gore's faction believed the Brotherhood's leadership had offered too many concessions in the consolidation process and threatened to splinter off into yet another brand-new league run by the players. The *Times* painted these players in an extremely unflattering light: "Ball players, as a rule, are very hard men to suit. They devise all sorts of means to keep up their salaries, and the present row may be a ruse to have the clubs engage the players early at a stipulated figure before the cut in wages comes along. It is bound to come, and they know it."[51]

Players League capitalists weakened their position by foolishly sharing their financial data with representatives of the National League during reorganization talks, making it a great deal easier for the National League magnates to wait out the Players League capitalists until they offered total surrender.[52] The financiers of the Players League began to fold, one by one, selling off their Players League stock to the National League owners. This continued until mid-November, when all but the colorful A. L. Johnson had sold out their interests. Johnson, the most outspoken critic of his fellow Players League capitalists "who sold themselves for League gold," found himself in a precarious situation. He promised the players he would represent their interests in the negotiations with the National League no matter the outcome. As the other Players League owners sold off their capital, Johnson, now the owner of a team essentially without a league, was left to bear the brunt of the punishment National League magnates had in store. They hung Johnson out to dry, leaving him as the sole Players League owner without a buyout offer. Johnson responded by berating the National League in the press. The cantankerous owner declared he would bring the other magnates to their knees, even if it cost him $50,000.[53] Johnson remained the only hope for the Players League throughout the winter months, though as far as the press was concerned the final verdict was in: the organizational strength and capital substance of the National League had simply overwhelmed the upstart Players League.[54]

The great baseball war left in its wake a fair amount of pessimism regarding the prospects for baseball's long-term success.

Columnists placed blame for the baseball situation not with the greed of the magnates but instead firmly on the heads of the players, specifically those who "bolted for the Brotherhood." One *New York Times* column, in January 1891, was particularly scathing. The columnist argued that the players, motivated by little more than financial greed and a desire to destroy the National League, had done nothing but degrade the very enterprise that they depended on for their livelihood. The writer posited that the conflict between the Brotherhood and the National League had served to greatly diminish public interest in baseball. He pointed out that the combined total gate receipts of the National League and the Players League in 1890 were less than the receipts of the National League alone in 1889. In the minds of baseball's public, the game needed a significant revival in order to get back on the right path.

After the turmoil of the 1890 trade war, this column offers a more settled picture of public perception regarding a professional baseball player's position in the greater labor market: "The most aggrieved player at the beginning of last season could not have denied that his earnings at baseball were very much larger than his earnings at any other occupation that was open to him, while his own method of righting his grievances left him very much worse off than if he had not attempted to right them."[55] This widely held view typically contends that the player ought to feel fortunate to make such a large salary for "playing a child's game," since he is after all, a man with few other options. Missing almost completely from this traditionalist public view is the idea that players possess highly specialized skill sets, which could be put to work generating huge profits for the right organization of capitalists. Convincing the public that this latter view was, indeed, the case would be a major challenge for baseball players moving forward. Also quite evident in the column's analysis is the belief that players were typically ill suited to understanding the business aspects of the game and should be grateful that the game's financiers were so willing to generously share their profits. That being the case, in the view of the baseball public the bottom line was that further labor action by the players had only one possible end result: further damage to the institution of baseball, leading to the possible death of the game. This public perception painted the players into a corner, one they would attempt to fight their way out of for more than seven decades to come.

Lessons Learned

The Brotherhood War of 1890 set the stage for more than a century of labor-management battles in the business of baseball. The owners continued to use the reserve system and their subsequent ownership of their players' services to maintain a monopoly over the professional game. Time and again, when challenged about these practices, the owners pled poverty, or the need to maintain competitive balance, or the importance of maintaining a level of paternalistic control over the players in the best interests of the game. They successfully cast themselves as the game's protectors, the only group worthy of the public trust to preserve a national institution in the face of constant challenges from the players, a group who saw the game only as a means of personal enrichment.

The players remained frustrated with life under the magnates' thumb. Hamstrung as they were with the form of involuntary servitude imposed on them by the reserve system, they remained unable to successfully organize collective action to resist magnate control. The competitive nature of baseball served to divide the players, and, over time, the magnates became even more skilled at nurturing and exploiting these divisions. By the mid-1960s the magnates were experts at the use of a wide variety of tactics that compounded the difficulties faced by players whenever they tried to organize. The owners used blacklists to squelch disobedience, big individual contracts to turn well-paid stars against their everyday counterparts, and the exertion of public pressure on players fearful of damaging a national institution in order to keep their players in line and maintain their monopolistic hold on Major League Baseball.

2

Monopoly and Trade War

The Players League's failed challenge left professional baseball players in dire straits, as over the next three years National League magnates easily reestablished monopolistic control over Major League Baseball. This monopoly stood unchallenged until 1900, when the upstart American League mounted a successful challenge to the National League and forced the "senior circuit" to accept its teams as Major League equals. The players initially benefited from this trade war, as competitive bidding for talent drove up player salaries. In the end, however, they were frustrated, as the American League successfully co-opted the players' newly formed union, the Protective Association of Professional Baseball Players. Over the next twelve years the American and National Leagues enjoyed their own monopoly, until the upstart Federal League started yet another baseball trade war in 1913. Once again, the players briefly benefited, only to have yet another union, the Fraternity of Professional Baseball Players, rendered ineffective by baseball's third trade war in twenty-five years.

The New Brand of National League Ball: 1891–1900

In the wake of the 1890 Brotherhood War, the owners, primarily under the leadership of Abraham Mills and Albert G. Spalding, set up a new National Agreement with the American and Western Associations. The new agreement strengthened magnate control by establishing a national board, comprising three owner representatives, or one from each league. The board's primary purpose was to preside over all manner of disputes, from player grievances against ownership to contract violations to interclub disputes over player signings.[1] Such occurrences were commonplace, as the National League and the American Association engaged in close competition for the services of the most talented Brotherhood members. The National League magnates made an effort to appear as if they sought peace with the other associations, but their aggressive pursuit of "refugees" from the Players League doomed this new National Agreement right from the start.

The bidding war for Players League refugees proved almost fatal to both leagues, until they final consolidated as the new, twelve-team National League in 1892.[2] In a final concession to the old American Association, the National League magnates agreed to Sunday baseball in some markets and the sale of alcoholic beverages at games, a small price to pay for the return of monopoly control. The new baseball monopoly provided National League owners with ideal conditions for driving labor costs to new lows. Club owners cut player salaries by as much as 50 percent, across the board. Players occasionally threatened to strike or form their own league, but the National League's threat of permanent blacklisting quickly scared the players from following through on their threats.[3]

Magnates had other methods, beyond the blacklist, for controlling players and their salaries. Throughout the 1890s, owners tinkered with the rules of the game in an effort to sell more tickets and help limit salaries. First they moved the pitcher farther away from home plate to help generate more offense. This generally meant more ticket sales, which was good for a time, but not after the newly minted offensive stars began to demand higher salaries. The owners stemmed the tide of these demands by once again changing rules, this time in favor of the pitchers.[4] As a result, the National League made large financial gains throughout the first half of the 1890s, but those gains began to vanish by 1895. Other challenges quickly appeared in the wake of these financial concerns. The relatively small number of roster spots in the consolidated league led to great divisiveness among the players. They gladly reinforced the National League's unofficial color barrier to help keep the potential labor pool small and literally fought tooth and nail to keep newcomers from taking their treasured place on a team roster. Frustrated players also increasingly abused umpires during games, a practice known as "kicking." Owners were torn between staying true to their promise to run a respectable game and allowing the rowdy on-field behavior to continue, fearing that fans were, in large part, drawn to the ballpark by the entertainment value of the on-field mayhem.

The National League faced challenges beyond the players' on-field antics. The league rarely enjoyed anything remotely close to competitive balance, despite strictly enforcing the reserve clause, which the magnates claimed would guarantee such parity. The financial and competitive interests of league owners became increasingly intertwined. Financially strapped owners' obligations often forced them to make extremely unbalanced sales and trades of players. Through these transactions strong teams often got stronger at the expense of their weaker counterparts. Sunday baseball was extremely lucrative, but some cities banned Sunday games, leaving clubs in those cities, such as the Cleveland Indians, at a huge disadvantage in their ability to generate ticket revenue. Infrastructure was also breaking down. Old wooden grandstand facilities were in constant need of repair and, in some cases, needed to be demolished and replaced with new steel and concrete grandstands. This meant that, in order to remain profitable, many owners faced the prospect of sinking unheard-of amounts of capital into the business of baseball. This new level of capital outlay went well beyond the comfort levels of most baseball magnates, especially given the national economic uncertainty so common throughout the decade.

Ultimately, the 1890s' brand of monopoly ball created precisely the kinds of conditions necessary for another baseball trade war. The National League magnates' interlaced financial structure, restrictive labor practices, and inability to maintain competitive balance paved the way for a new league to rise, a league fittingly molded in the spirit of the Progressive Era.[5] *Sporting Life*'s editor Francis Richter said it best. He believed the National League magnates opened themselves up to an outside challenge through their "gross individual and collective mismanagement, their fierce factional fights, their cynical disregard of decency and honor, their open spoliation of each other, their deliberate alienation of press and public, . . . and their tyrannical treatment of their players."[6] The National League capitalists were being taught once more not to underestimate the significance of fan and media support. The opportunity for a rival Major League was, of course, great news to players. They knew a trade war between two Major Leagues meant more jobs, increased salaries, and the potential for better working conditions and more freedom of contract.

A New Rival: The American League

The National League's new rival emerged under the leadership of one of the "senior circuit's" many detractors, Western League president Bancroft "Ban" Johnson. Johnson was a progressively minded former Cincinnati sportswriter, best known for turning the Western League into the "best run league in the game." Johnson constantly criticized National League baseball as ill-suited for women and families because of poor sportsmanship, gambling in the stands, and a lack of respect for umpires and other officials.[7] Johnson believed he and the Western League could take advantage of National League contraction by putting new clubs in each city abandoned by the National League, as well as in new markets like the south side of Chicago, where recent immigrants would quickly fall in love with the national game.[8] With this expansion the Western League was rebranded as the American League and quickly filled its rosters with talented players whom the National League had cast aside in its contraction process.

Immediately following the close of the 1900 season, Johnson announced that American League clubs would not renew their membership in the existing National Agreement. He declared that the American League would not consider cooperating with the National League until it agreed to major revisions in the National Agreement and acknowledged the American League as a Major League of equal standing.[9] Johnson knew the baseball public, and his efforts to establish a second Major League, one on equal footing with the National League, underscore the importance of the relationship between baseball and its public. The *Sporting News*, by this time already regarded as the "bible of baseball," welcomed the American League's expansion into the eastern market, proclaiming the new circuit to be "baseball's only hope." The paper pleaded with American League management to make the reforms necessary to bring quality baseball back to the American public: "The weakness of the [National League] magnates, their bickerings and the ceaseless kicking and senseless delays on the field helped irritating conditions already bad. Besides the clubs were so evenly matched that for most of the season the people of the seven [league] cities regarded their teams as losers. It was four months before the people of Pittsburg realized that the team was a winning one."[10] Less than a decade into the new "monopoly ball" era, the National League had already lost touch with the very baseball public it claimed to know so well.

Such criticism of the National League was rampant. The *New York Times* ran an editorial containing a laundry list of the National League's major problems. *Times* writer William Cauldwell conceded that, while the National League contraction plan provided a more compelling pennant race, as the owners intended, it did little to solve the league's larger problems. The plan did not, as hoped, bring about a great increase in the economic demand for baseball. Cauldwell argued that several factors played important roles in the National League's failure to improve the game's public appeal. The writer called for improved sportsmanship on the part of players and owners. He believed the public had tired of players "kicking" and constantly complaining about poor umpiring. Cauldwell called on

National League magnates to show they were indeed serious about improving the game:

> It is in the power of the club owners—"magnates" as they are called—to effectually remedy this menacing evil to the national game, and yet they remain supine and let it go on. There has been spasmodic legislation against kicking and rowdyism, but it was never enforced. If the club owners are so short sighted or such poor sportsmen—most of the present league owners appear to be both—that they won't throttle unmanly tactics by their employees, then they are chiefly to blame for this source of the declining prosperity of baseball. If they are so anxious to see their team win and thus swell gate receipts that they will condone and even encourage unsportsmanlike behavior by their players, then their presence as "magnates" is a menace to the welfare of the game, and the sooner they are out of it the better for the game.[11]

Cauldwell also criticized the National League magnates for their syndicalism, arguing that their push for monopoly had, by its very nature, drawn outside competition to the industry. Ban Johnson could not have asked for a better proponent for the American League. True to his progressive spirit, and in line with the growing progressivism of the coveted middle-class baseball fans, Ban Johnson set out to bust the National League trust.

Enter Baseball's First Craft Union:
The Protective Association of Professional Baseball Players

As was the case during baseball's earlier trade war, the National League had more than Ban Johnson to worry about. Many players were fed up with the $2,500 salary limit and the specter of job losses due to contraction. Moreover, players knew that a potential trade war made this moment a critical time for collective action. During the 1900 season, a group of players formed the Protective Association of Professional Baseball Players. The association's chief goals were protecting players' rights and increasing salaries, all while taking great pains to distance itself from the Brotherhood's failures, just ten years earlier.

Careful to seek counsel from outside the Brotherhood's circle, the Protective Association chose attorney Harry Taylor, a former player in both the Major and Minor Leagues, as its primary legal counsel.[12] Foremost among the Protective Association's demands were basic medical coverage for players injured while playing, an end to the practice of reserving players at a lower salary than the previous season, and the establishment of the player's right to approve all sales and trades. Finally, it asked for the institution of a formal arbitration system to settle all ongoing disputes between players and management. Organizationally the association distanced itself from the Brotherhood, but it was quite similar in identifying goals designed to resonate with progressive, fair-minded, middle-class fans, as well as working-class fans well aware of the perils of workplace injuries and plummeting wages.

These demands tell us a great deal about the shifting labor consciousness of professional baseball players at the turn of the century. Gone were the sweeping, industry-wide reforms proposed by John Montgomery Ward and the Brotherhood of Professional Baseball Players. In their place was a set of pragmatic requests from a group of men clearly unwilling to take a dramatically new course of action. The Protective Association was a group of workers that understood the place of the highly skilled worker in the management-labor hierarchy, hammered out as it was by the market and the courts in the late nineteenth century. Their proposed reforms fit well with other workplace reforms characteristic of the Progressive Era.

Like the Brotherhood, the association made requests rooted in fairness and liberty. It differed from the Brotherhood in is caution. The Protective Association was much more willing to accept the kinds of gains made by the skilled workers in the American Federation of Labor. In fact, the Protective Association briefly considered associating with the AFL, but after hearing out AFL representative Dan Harris at an early meeting, the association decided against an official affiliation for fear of antagonizing the magnates. This was one of the association's greatest fears; it wanted to extend absolute assurances to the owners that the new organization was completely without radical intentions.[13] Ideologically, this was a major step backward and set a nasty precedent. For more than sixty years to come, player unionism foundered on this intense fear of antagonizing the powerful capitalists and of falling out of favor with middle-class fans who feared radicalism of any kind. Perhaps even more importantly, the players essentially conceded that it was the owners who were indeed most deserving of the public trust. This concession amounted to a substantial self-imposed obstacle to unionization moving forward.

The Protective Association's requests unmistakably reflect the Progressive Era context. The players no longer saw themselves as free-labor republicans seeking a fair share of the fruits of their labor. Instead, the players asked for what was rightfully theirs in a more reasonable relationship between worker and capitalist. The players rightly assumed this strategy would resonate with the greater baseball public, as the open support they received from the media demonstrated. Francis Richter of *Sporting Life* said it best: "The wonder is that the union for the self protection against intolerable oppression has been so long delayed."[14] Richter's sympathies were echoed across the sporting press. There was almost a complete absence of shock or outrage in the public response to baseball's cautious and respectful new players' union. The players took relief in striking just the right chord with the public.

The Protective Association certainly also understood the attractive nature of its demands to a progressive baseball reformer such as Ban Johnson. But while demands for protections such as medical coverage and an arbitration board may have appealed to Johnson's progressive leanings, he had more pragmatic reasons for seeking the players' favor. Johnson had an immediate need to woo the established star players required to raise the profile of his new league, and he very publicly agreed with the Protective Association's demands right from the start.[15] Just as the players sensed the time was right to organize, Johnson knew he needed the support of these players in order for the American League to succeed. It was no coincidence that Johnson established ties with many key members of the Protective Association, including the likes of association vice president Clark Griffith. Johnson understood the value of men such as Griffith who had the players' trust. Griffith, and others like him, proved invaluable as recruiting agents for Johnson's new league.

Since Johnson was in open agreement with the Protective Association, the shared demands of the players and the American League were the talk of the annual National League owners' meetings in December. The magnates wasted little time; they rejected the players' petitions for changes in the National Agreement and refused to officially recognize the American League.[16] Immediate public reaction to this course of action was decidedly negative. The *Chicago Daily Tribune* believed this was a war the National League could ill afford: "It [the National League] has estranged the public. . . . The players have not to contribute any backing this time. Theirs is a defensive rather than an offensive alliance, and their part will be largely to help someone else fight their battles for them."[17] The *New York Times* said that the players' requests "seem only reasonable and in accord with accepted ideas of individual right, but the [National] League managers . . . did not agree, rejected the players' overtures in positive terms, and practically defied the ball-tossers to better their condition by carrying out the talked of strike or affiliating with 'Ban' Johnson and his new American League."[18] The "Bible of Baseball" joined the *Times* in its criticism of the owners, fearing that this situation might bring about an end to the game: "Had they [the National League magnates] been men of fairness and wisdom they would have granted nearly every request made by the players, because every one was founded on reason and justice. Such action not only would have been just and right, but it would have improved the business, pleased the players and made them feel that as justice had been shown them, they ought in return to do all they could for the game and their employers interests. But of course, the 'magnates' took the wrong course—they always do."[19] The Protective Association's caution and respectability won its members the support they expected from Ban Johnson and the baseball press, and their efforts to align their plans with the public interest paid off with increased public pressure on the prevailing baseball power structure. The next course of action, for Johnson and the players, was far from clear.

The Protective Association found itself in an interesting predicament. Public support for the new American League grew daily, and Ban Johnson seemed ready to welcome it with open arms. Additionally, the sporting press clearly approved of its cautious approach. The National League magnates, on the other hand, were confident in the ironclad nature of the reserve clause. Their response was to threaten an overall reduction in player salaries for the 1901 season. These men remained absolutely rigid in their resistance to any kind of players' union. John Day even claimed that he would "raze his park before he would deal with a union."[20] For the Protective Association to truly be effective, it needed to find a way to work with owners in both leagues.

The Protective Association's by-laws and leadership philosophy compounded the players' dilemma. Again shying away from the Brotherhood's slightly more radical shadow, the Protective Association was determined to remain blame free in the event of a baseball war. The association publicly declared its refusal to legally challenge the reserve clause and insisted that all members honor any existing contract, including those with National League clubs. Association members were honor bound not to enter into any contractual agreement with a baseball club without the approval of the Protective Association's leader, Harry Taylor, and its legal counsel. This left the majority of current National League players with little control over their personal circumstances. As the Protective Association's president, Charles "Chief" Zimmer, said, "We have refrained from declaring war because we don't want to hurt the game."[21] Within a week of the owners' rejection of the players' requests, the association's leadership sent out a circular warning players that National League owners were indeed on the move toward cutting salaries. Zimmer and the association leadership cautioned members against "jumping leagues at this time."[22] The Protective Association remained so apprehensive about negative public response to any kind of radicalism that it essentially surrendered its biggest bargaining chip, the threat of desertion. The association found itself promising to honor the very contracts, allowing salary cuts and player sales, that had stirred the players to action in the first place.

As the players stood confounded by their next step, American League expansion plans for eastern markets such as Boston, Baltimore, and Philadelphia remained on track. Ban Johnson was further encouraged by the National League's lack of the same will it showed in 1890. There was little talk in 1900 of National League magnates raising a war chest to fight side by side against the American League threat.[23] Johnson's sound business sense, tough talk on reforming the ills of the National League, and public support of the Protective Association's demands made him out to be the players' ideal ally.

Not all the players, however, were eager to jump into Johnson's camp. Some men feared the blacklist, either from the National League or their own Protective Association. Many veterans, old enough to remember the Brotherhood War, remained cautious. These men knew it was likely that the American League would court them and then leave them out in the cold once Johnson's new circuit had won its war with the National League. Additionally, if Johnson was right about the National League's inability to mount a war chest, the likelihood of a huge trade war serving to boost player salaries was minimal.

By the start of the National League's spring meetings in late February, the Protective Association still sought league action on its proposals. The only change in the players' favor was that National League magnates now seemed to understand the need to placate the players in the face of the upcoming challenge from the American League.[24] National League magnates were even desperate enough to actively consider reconstituting the American Association as a National League puppet. This strategy was intended to increase competition with American League franchises in cities without an existing National League club.[25] Desperate as they were, there was little doubt that National League magnates required the players' support. Having pinned themselves into a corner with their own unwillingness to desert or strike, the Protective Association members hoped this was the opportune moment to recover momentum and gain key concessions from their masters.

Chief Zimmer went into the National League meetings as the players' sole representative. Zimmer succeeded in gaining concessions from the National League magnates in regard to the farming of players and the use of the option clause, but the price for these gains was steep. Zimmer promised the National League that the Protective Association would blacklist all players who "jumped" from the National League to sign with American League clubs.[26] Many players believed that Zimmer, desperate for any kind of concession, had sold them down the river. Zimmer stood strong in the face of this criticism. He made a public statement in early March, promising to uphold his part of the bargain. According to Zimmer, any Protective Association member who violated the reserve clause and signed an American League contract would be immediately suspended.[27]

This did little to stem the tide, and players continued to publicly criticize Zimmer. In spite of the threatened consequences, a few began to jump to the American League, partially in an effort to show their contempt for Zimmer and the Protective Association. Zimmer and Taylor stayed the course, and issued a joint statement to make their position: "The Protective Association was formed primarily and mainly to destroy the disposing of the services of professional baseball players without their consent. Its first recognition came from the American League, which months ago granted nearly all the players' demands, and the players, to a man, appreciate the value this action has been to them. The National League . . . having a system of 'farming' in vogue, was harder to deal with; its reports ignored the players at a conference in December."[28] Its cautious approach and fear of a trade war served the Protective Association poorly. It exchanged small gains for a promise to uphold many of the important tools of owner control. This was an early test of solidarity for the new craft union, one that offered a less than promising picture of the Protective Association's future success, especially if the players would continue to allow the fear of negative public reaction to affect their approach to collective action.

The apparent peace pact between the players and the National League did not faze Ban Johnson. He continued to demonstrate shrewd business sense and an ability to walk a very fine line in his dealings with former National League players. Johnson, in agreement with the Protective Association's original demands, declared himself opposed to the practice of "farming" and the National League's abuse of the reserve rule. The American League would not violate any existing National League contract, but that did not mean it would honor the National League's reserve clause and option rules. This left any player not already under contract for the 1901 season open to sign with an American League club. Many players, under these circumstances, showed their dissatisfaction with the National League monopoly by signing with an American League team. Impressed with the way in which Johnson ran the American League and drawn by the prospect of slightly higher salaries and the chance to get out from under the National League's oppressive control, more than seventy players jumped from the National League to the American League in the months leading up to the 1901 season.[29]

Despite their official proclamations against "jumping," the officers of the Protective Association provided a fair amount of aid to the American League's efforts. Clark Griffith, a high-ranking Protective Association official, did yeoman's work in recruiting players for Johnson's new league. Philadelphia player-manager Connie Mack joined Griffith in his efforts. These men played a key role in the early success of the American League and were later rewarded for their efforts, as they rapidly ascended baseball's management ladder. Mack and Griffith were among the game's early pioneers who made the transition from player to manager to magnate. Once they made the transition to management, their views on players' unions changed dramatically. Both men later became outspoken opponents of unions in professional baseball. In the early years of the American League, however, they were all for the Protective Association and any assistance it could provide in bringing top-quality talent to the American League.

True to form, the National League magnates resorted to the legal system and rule changes in a final effort to hold onto their players and suppress salaries. First they turned to the Pennsylvania courts in search of an injunction preventing Phillies star second baseman Napoleon "Nap" Lajoie from jumping to the American League's Philadelphia Athletics. Ban Johnson outmaneuvered his National League counterparts by assigning Lajoie to the Cleveland club, outside of the jurisdiction of any court in Pennsylvania.[30] Foiled in the courts, the National League magnates turned to the already oft-used tactic of manipulating the rules of the game in order to keep salaries in line. They introduced a wider, five-sided version of home plate designed to help umpires more easily "see" strikes. The National League owners also decided that the first two foul balls in each at bat would be counted as strikes, common practice in today's game. By making it easier for the pitcher to generate strikes, the National League was, in fact, making it much more difficult for the batter to reach base safely. The owners knew this change would result in lower batting averages and fewer runs batted in, the two key offensive statistics used to determine a player's salary.[31]

The American League went along in adopting the five-sided plate but waited a year before adopting the foul strike rule. These seemingly minor rule differences meant that American League baseball was a much more offensively oriented, and exciting, brand of baseball during the 1901 season. American League offensive fireworks went a long way toward establishing it as a legitimate "major" league in the eyes of fans. The impact on ticket revenue was also significant. Once the only show in town, the National League outdrew the American by fewer than 250,000 fans in 1901. Conditions worsened for the National League clubs the following season. They watched helplessly as the "junior circuit" outdrew them by more than half a million fans in 1902.[32] Ban Johnson not only outmaneuvered the National League magnates for the favor of the players, he also understood what was necessary for the American League to attract a new generation of American baseball fans. In no time at all, Johnson's appreciation for the necessity of public appeal and approval propelled the American League to the forefront of the national game.

The American League built on its early success by continuing its assault on National League rosters and markets. Ban Johnson moved a franchise from Milwaukee to St. Louis in order to establish an American League foothold in one of the best baseball markets in the nation. When American League magnates signed key stars such as Rube Waddell, Joe Kelley, and even the Protective Association's president, Tom Daly, Johnson had successfully made "jumpers" out of almost the entire Protective Association leadership. Individual members of the association benefited from the boom in salaries caused by this trade war, but ultimately the American League's success spelled doom for the Protective Association. The rising profile of the American League meant Ban Johnson would soon have little use for the favor of the Protective Association. A monopsonistic baseball labor market was once again on the horizon.[33]

By the end of the 1902 season, even the most dyed-in-the-wool National League magnate could not deny the American League's new place in the baseball universe. National League magnates had little choice but to sue for peace. The only real issues of contention were the Pittsburgh and New York markets. Johnson renamed the American League's Baltimore club the Highlanders and moved them to New York at the end of the 1902 season. This was widely believed to be in direct response to the traitorous behavior of the Highlanders' last manager in Baltimore, John McGraw.[34] McGraw was a player-manager notorious for running a rowdy operation. He lived in constant fear that Johnson, ever the progressive reformer, was out to remove him and some of his more disreputable players from the game.

McGraw decided to be proactive and not wait for the 1902 season to run its course. He conspired with New York's National League owner, John Brush, to jump, along with four of his key players, to the Giants. Johnson responded by propping up the Baltimore club just long enough to finish the season and then moving the club to New York to be in direct competition with the Giants. In the short term the Highlanders were a baseball laughingstock, but in the long run they got the last laugh in the five boroughs. The Highlanders later changed their name to the Yankees and went on to become baseball's most storied franchise in baseball's largest market, to the chagrin of both the National League's New York Giants and the Brooklyn Superbas, the club that would become better known as the Dodgers.[35]

Peace between the leagues came in the form of yet another new National Agreement, a pact that demonstrated the clear return to the days of "monopoly ball." With the establishment of the American League as a true second Major League, Ban Johnson's days of paying high player salaries were over. The new agreement created a national commission composed of the two Major League presidents and a third party of their mutual choosing, a position that evolved into the commissionership of baseball. This commission served as the final authority in all interclub and interleague disputes, as well as the final appellate body for player grievances against a league or club. Finally, this new commission was responsible for classifying the Minor Leagues and setting "draft prices" for each classification. These prices indicated the amount a Major League club would pay a Minor League club for the rights to a particular player.[36]

The first draft prices set by the commission were bad news for the players and indicated that the trade war boom days were over. At the end of each season, Major League clubs could now draft as many players from the Minors as they pleased. The national commission set draft prices so low that no owner could resist the temptation to stock up on prospective talent. Draft rates ranged from $750 for a player from the Class A, or top-ranked, Minor Leagues, down to $200 for a player from a Class D club. The ease with which clubs could stockpile talent was an obvious threat to the job security of Major League veterans, who knew their clubs now had long lists of players waiting in the wings for their own shot at baseball stardom. The magnates now enjoyed just the position of strength they needed to reimpose the monopolistic labor practices of the late nineteenth century.

With the national commission under the firm guidance of Ban Johnson, labor peace reigned, and the baseball magnates began the business of cutting salaries in earnest. None other than the former Protective Association vice president Clark Griffith, now firmly installed as the manager of the New York Highlanders, defended the practice of reducing player salaries for the reserved years of their contract. Salary cuts were especially deep on the rosters of smaller-market teams trying to recoup their trade war losses. Cleveland owner Frank Robison pressured Johnson to adopt a series of reductions designed to drive the average player salary down to $2,400. Some clubs, such as Philadelphia, drove their entire payrolls below $40,000, even though many rosters had by then grown in size to as many as twenty-one or twenty-two players.

Lower labor costs made the game profitable again, and a fresh infusion of owner capital reinvigorated the game. The new National Agreement provided a stable environment for ushering in the game's "modern era." A wave of new stadium construction began, with concrete and steel ballparks replacing many of the old, haphazardly built wooden parks. From Ebbets Field in Brooklyn to Fenway Park in Boston to Wrigley Field in Chicago, big league baseball games unfolded on grand new stages; however, storm clouds loomed. Just as the stadium boom drew to a close, attendance took a turn for the worse. Major League attendance fell by more than 20 percent between 1910 and 1912.[37] The industry suffered, especially since almost all team revenues were generated by ticket sales. As always, tough times meant a baseball trade war.

Fraternity, not Brotherhood

The magnates took two steps to try and fend off this economic downturn. The first, of course, was an effort to minimize labor costs by cutting back on player salaries. The second was an attempt to make baseball more attractive to fans by once again boosting offensive production. The owners introduced a new baseball with a cushioned center made of cork. This livelier ball quickly boosted batting averages by 15–20 percent. Both measures were countered quickly by those most affected, the pitchers, who learned they could regain the upper hand against batters by modifying the baseball. The resulting pitches, like the spitball and the scuffball, dove and danced in a way that made them much more difficult to hit than pitches made with an unmodified ball. Faced with rule changes designed to further manipulate the baseball labor market, star players, who suffered most dramatically in the new salary structure, sought to organize their fellow players in an effort to recoup their financial losses.

The new organizational momentum came from unlikely sources. Popular players, such as Detroit second baseman Ty Cobb and Washington pitcher Walter Johnson, quickly tired of stagnating salaries. These men sought to cash in on their celebrity status through product endorsements, barnstorming tours, and other types of exhibitions.[38] Barnstorming was extremely popular in this age before radio and television brought the exploits of America's ball-playing heroes into living rooms across the nation. Not surprisingly, the magnates were opposed to these activities. They believed they held the exclusive rights to the on-field activities of their players and resisted the idea of a player generating baseball-related income without returning any benefit to his owner. Moreover, owners feared their players might be damaged by a career-ending injury while participating in one of these exhibition games. The owners took forceful steps, such as denying the use of National Agreement parks for barnstorming events, in order to limit these types of activities by their players.

Understandably, the players grew increasingly disgruntled

with the owners' prohibitions. The owners wanted to limit barn-storming for fear of injury, but many players felt the magnates' interest in this regard was completely one-sided. The players believed the owners cared about injury only as it related to a player's value. They were sure the owners had little interest in the health and welfare of the players for their own sake. This was most evident, players felt, in the lack of club-provided health or pension benefits, especially for players permanently disabled by their participation in the game. This concern over health and pension benefits was significant, as these issues were later critical to garnering public support for the players' future unionization efforts.

Restricted pay, the absence of health and pension benefits, and the magnates' continued farming and optioning of players pushed the players to form the Fraternity of Professional Baseball Players in 1912. Under the leadership of David Fultz, the Fraternity quickly signed up 288 players, enough that its members formed a majority on all but three Major League rosters.[39] Like the Protective Association, this organization started with less than revolutionary goals. According to the *Chicago Daily Tribune*, these men "are wise enough to . . . avoid the idea of unionism and wage scales. It was decided to avoid calling the organization anything that savored of 'players' union'." Following the established pattern, the magnates initially tried to appear welcoming to the Fraternity, all while attempting to set acceptable parameters for Fraternity activity. Chicago White Sox owner Charles Comiskey said, "It looks to me as if a lot of good might be done [for] both the players and the owners with such a body at the head of the men engaged in the game. I don't think any unreasonable demands will be made, and I don't believe the players intend to wreck the game."[40]

Like the leadership of the Protective Association a decade earlier, Fultz and the Fraternity stopped well short of the kinds of more radical demands associated with the Brotherhood. Fultz made it plain that, while the Fraternity had no love for the reserve clause, its primary purpose was not to tear the clause down:

"When a player signs a contract he enters into an agreement which binds the owner only for ten days, while the player is bound for the remainder of his professional career. Never again has he the power to contract." The Fraternity wanted to change this aspect of the reserve clause, not eliminate the reserve system altogether. Fultz continued, "With these rules, however, we have no fault to find; we realize their necessity. Baseball is a peculiar business and must be governed by peculiar laws. We simply mention them to show the opportunity for grave injustice when this abnormal power falls into the hands of an overreaching magnate."[41] The Fraternity made clear its willingness to work within the boundaries of acceptable reform clearly delineated by the baseball public, who, at this time, accepted the necessity of the reserve clause for the business of baseball.

Fultz clearly outlined the players' demands. First and foremost, the magnates needed to follow the contract to the letter. Second, salaries needed to be improved dramatically. The baseball press made a great stir about the exorbitant money, in some cases more than $4,500 annually, paid to star players. In contrast, Fultz wanted to call attention to the many players making less than $1,000 a year. The Fraternity leader argued that baseball players should not be thought of simply as grown men fortunate enough to make a living at a "kids' game." Instead, Fultz believed, the salaries of Major League Baseball players should be viewed in the same light as the salaries of the top three hundred men in any given industry. This was Fultz's primary approach. Baseball was an industry, a business. As such, it should honor its contracts and treat its employees with fairness and respect. Fultz also countered owner claims of poverty, remarking that "a glance around league circuits at the stupendous equipment recently completed or now under construction, would convince the most casual observer that after paying salaries the magnate still has enough left to keep the wolf out of the garage."[42] Fultz's comments further demonstrate a growing understanding, among the players at least, that players were more than mere laborers; they were, at a minimum, highly skilled workers, and they deserved compensation in accordance with their unique talents and abilities. Convincing the public of this would remain a major challenge for players over the next six decades.

Beyond contractual questions and salary issues, the Fraternity wanted greater protection for players from abusive spectators. It demanded that player grievances be heard and ruled upon in a fair and open manner. Fultz publicly criticized the owners for their continued abuse of contracts and arbitrary disciplinary actions. He complained specifically about the way owners used reassignment to the Minors as a way of arbitrarily reducing a player's salary. Fultz argued that baseball needed a better record on safety. At this time there were as many as forty fatalities a year within the professional ranks alone, primarily from batters being struck in the head by a pitch. Finally, Fultz also objected to the fact that players who were reassigned often had to pay their own travel expenses, even though they were being moved at the whim of the magnate.[43]

In keeping with the progressive spirit of the age, the Fraternity sought to protect its members from unsafe and unfavorable conditions in the workplace. Like good Progressives, Fraternity members asked more of their employers and more of themselves. One of their principal aims, they insisted, was to help put an end to player rowdyism. This could be best achieved, they believed, by helping curb the behavior of abusive fans, like those who deliberately provoked an attack by Ty Cobb during the 1912 season. Fultz wrote, "We believe that rowdyism in the stands is often a potent factor in causing trouble on the field. We trust that you will cooperate with us in our endeavor . . . to make baseball more wholesome and attractive to the better classes of the sport loving public."[44] This campaign was a large part of the Fraternity's efforts to portray its members as responsible men looking out for the interests of the game. It hoped this responsible approach would generate public pressure on the owners to compromise.

Things got decidedly more interesting when several members of Congress announced they would be looking into the possibility that the National Agreement essentially made Major League

59

Baseball a trust. With congressional pressure on, the magnates decided to lay low in their dealings with the Fraternity. This situation became even more complex in late 1913. A newly formed Minor League, the Federal League, announced its intention to pursue Major League status, in direct competition with both the American and National Leagues. Just as Ban Johnson had done a little more than a decade earlier, the Federals announced they would aggressively expand into eastern Major League markets in time for the 1914 season. Johnson, who had successfully co-opted the Protective Association of Professional Baseball Players to his advantage in 1901, completely understood how the new league might use the Fraternity to its advantage, especially if the established leagues condemned the players' group. Johnson convinced the National League magnates to join him in embracing the Fraternity.[45] The National Agreement clubs officially recognized the Fraternity in January 1914 and agreed to eleven of the seventeen points on the Fraternity's platform.[46]

Just as he had used the Protective Association to launch the American League, Johnson intended to use the Fraternity to thwart the threat of the Federal League. Immediately after recognizing the Fraternity, the magnates' unofficial commissioner, Garry Herrmann, turned to Fultz and said, "Now what are you going to do for us?"[47] The primary answer was that the Fraternity's leadership came out strongly against any form of contract "jumping." The magnates claimed it was, after all, the Fraternity men who were so insistent that all parties follow contracts to the letter. The magnates knew that, without "jumpers," the Federals would be unable to sign any of the top-flight talent needed to draw fans to their new league.[48]

For the most part, the magnates' plan worked. Jumping was limited to a select few stars, and oftentimes these were men already of questionable repute. The Federal League threat did a fair amount to boost salaries all over baseball, especially for established stars like Ty Cobb who felt they were being short-changed. During the two-year trade war, player salaries jumped as much as 50 percent. Many players knew the Federal League threat would be short lived and simply used negotiations with the Federals as leverage with their existing Major League club.[49] The Federals made a big dent among the ranks of more talented Minor League clubs, a move that also played into American and National League hands. The Minor Leagues had no alternative other than to turn to the American and National Leagues for protection, a move that pushed the Minors even further into the National Agreement fold. With the Minor Leagues thus committed to the National Agreement, the Federals had even less access to the Minor League talent stockpile.

The Federals Sue for Relief

Cut off in their efforts to lure star talent to their new enterprise, the Federals struggled at the gate. In the end, it was the battle for ticket revenue that mattered most. As the 1914 season drew to a close, the Federals were close to financial ruin. The National Agreement magnates reacted accordingly. No longer concerned about the Federal League as a legitimate financial threat, the owners immediately dealt sternly with the Fraternity. The magnates refused to consider any new Fraternity requests and backed off several of the concessions granted prior to the 1914 season. The Federals, now more convinced than ever that the National Agreement constituted a massive baseball trust, asked for a nine-count federal injunction against the National and American Leagues.[50] They filed their request with the federal court and it was heard by Judge Kennesaw "Mountain" Landis, who was well known as a trustbuster. Landis was the man who fined Standard Oil $29 million in 1907 for a host of antitrust violations. The Federal League owners, optimistic about their chances of relief from Landis, failed to consider the fact that he was also a huge baseball fan and viewed the game as an important national institution.[51]

There was much hue and cry, especially in the baseball press, in response to the Federals' suit. After experiencing three trade wars in the previous twenty-five years, most sportswriters accepted the truth as proclaimed by the owners: Major League Baseball was not a trust. It was a unique business in which all operators must share a common understanding and honor each other's contracts. "The player's contract, the main point assaulted in the suit, is the foundation of base ball," sportswriters argued. "Without it all would be chaos."[52] With Landis on the bench and the baseball press in their corner, the magnates had little to fear from the Federals' suit. Most importantly for the owners, belief in the unique nature of the business of baseball and the necessity of the reserve clause was now firmly entrenched in the hearts and minds of the baseball public.

Landis delayed judgment, hoping that the two sides would eventually reach a settlement. His hopes were realized. By the end of the 1915 season, nearly every magnate was clamoring for peace. The American and National Leagues effectively bought out the remaining Federal League magnates for $600,000. As was the case with the Players League owners in 1890, many of the Federal League magnates received stock in the surviving Major League franchises. Most of the owners left out of the settlement were able to recoup their losses by selling players back to the American and National League clubs. The one exception to this was the ownership group of the Federal League's club in Baltimore; they were left with nothing but shares of stock in a now worthless enterprise. For his part in all of these dealings, Landis received favorable reviews from league leadership, reviews that no doubt played a role in his ascension to the commissionership of Major League Baseball in 1921.[53]

The Gift of Monopoly: The 1922 Antitrust Exemption

Baltimore's Federal League magnates decided to pursue continued legal action in an attempt to regain their losses from the 1915 baseball war. The end result of their suit was the greatest gift the American and National League owners could wish for: a federal antitrust exemption for Major League Baseball. In their suit, the Baltimore Federals alleged that the rival leagues had conspired to ruin the Federal League, in violation of the nation's antitrust laws. The trial court ruled in favor of the Baltimore club and awarded $80,000 in damages, an amount that automatically tripled to $240,000 under the provisions of anti-trust laws. Attorneys for the Baltimore club used language very much in concert with that used by Brotherhood members more than thirty years earlier. They declared that baseball magnates were "highwaymen" who "bought and sold players like chattels and slaves." They argued that this case was about more than the Baltimore club's specific grievances, it was about whether or not organized baseball was in fact "above the law."[54]

George Wharton Pepper, lead counsel for the National League, relied on appeals to public emotion. He decried the Baltimore suit as an attempt to bring ruin to baseball by forcing cancellation of the World Series. Pepper's strategy, throughout the appeals process, was to make baseball out to be a completely local enter-prise, actually quite small in nature. In the process of doing so, he worked to erase ties between Major League clubs and their Minor League counterparts. His was an effort to portray each Major League club as a small, local operation with merely forty employees (the players) instead of a national organization with subsidiaries (Minor League clubs) in several states. The appeals court ultimately agreed with Pepper. It ruled that baseball was not subject to federal antitrust laws, reversing the original trial court's decision.[55]

The case made its way to the Supreme Court, where Oliver Wendell Holmes wrote on behalf of a unanimous court that Major League Baseball was essentially a collection of small, local businesses that put on exhibitions of baseball. It was not, in the view of the court, interstate commerce:

> The business is giving exhibitions of base ball, which are purely state affairs. It is true that in order to attain for these exhibitions the great popularity that they have achieved, competitions must be arranged between clubs from different cities and States. But the fact that in order to give the exhibitions the Leagues must induce free persons to cross state lines and must arrange and pay for their doing so is not enough to change the character of the

business. According to the distinction insisted upon in Hooper v. California . . . the transport is a mere incident, not the essential thing. That to which it is incident, the exhibition, although made for money would not be called trade of commerce in the commonly accepted use of those words. As it is put by defendant, personal effort, not related to production, is not a subject of commerce.[56]

The court ruled that transporting players across state lines was incidental to the local nature of the exhibition. Moreover, antitrust law of the day declared monopolies to be illegal only if they dealt with the manufacture, transportation, mining, or sale of commodities. Labor was not considered to be a commodity or an article of commerce.[57] This ruling was a product of the age just prior to the dawn of modern media and entertainment. The court failed to see a baseball game as a "production" actually consumed by the fans, or customers, of Major League Baseball. The Supreme Court's finding may seem somewhat questionable now; especially in a media age when writers and producers wrangle over Internet-based broadcast royalties. In the early 1920s, however, the scope of the definition of interstate commerce was much narrower than in the years following the Depression. The court's ruling was in line with other rulings made during this period. The decision paved the way for a virtually unrestricted monopoly on the business of Major League Baseball. Even when the issue was revisited in 1953 and 1972, the court ultimately ruled that while the decision was an anomaly, it would not overturn it. These decisions left it to Congress to legislate otherwise, and despite many committee hearings and investigations in the intervening period, baseball still enjoys this exemption today. This special treatment remains in place because such a large share of the baseball public revels in baseball's unique position in our society and fears large structural changes that might weaken the game's status in the nation's consciousness.

The years between 1891 and 1922 were marked by two baseball trade wars and as many attempts at collective action by the players. In each situation the players were unable to find the solidarity and public support they needed to overcome owner attempts to co-opt their organizations. They remained cautious in the face of owner intimidation. Lacking solidarity and fearful of a backlash in public opinion, they assumed a careful, cooperative stance in their dealings with the magnates. This approach failed. The players were unable to take advantage of these tumultuous times and found themselves just as tightly controlled by the magnates in 1922 as they had been in 1891. If anything, conditions for the players had become even more desperate. The antitrust exemption gave the American and National Leagues unprecedented hegemony over the business of baseball.

3

1946, a Year of Postwar Tumult

The two decades following the antitrust exemption are widely thought of as the first golden age of Major League Baseball. The 1920s saw the birth of the Yankee Dynasty, which began with New York's acquisition of slugging outfielder/pitcher Babe Ruth from the Boston Red Sox. Public interest in the game remained high throughout the 1930s, even though the Great Depression took its economic toll. The Yankees remained strong and were joined by a host of other well-known clubs. Mickey Cochrane's Detroit Tigers, Charlie Grimm's Chicago Cubs, Connie Mack's Philadelphia Athletics, and Dizzy Dean's "Gas House Gang" Cardinals all helped make this a memorable and colorful era in baseball history. Baseball's success in this era was due in large part to unprecedented roster stability, made possible by the antitrust exemption, which gave owners near-total control over their players while all but eliminating the threat of further trade wars. Players on successful teams often stayed in one place for the length of their careers, building a comfortable familiarity with their hometown fans and reinforcing the notion that players belonged to a team, and its city, for life.

The magnates used this period to forge an increasingly paternalistic relationship with the players, or "their boys." This paternalism took a variety of forms, ranging from owner efforts to mold their players' off-field behavior through fines and public scolding to the magnates' insistence that the complex financial dealings of Major League Baseball were beyond the understanding of mere ballplayers. Owners used a variety of tactics to mislead their players regarding the salary and benefits received by their peers, a masterstroke designed to keep the players at odds with one another. As a result, players were reluctant to share key financial data among themselves and remained further away from any sort of collective labor action. At the slightest whiff of player unrest, Major League magnates used the reserve clause and the threat of blacklisting to keep their "boys" in line. This was the nature of the player-owner relationship at midcentury.

U.S. entry into World War II tore apart Major League Baseball, along with all the other trappings of "normal" American life. The war placed nearly all able-bodied young men into the service of their country, drawing the vast majority of baseball's talented young players into the armed services. Some of the most notable players in the history of the game, Hall of Famers like Ted Williams, Joe DiMaggio and Bob Feller, left to fight abroad. The men available to play were either too old for service or otherwise deemed unfit. Baseball's popularity was put on hold, as the quality of play on the field took a significant turn for the worse. As a result, these wartime years are still treated as something of an oddity in the history of the game.

After the war's end in 1945, baseball faced a significant period of readjustment in 1946. During the war, while many of their heroes were fighting overseas, baseball fans stayed home rather than head out to the park to watch what many considered to be an inferior brand of ball. Most teams, including the mighty Yankees, drew less than six hundred thousand fans a year, or an average of less than ten thousand per game. Some teams drew as little as three thousand fans per contest, a figure that represented a significant decline in attendance, even from the tough years of the Great Depression.[1] Teams and fans eagerly anticipated the return of their prewar heroes, as well as the discovery of many new, exciting, younger players, forced by the war to put their baseball aspirations on hold. This anticipation, though, was accompanied by a tinge of justifiable uncertainty regarding the specific ways that this new player labor surplus would sort itself out. The magnates, for their part, began to make very public warnings about their need to resist inflationary pressures and keep player salaries low. Otherwise, the owners argued, they would be forced to institute higher ticket prices in order to recoup skyrocketing payroll costs.[2] League management rarely missed an opportunity to try to persuade fans that one likely outcome of higher salaries would be higher ticket prices.

Baseball, as it turned out, was little different from the many other industries that went through a period of labor turmoil in the years immediately following World War II.[3] Within five months of v-j Day, changes in the baseball labor market brought two distinctive challenges to the business of baseball. One came in the form of international raids on Major League rosters; the second was the most successful player unionization campaign since the days of the Brotherhood more than fifty years earlier.

Baseball Banditos: The Pasquel Brothers and the Mexican League

The first challenge came from south of the border. Five Mexican baseball magnates, the Pasquel brothers, mounted their own assault on the reserve clause and Major League rosters. The Mexican professional league was a long-established haven for the best Latin American players as well as some of the biggest stars of the American Negro Leagues. Founded in 1924, the Mexican League boasted teams in eight cities and counted among its owners some of Mexico's wealthiest entrepreneurs. The Pasquel brothers, perhaps the most influential of these men, recognized the American baseball labor surplus as an opportunity to draw some of the most recognizable big-league stars south of the border. The Pasquels believed the acquisition of American talent could be the first in a series of moves designed to put the Mexican League on par with the American Major Leagues.

The Pasquels began aggressively pursuing some of the more prominent stars from baseball's largest markets during the late winter and early spring of 1946. The brothers intentionally targeted players who felt especially underpaid, exploited, or just underappreciated by their respective Major League clubs. In a time full of concerns over postwar inflation and housing shortages, players' salaries often failed to keep pace with living expenses. In many cases, Major League players took second jobs in factories and filling stations during the off-season in order to make ends meet. The Pasquels knew their target market well. In addition to offering these disgruntled players significant pay raises, they addressed players' family concerns by willingly subsidizing living and travel expenses and securing housing in Mexico. When questioned about the sincerity of their long-term commitment to these contracts, the Pasquels offered to pay the money for the entire length of a contract up front, placing it in an escrow account. In this way the Pasquel brothers demonstrated both a fair amount of media savvy and a keen understanding of the weaknesses of the player-management relationship in Major League Baseball. Their actions paid off in the American baseball press, which enthusiastically covered the Mexican League's recruiting efforts right from the start.[4]

The Pasquels' raids wrought havoc with the plans of American magnates, some of whom were eager to use the postwar talent surplus to drive player salaries down further, all while realizing a resurgence of ticket revenues from fans eager to see their heroes retake the field. The Pasquels also raised the hopes of established players, many of whom were anxious about their postwar status, and willing to explore alternatives. The Pasquels and the Mexican League provided just that, and for the first time since the rise of the Federal League, many star players happily found themselves the targets of a bidding war.

The Pasquels started with midlevel talents like Danny Gardella, Sal Maglie, and Luis Olmo. Throughout the spring of 1946, the baseball public was gearing up for a return of their national pastime in its purest form, and news of the Pasquels' attempts to sign these players shocked the baseball public. The American magnates felt compelled to respond. The Giants' Mel Ott told the *New York Times*, "The time has passed when we have to worry about players like that [Gardella and the other defectors]. It was different in the days [during the war] when we often didn't know when we would be able to put nine men on the field, but now we have a camp full of fine players, and I don't think any of the others will be missed."[5] The Dodgers' Branch Rickey pinned the problem on the defectors' immaturity, impulsiveness, and greed.[6] Major League management fashioned a bold "good riddance" stance but in fact was very nervous about the public exposure the Pasquels' raids gave to the manner in which many Major League Baseball players were treated. The American magnates knew they could little afford to have some of their more restrictive labor practices exposed at a time when union membership across the United States was booming and when so many members of the baseball public were increasingly aware of the contractual conditions imposed on professional ballplayers.

The Pasquels continued to make noise throughout the spring. They signed the beloved Dodgers catcher Mickey Owen and the star St. Louis Browns shortstop Vernon Stephens. Owen's signing further exposed the management practices of the Dodgers, perhaps the most controlling club in baseball under the guidance of Branch Rickey, while Stephens's circumstances highlighted the tightfisted ways of the Browns, a team that had difficulty generating income because it competed for ticket revenue in St. Louis with a very successful Cardinals franchise. Mexican League management clearly reveled in the publicity won for their cause; they made runs at signing top American stars like Ted Williams and Bob Feller, even though they knew they had little chance for success. They loved exposing the hypocrisy of Major League magnates and further tweaked Rickey's nose by going after Jackie Robinson, a player Rickey had recently lured away from his Negro League club, the Kansas City Monarchs. The Pasquels went right for the jugular, portraying Rickey as a thief who criticized others for committing the same crime. The Pasquels proved expert at exploiting weaknesses in the Major League player-owner relationship. American owners demanded loyalty yet offered limited job security. They claimed to run the game with an eye to the best interests of the players and the public but sought to limit salaries and maximize profits at every turn, all within the framework of a legal monopoly. The Pasquels knew how badly many American owners wanted to keep these practices out of the public eye, and they also understood the enormous public reaction they could generate with their well-publicized raids. By the time the raids had fully run their course, the "baseball banditos" had put on quite a demonstration regarding the significance of public favor in the player-management relationship.

The Mexican League raids ultimately flamed out, especially after the Pasquels' cousin, Miguel Aleman, won the Mexican presidency in July. As it turned out, the Pasquels' primary goal was to increase Aleman's popularity by weakening the uniquely American institution of Major League Baseball. Jorge Pasquel not only helped win the Mexican presidency for his cousin, he exposed the underbelly of the business of baseball. His efforts to raid American rosters exposed many of the Major League's monopolistic practices, from the restrictions of the reserve clause to the use of punitive blacklists. As a result, many observers in the United States took note of the one-sided relationship between players and management. This increased public awareness paid off for the players, as they ultimately received the first serious management concessions of any kind since Ban Johnson founded the American League in 1900.

The American Baseball Guild

The Mexican League's challenge was not the American magnates' only source of labor anxiety at the start of the 1946 season. In mid-April, right at the peak of tensions with the Mexican League, labor organizer Robert Murphy announced the formation of the American Baseball Guild. Like the craftsmen of the Middle Ages before them, and more recently their contemporaries in the Screen Actors and Newspaper Guilds, baseball players now had a craft union designed to represent their interests in the complex postwar labor market. Murphy, a former Harvard athlete and examiner for the National Labor Relations Board, believed his organization stood poised to bring about permanent change in the business of professional baseball. "Organized baseball no longer can rule with the iron hand of an absolute dictator," Murphy argued. "Now it must deal with organized baseball players in the form of the American Baseball Guild. The Guild's purpose is to right the injustices of professional baseball and to give a square deal to the players, the men who make possible big dividends and high salaries for stockholders and club executives."[7] Murphy's statement, more than a half century after the failure of the Players League, echoed many of the themes and ideas so dear to the heart of John Montgomery Ward and the leadership of the Brotherhood of Professional Baseball Players. Murphy firmly believed that the primary value of the game lay in the players' on-field labors, not in the management and organizational skills of the ownership and front office staff. While Murphy's efforts to form a union ultimately proved unsuccessful, the guild's story does much to strengthen our understanding of midcentury relations between players and owners and the challenges facing ballplayers as they sought to create a union of their own.

Like the Pasquels, Murphy understood the importance of making a big public splash, and he expressed great optimism regarding the guild's chances for success. He claimed that a majority of the players from three or four clubs already belonged to his organization. He worked diligently to cast club ownership in a sinister light and to stop the magnates short in their efforts to use their paternalistic relationship with the players to co-opt the Baseball Guild. On April 18, fearful that the owners would use the blacklist and the reserve clause to put a damper on player militancy, Murphy charged several clubs with intimidation tactics in violation of the Wagner Act. He issued a public reminder to club management that it was illegal to discuss issues related to the formation of a union with potential union members. Like many organizers of his era, Murphy wanted to assure his workers' right to free speech on all workplace matters. Murphy's approach signaled a new, more militant and formal tack on behalf of the players. For perhaps the first time, ballplayers had a labor organizer who made no bones about his efforts to create a serious craft guild–style union for professional ballplayers. Murphy believed the time had come for players to shed the bonds of paternalism and assert themselves in the same way as workers in other industries.

As was the case with many of his predecessors in the baseball labor movement, Murphy attempted to gain greater public support through the press. Public support in the press was always critical to the success of a baseball players' union, but it was especially important during the years of postwar transition, when capital would move to put labor "back in line." Murphy endeavored to build up the guild's prospects in the public eye by claiming he understood the reasons why Major League management was so concerned. He speculated that national organizations such as the AFL and CIO were happy to have professional baseball players considering joining their ranks, and he understood why magnates would naturally fear the collective strength of these groups. Murphy continued to claim that some of the game's most prominent players belonged to the guild. Such threats compounded the worries of clubs everywhere, which were busily trying to keep their rosters intact in the face of the Mexican threat. Murphy's claims led to a great deal of speculation, as he declined to identify specific players when pressed, saying, "Naturally I can't say at the moment what players are affiliated with the Guild, you know as well as I do where they'd land—in Peoria in about three hours."[8] This argument made a certain amount of sense but also left the guild organizer open to speculation that his efforts were more bluster than substance.

Murphy wanted to put the magnates on notice that the Baseball Guild was watching out for players who might be demoted to the Minor Leagues as reprisal for their union involvement. This was a real fear for the guild, especially in a workplace environment such as baseball's, in which talent evaluation involved a fair amount of subjectivity. A club could easily claim that a player did not fit into its "immediate plans" and ship him back to the Minors. Such a move was not just a blow to the player's immediate prospects, it also cost the player one of his precious "options," or opportunities to move between the Major and Minor

73

Leagues. A player without any remaining options could play only at the Major League level; otherwise his playing days were over.

These options, therefore, were extremely dear to the players. If a wasted option was not enough of a threat, players knew that banishment to the Minors could mean they might never fulfill their dreams of playing Major League Baseball. The owners proved eager to use the abundance of talented young players in the Minor Leagues as leverage against Major League veterans who might be tempted to form a union. This, of course, was especially true in light of the influx of new baseball talent as young men returned from military service. As was the case with the Mexican League defections and the formation of the Players League, baseball's owners had significant leverage on their side. If he so desired, an owner could easily play on the fear shared by many existing stars that their club could easily replace them with talented younger players. Veteran players, who had been rookies themselves in the years before the war, knew just how quickly the public could forget about their old favorites, making them reluctant to risk public disfavor by leaving for Mexico or vocally supporting the Baseball Guild.

Murphy's attempts to mount a successful public relations campaign met with a fair amount of backlash in the baseball press. Typical were the comments of *Los Angeles Herald* columnist Vincent Flaherty: "$40,000 players cannot be expected to up and walk out simply because a mediocre performer wants $10,000. Professional baseball is too individualized for that. The St. Louis Cardinals cannot afford to fork over salaries comparable to the New York Yankees. Moreover, baseball is conducted upon a much too competitive basis to lend itself to competitive organization. It is . . . a constant battle for survival among players—aging and fading stars fighting to stave off the rush of up and coming rookies."[9] Flaherty's writing reflects the widely held view among baseball traditionalists that unionism was solely suited for large industry. He also clearly expresses what, by 1946, the common wisdom held to be the case regarding the mix of unions and baseball: in the end, self-interest would prevent the players from effective collective action. H. G. Salsinger of the *Detroit Free Press* reinforced this notion: "Baseball is a profession and not a trade. That is one reason why a players' union is impractical. No two ball players are of precisely the same ability, therefore it is impossible to set a maximum wage scale. . . . Would they want [Tigers First Baseman] Hank Greenberg to slash his salary to strike an average for first basemen, or would they demand that all first basemen receive the same pay?"[10] Such a view perpetuated the image of players as selfish and childish, men badly in need of paternal guidance from the magnates. Changing this perception continued to present a major challenge for ballplayers interested in moving forward with collective action.

Murphy and the Baseball Guild did not wait long before bringing their first set of specific charges against a Major League club. Just ten days after going public with his plans for the guild, the labor organizer filed unfair labor practice charges against Washington Senators owner Clark Griffith. Murphy claimed Griffith "did counsel and urge the players against joining the guild; and, further, did make statements calculated to intimidate and coerce the players on the club from exercising their rights to self organization."[11] Murphy was clearly a product of the Depression-era school of labor relations. He filled his arguments with references to the National Labor Relations Act, management intimidation, and the workers' right to organize.[12] Griffith's response, on the other hand, was typical of baseball owners dating back to the days of the Players League. Griffith argued that the formation of a union threatened to destroy the reserve clause, without which professional baseball would cease to exist. He further claimed that Murphy's charges were baseless. The owner said he intended his statements regarding the guild to be a public response to its proposals, not a specific statement of instruction to the players on his club. Griffith, the former vice president of the Players Protective Association and a recruiter for Ban Johnson's American League, now fully embraced the role of small-market magnate and assumed that any structural changes to the game would render him unable to keep the Senators financially afloat.

Unfortunately for Murphy, the Baltimore Labor Relations Board rewarded Griffith's faith in the power of the antitrust exemption and refused to hear the guild's complaint.[13]

Undeterred, Murphy and the guild continued to press forward by announcing an eight-point program. The primary provisions of this program were a minimum player salary of $7,500 and the agreement that there would be no maximum limit on player salaries, whether official or unofficial.[14] This first point alone set the guild apart from earlier players' unions in that it pushed directly for specific improvements to player salaries. Other provisions of the plan also reflected longtime concerns of Major League Baseball players. Any player sold to another club would personally receive 50 percent of his sales price. Players also demanded the right to salary arbitration, greater freedom of contract, increased provisions for performance bonuses, and medical insurance policies. In return, they promised the peaceful resolution of all labor disputes and a no-strike guarantee once the league officially recognized the guild. The guild believed that this program, by providing a "floor" for compensation and benefits without setting a ceiling, would help lure younger players into the fold without alienating veteran star players, who were likely to oppose unionization on the grounds that the movement limited player salaries on the top end. This strategy proved very effective for Marvin Miller twenty years later, but it would prove to be a tough sell for Robert Murphy in the summer of 1946. The guild's goals were similar to those of traditional unions across the nation in the postwar years, but average baseball fans would need to have these kinds of benefits in hand themselves before they would support professional ballplayers in their push to make similar gains.

Murphy continued to prove he was a man prepared to strike quickly. He announced on May 15 that "an overwhelming majority" of the players with the Pittsburgh Pirates were in the guild, making it the first team in which players were prepared to collectively bargain with their management. Murphy deliberately chose Pittsburgh for his opening campaign. He understood that a history of poor treatment by Pirates management made the Pirates players a likely target for organization. Additionally, he hoped for greater public support in Pittsburgh, as it was "a highly unionized city covered by both National and State Labor Relations Acts."[15] Murphy knew that a group of players in a labor-friendly city would be much easier to guide through the organization process than those who faced stiff opposition from fans in less labor friendly cities.

The guild's leader believed that a club-by-club approach was more workable than trying to gain a majority within the total membership of the players. He believed success with one club would open the door to organizing other clubs, and Pittsburgh was a good place to start because the Pirates did not have as many highly paid stars as teams like the Tigers, Yankees, and Red Sox. These teams, Murphy conceded, were more resistant to unionism because their higher-salaried players worked to keep unionism out of their clubhouses. Local fans had strong connections to these beloved stars, and dueling with them in the court of public opinion was not a worthwhile enterprise for the guild. Murphy formally informed Pirates management that the guild now served as the collective bargaining agent for all Pirates players and hoped that the union-friendly location and relatively small number of star players in Pittsburgh would work to his advantage.[16]

Pirates president William Benswanger initially proved more diplomatic in his dealings with the guild than some of his peers, like Clark Griffith. Benswanger agreed to begin talks with the players, providing they met the criteria for official certification. Murphy and the Pirates players quickly announced some rela-tively modest goals for the upcoming negotiations. In fact, many of the players' requests actually fell well short of the guild's eight-point program.[17] The Pirates players hoped for a $6,000 minimum player salary, management contributions to a player pension program, basic disability insurance in case of accident, and a small percentage of the proceeds of player sales. The fig-ure mentioned in the New York Times was 10 percent, so that a player sold for $10,000 would receive $1,000 in exchange for the inconvenience of being sold on the open market.[18] These demands offer a number of valuable insights into the emerging labor consciousness of Major League Baseball players. The Pirates players recognized baseball's potential profitability in a prosperous postwar economy and sought to increase their personal gain from this likely boom. Additionally, these men were wary of the profound economic impact of a career-ending injury as well as the financial difficulties suffered by former players in their years after baseball. Finally, the players understood the importance of staking a claim to at least a small portion of their value as a commodity to the franchise. Much as the Populists paved the way for the Progressives by pushing their vision for reform out into the American discourse, the guild's efforts in Pittsburgh called the reasonable demands of ballplayers to the attention of the mainstream sports media at an important time in the development of postwar sports culture.

Pirates president Benswanger's cooperative mood did not last long. By late May it was clear that he hoped to use the certification issue as a way to get around dealing with the guild. The Pirates front office began to drag its feet in setting up a certification election. When Benswanger and Pirates attorney Seward French met with players as promised on June 5, they announced that the front office would entertain a certification election only at the completion of the 1946 season. Murphy was outraged by the request for a delay. He accused Benswanger and French of "just stalling until the end of the year when they know the players will all be home [spread out in their various hometowns across the country] and we [the Guild] can't reach them." French denied that the club was trying to stall the guild, claiming the delay was necessitated by three key questions: "Whether the Guild is an appropriate union, whether unions have an appropriate place in baseball, and settling conditions under which an election would be held."[19] French's comments demonstrate the mood of that portion of the public distrustful of unions in the postwar period. During 1945 and 1946, nearly every major industry experienced work stoppages driven largely by fear of inflationary pressures. French's remarks not only question the place of a players' union in baseball, they reflect the notion, shared by many, that perhaps unions had gained enough during the Depression and war years.

Murphy, who had been very diplomatic up to this point, decided to take off the proverbial gloves. He called French's remarks "talk and window dressing" and told reporters he was on his way to tell the Pirates players "just what kind of owners they'd got." The guild leader asserted that the players would be much happier, and would play better baseball, if the Pirates management allowed them to pursue the kind of representation they so badly wanted. Finally, in an obvious attempt to further frame the conflict in terms with which the working public would sympathize, Murphy began referring to the Pirates players as "the club" and Pirates management as "the company." This was a distinction clearly intended to remind the public that the value of baseball lay with the on-field efforts of the players, not with the financial backing and organizational skills of the capitalists. Much to Murphy's satisfaction, organized labor began rallying to the guild's cause. He won the support of the CIO's 210,000-member Steel City Industrial Union Council, whose regional director, Anthony Federoff, told Murphy, "No red-blooded American man or woman carrying a union card will go to a ball game while there is a strike of players."[20] This was music to Murphy's ears, but a very threatening tune to the baseball establishment. Comments like these threatened to scare off the type of fan who saw little place for militant labor action in the national pastime. Labor strife was one thing in the factory or the mill, quite another on the playing field.

Murphy's commitment to the cause and the CIO's backing were not enough to fully mobilize the Pirates players. On June 7 the players voted not to strike in response to Pirates management's attempts to avoid official certification of the guild. The final strike vote tallied twenty Pirates players in favor of striking, while sixteen voted against. This constituted a simple majority but fell short of the two-thirds necessary to approve a strike.

The vote, which took place at the end of a tense two-hour meeting held prior to a game with the New York Giants, received a great deal of media attention. The press emphasized the fact that Pirates management kept Murphy from attending the meeting, while a representative of the club's management was allowed to address the players prior to their vote. Regardless of this obvious breach of protocol, members of the baseball press saw the vote as a litmus test of player solidarity and willingness to sacrifice. Even in a time of great forward momentum for labor, most writers concluded that baseball players were incapable of meaningful collective action.

The failed vote dealt a harsh blow to the guild's forward momentum. Players acknowledged that a vast majority of them were indeed guild members who believed in Robert Murphy's abilities and intentions. But, despite their frustration with the ownership's stall tactics, they remained unwilling to take a step as "severe as a strike."[21] A common sentiment expressed by the players was that they did not want to take such a strong action against Pirates owner Benswanger, who the players agreed had always treated them well. It is also understandable that, as a small-market owner, Benswanger had a strong interest in maintaining the business status quo in Major League Baseball, especially given the widely held belief that the reserve clause was essential to competitive balance and even financial survival for clubs like the Pirates and Senators. Clearly Benswanger had successfully cultivated his players' loyalty over the years, to a point that may have bordered on dependency. Pirates players were taught to believe that all good things came from the owners and they should be grateful for any benefits that came their way. A prime example of this sort of thinking was Pirates pitcher Rip Sewell. An All-Star in 1943 and 1944, Sewell was one of the team's best pitchers. He proudly claimed almost total responsibility for turning the strike vote in management's favor. Sewell insisted on the requirement of a two-thirds majority as soon as Murphy began calling for a strike. He told his teammates he was "going out to pitch against the Giants whether you go out there with me or not." This threat, Sewell argued, was critical to gathering the votes needed to defeat the strike.

Sewell, a southerner from a nonunion background, maintained for many years, "I'm for unions where they belong, like coal miners and truckers and people who can't help themselves. In sports it [a union] will eliminate the competitive incentive." As to the type of association that might benefit the players the most, Sewell was all for what amounted to a company union: "You don't need some outside lawyer from Boston who doesn't know first base from right field organizing a union. Bring in a club lawyer to do it."[22] As a baseball man who firmly believed he had rightfully earned his place, Sewell, like many others, was distrustful of people outside the game. Interlopers like Murphy, to Sewell's way of thinking, simply did not understand the exceptional nature of the business of baseball.

This attitude was not uncommon throughout clubhouses across the Major Leagues. Much like the political bosses of the late nineteenth century, baseball owners worked in many ways to keep their players feeling dependent on their generosity and goodwill. Pirates infielder Lee Handley spoke to this sentiment: "The reason we didn't strike was that we hold President Bill Benswanger in high regard. His record in dealing with the players is so fine we fellows thought twice before doing anything so drastic."[23] Baseball owners built this blind player loyalty despite the business realities of Major League Baseball. In many cases, owners reaped huge financial profits and shared a relatively small percentage of these profits with their players.

Benswanger's public statements in the days immediately following the strike vote further reflect this paternalistic attitude. "I am awfully glad the boys acted the way they did tonight," he told the *New York Times*, "and I think it was to the best interest of the game and the public."[24] By referring to the players as "boys" and commending them for doing the right thing, Benswanger sounds a great deal like a concerned parent discussing his potentially rebellious children. Ultimately, the Pittsburg owner appeared to be a man relieved to hear that his children had again come around to understanding that "father knows best." The baseball public, especially eager for a return to normalcy after more than a decade of war and depression, appeared to share Benswanger's sense of relief.

The baseball press, already less than charitable in its discussions of the guild, became even more so in the aftermath of the Pirates players' failed strike vote. *Los Angeles Times* columnist Al Wolf raised questions about the impact of the guild on the "clean reputation" of the game, asking, "How long would the public continue to believe in baseball if such a players' agent [Murphy] lolled outside the jurisdictional limits of the game, where gamblers touts and racketeers roam unmolested?"[25] Wolf agreed with Rip Sewell. He called for the owners to establish what amounted to a company union, so that the public could still trust the integrity of the game. Along these same lines, Cincinnati general manager Warren Giles told the *Sporting News*, "If the time does come when the ball players . . . resort to collective bargaining which wrings a lot of concessions out of their employers, I believe baseball players will lose a lot of concessions which have become part of baseball tradition."[26] Giles was referring to interest-free salary advances and the fact that teams often paid for their players' health care, even when the clubs were not contractually required to do so. Giles's comments further reflect the patriarchal nature of the player-management relationship. The remarks demonstrate the techniques owners used to foster this relationship as well as the notion that the average player would be hopeless if he had to fend for himself and weigh the risks and rewards of union membership without the guidance and protection of the magnates.

The guild's inability to convince its Pittsburgh members to strike called into question the strength of Murphy's leadership. Opinions varied; however, most members of the baseball press agreed that Murphy's position was quite precarious and that the time was not right for unionization of the national pastime. Tommy Fitzgerald of the *Louisville (KY) Courier Journal* wrote, "I don't like the idea of sports being unionized. Sport is a pleasant escape from the cares of the business world. The farther sports stays away from the coldness of business, the more warmly it will be received." Despite Murphy's efforts to maintain the image of a strong guild presence among the Pirates, more than one player reported that the players were "saying good bye to the Guild, but not to some of its principles." Writing of the notion that outsiders would come in and threaten the structure of the game, *Detroit News* columnist H. G. Salsinger wrote, "Most of these strangers . . . are fellows who had nothing whatever to do with the development of the business or industry that they invade. They are rank outsiders who have decided to participate in the profits of the business."[27] In an industry where so many of the most influential insiders started out as players and later made the transition to management and even ownership, there was little trust in "meddling outsiders" like Murphy. Getting past the mistrust of outsiders would continue to prove a significant obstacle to player unionization efforts over the twenty-five years to come.

The press acknowledged the challenges players faced, but it was obvious to them that an outside labor organizer like Murphy was not the answer. Pirates manager Frankie Frisch barred the press from his clubhouse in the wake of the strike vote. When the news spread that Murphy was next headed to Philadelphia to organize the Athletics, word came that the venerable Athletics owner Connie Mack, himself a former player who became a magnate during the late nineteenth century, had closed the Athletics clubhouse to all visitors.[28] Murphy promised to move on to New York instead of going to Philadelphia as planned, but in the wake of being essentially shut down by the Pirates ownership and forced off course by the Athletics, his guild's prospects were less than promising.

Murphy sought to regain some momentum by filing charges against the Pirates with the National Labor Relations Board on June 10. His petition charged the Pirates with replacing the guild with what was, in effect, the very kind of company union so favored by Rip Sewell and the baseball press. He argued that the

Pirates had violated the National Labor Relations Act by forcing players to deal with management through an informal players' committee instead of the guild. These actions, Murphy maintained, were a clear violation of the players' rights as protected by Section VII of the National Labor Relations Act. Murphy's attempts to rebuild momentum were short lived. Two days after he filed his petition the National Labor Relations Board ruled that professional baseball did not qualify as interstate commerce and therefore did not fall under board's jurisdiction. There was no escaping that the national board's decision was a clear blow to the guild.[29] Five days later the guild withdrew its National Labor Relations Board charges against the Pirates, and Murphy announced official plans to take up the guild's claims with the Pennsylvania Labor Relations Board (PLRB).[30] The Pennsylvania board rewarded Murphy for this move almost a month later, on July 16, when it agreed to hear the guild's charges against the Pirates.[31]

The Pirates' response to the guild's charges is indicative of how firmly team executives believed in the power of baseball's past antitrust exemptions. Pirates attorney Seward French urged the PLRB to hold an immediate hearing to determine the board's jurisdiction in the Pirates case. French held fast to the idea that baseball was not everyday interstate commerce but instead a more sacred national pastime. He based his argument on the idea that baseball relied on small groups of highly skilled workers, not large masses of semiskilled workers like the steel industry or automakers. Therefore, French argued, baseball could ill afford to have any discussion of industrial-style unionism within its player ranks.[32] French further built his argument around the idea that the law establishing the PLRB was intended to deal with "sweatshops and industrial unrest and strife," "evils" that did not exist in baseball.[33]

To the great surprise of French and the Pirates, the jurisdiction argument failed them badly. The PLRB not only agreed to hear the case but went ahead and ordered a second certification election to take place on August 20. Murphy, who continued to claim that twenty-six of the thirty-one Pirates players held guild membership cards, was ecstatic about the upcoming election. The organizer used the decision to further cast the guild's certification struggle in the language of worker-capitalist struggle. Murphy declared, "The PLRB used good judgment in holding that baseball players, as any other working or professional men or women, have the right to organize" and went on to say that "I have felt all along that baseball is big business. Club owners have evidenced that baseball is a big business by their precipitate attempt to form company unions in their strenuous efforts to defeat the American Baseball Guild, a legitimate players' organization. This tactic has been used often by industry."[34]

Players' Relations and Pensions

Murphy was not referring solely to the Pirates' attempts to insert a "players' committee," which was essentially a company union, in the place of the guild. He spoke of the active steps taken by Major League Baseball's leadership at the All-Star Break in July to form an organized Player Relations Committee (PRC). This committee, formed by the owners, was intended to represent all owners and players in the drafting of the new Major League player contract. The owners agreed on six representatives to act on their behalf. The magnates indicated that they would accept nominations from each of the sixteen clubs for player representatives, although it was up to Commissioner Chandler to make the final decision on player representatives. The baseball press widely acknowledged that the formation of the players' committee was a direct move to counter the guild's unionization efforts. As the *Los Angeles Times* put it, "In all the moves made by the American Baseball Guild . . . the reserve clause was a target for attack. Most baseball and legal observers believed major league officials shied from a court showdown because of the doubtful legality of the reserve clause."[35] Baseball management did its best to put the most positive spin on the process, although Murphy was highly critical, insisting that the players' committee was nothing more than a "company union" and therefore was a violation of players' rights as protected by the National Labor Relations Act.[36]

Murphy attempted to further turn the press against management efforts to forestall the guild. He argued that management was seeking to institute a higher minimum salary and give the appearance of greater player representation only in an effort to avoid a court battle with the players over the reserve clause. Murphy claimed the concessions on salary and representation were essentially an admission that "the Guild is correct in its claim that the baseball contract is unfair to the players. It is obvious that the efforts of the Guild to correct injustices to the player are in a large measure responsible for this action by the baseball barons. This is proved by the fact that never before in the long history of baseball was such a measure suggested by the owners." Murphy emphasized the fact that two concessions the owners were willing to discuss, a minimum salary and the idea that a player would receive a percentage of his sale price, were key planks in the guild's platform. Additionally, Murphy tried to raise public suspicion about the owners' lack of willingness to deal with the guild while they were proclaiming to be in a great hurry to consult with an owner-dominated players' committee.

Larry MacPhail, president of the New York Yankees and the owner-appointed chair of the joint player-management committee, told reporters that "from the beginning [the owners] were unanimous in the opinion that the players should have representation on all matters pertaining to players. In this way we believe the grievances voiced by the players from time to time could be easily satisfied and there would be no need for unionization."[37] MacPhail expressed confidence that what the players wanted was representation, a shift in tone perhaps designed to resonate with a public increasingly open to the importance of workplace representation for workers but still somewhat skeptical regarding unionization in industries such as Major League Baseball. MacPhail spoke in terms of a greater baseball community, a wise management move when it came time to assuage the players' fears and assure them they had an equal stake in the game. He also knew how to strum the self-reliant "Yankee Heartstrings" of the game's traditions. "I doubt the players ever wanted a union anyway. The average player is an individualist who wants to handle his own business."[38] MacPhail's comments called to mind the way that National League owners of the 1880s described their relationships with the players as a baseball community, not a contentious player-management relationship. He cast the American Baseball Guild, much like the Brotherhood of Professional Baseball players, as a disruptive outside force determined to break up the harmony of Major League Baseball, even though this was perhaps a false harmony, given its basis in the reserve clause and baseball's antitrust exemption.

It was not long before the owners' moves toward compromise had the intended effect. Many players expressed their satisfaction with the formation of the players' committee and seemed drawn to the safety and nonconfrontational setup proposed by league management, even though it clearly deprived them of a great deal of power at the bargaining table.[39] The players set themselves back further by choosing largely veteran players to represent their interests. The magnates had to be pleased that among those chosen were Rip Sewell and Lee Handley, men who had played key roles in heading off the Pittsburgh strike threat little more than a month earlier. The National League clubs opted to send two men each instead of the initially agreed upon single representative from each club. Some clubs, quiet during the Pirates' run toward guild certification, now eagerly joined the discussion with the owners' "permission." The Phillies were among the teams that presented an entire "platform": a $5,000 minimum salary, a sliding compensation scale for players who were sold or traded to another club, and full compensation for spring training expenses, including a five-dollar per diem to cover expenses beyond room, board, valet service, and laundry. The most noteworthy part of the Phillies' plan was its pension proposal. The Phillies called for regular contributions from each player, to be matched by the owners. All players with at least ten years of big league experience would be eligible to receive pension benefits under the Philadelphia plan.[40]

The proposed pension plan captured the imagination of the players, chief among them Marty Marion, shortstop of the St. Louis Cardinals. He proposed what became known as the Marion Plan. Marion built his plan around contributions by the players and the owners, as well as monies from the All-Star Game, the World Series radio broadcast rights, and a series of eight inter-league games.[41] Marion calculated that in ten years the fund would reach $4 million and would be ready to start paying benefits to players with at least five years of big league experience once they reached forty-five years of age. In terms of actual benefits, the payouts were modest, which says a great deal about ballplayers' expectations for their lives after the game. Players with at least five years of experience were to receive $50 monthly, and a player with at least ten years of experience would receive $100 monthly. The great fear for many of these men was that they might end up indigent and humiliated after spending the most productive years of their lives entertaining the public by playing a "boy's game." Marion expressed confidence that the pension issue was such a large player concern that its resolution would be a huge step toward stopping the exodus of talented veterans jumping ship in order to win big Mexican League contracts in the final years of their playing careers.

Marion's proposal drew a great deal of attention from the national sports media and effectively brought the pension discussion to the fore.[42] The pension issue was a great fit for the age; pensions were at the forefront of national labor relations during this time. Not long after 1946, unions such as the United Auto-workers staged massive campaigns to win pensions for their members. For the average player, the reality of being "too old to play but too young to retire" loomed on the horizon. Sentiments like these gave the pension issue great traction with an overwhelming majority of players. They understood that their most valuable skill set related to playing ball and lived in fear of a vastly diminished earning capacity once their playing days were over. Even staunch antiunion men like Rip Sewell were big proponents of a players' pension program in 1946.[43]

Marion was not the only player to take it upon himself to create a proposal. Within two weeks of the owners' announcement regarding the formation of the players' committee, several clubs had written and approved seven-point (or eight-point) programs of their own. Again, these bore a strong resemblance to the plan the American Baseball Guild had announced just a few months before. The Cleveland Indians called for a program identical to that of the guild, adding a request for the elimination of all restrictions on barnstorming and other off-season sports. The Indians also asked that players be allowed to take their salary over twelve months instead of only during the season. The Pirates, still in a holding pattern over the guild certification issue, called for a minimum salary of $7,500, a figure fully 50 percent higher than that proposed by most other clubs. The Bucs also demanded first-class travel throughout the season and an increase in the number of free game tickets allotted to each player.[44] By the time the owners and players began their meetings on July 29, four more teams had contributed their own plans to the debate. These players added concerns about locker-room conditions and called for an end to recalling the waiver list and a change in the definition of a "ten-year man" to allow that designation to be made once a player had signed to a contract for his tenth season.[45] Now that the owners had expressed openness to dialogue, these teams willingly put their demands, which were more than a bit bolder than the guild's original program, into the public eye. Such a brave public display seems to indicate that these men firmly believed that, because they had the magnates' permission, their new demands would not generate ill will among the baseball public. Given the similarity between the various players' proposals and the guild's original program, it appeared that the guild platform was on the right track but the players could not yet afford to use unionization as the path to achieving their goals.

Reaction in the press proved the players right. The *Sporting*

News headlines crowed, "Full Acceptance of Players' Demands Seen: All Points Viewed as Reasonable."[46] *New York Times* columnist John Drebinger wrote optimistically about the future of the proposed negotiating structure. Drebinger argued that it would set a wonderful example for workers and managers everywhere if baseball owners, with a monopolistic hold on their labor market, could reach a peaceful agreement with their laborers without any union involvement. Drebinger tipped his hat to Robert Murphy by acknowledging that none of this would be happening without the threat of unionization, and he posited that the new Player Relations Committee's structure would forever end the talk of unionization in baseball.[47]

The support of opinion makers like Drebinger was critical to the success of any effort to unionize the players. Like many columnists of the day, Drebinger often positioned himself as the voice of the fan. If he declared unions ill suited for the game of baseball, most fans would follow suit. One key obstacle to the acceptance of the union idea for men like Drebinger was their very narrow view of the role of unions. In the postwar context, they saw unions as large industrial organizations, designed to protect the rights of faceless, semiskilled masses. These writers had difficulty imagining that a craft guild of highly skilled workers might improve the lot of all players, from highly paid stars to rookies fresh from the Minor Leagues. Unions, in the minds of many, were great levelers. They were not the kinds of organizations that might help spur their individual members on to individual greatness. Baseball players needed to learn how to shift this public perception if they ever hoped to successfully organize an independent organization of their own.

For his part in all of this, baseball commissioner Happy Chandler seemed quite satisfied to play the role of the caring grandparent, scolding his children (the owners) for how they were treating his grandchildren (the players). Chandler, whether in response to the incursions made by the Mexican League onto Major League rosters or to the threat of unionization by the guild, pronounced his sympathies for the plight of the players and publicly supported calls for many of their demands. Chandler said, "I told the owners that they're going to make more money this year than at any time in the history of baseball and now's the time to give the men who play for them something which should have been granted long ago."[48] Chandler was wise to position himself as a man determined to acknowledge the wrongs of the past, knowing he needed to move baseball away from the types of conditions that might lead to unionization.

The PRC's actions reflected Chandler's attitude. The magnates rapidly made concessions on issues like the minimum salary, a five-dollar per diem during training camp, and modest total contributions of about $40,000 annually to the pension fund. It was the issues that remained out of the public discussion that were most telling. Players pushed hard for the modification of the reserve clause. They wanted improved severance pay and demanded that a player sold from one club to another be awarded a small percentage of his sales price. These issues stayed out of the owners' public discussions of their negotiations with the players. The owners seemed content to allow the press to cast these as "minor issues to be discussed," when in fact such changes would surely bring about major changes in the business of the game.[49]

The PRC's concessions on salary and the pension allowed the reserve clause to come through the tumultuous 1946 season unscathed. The *Sporting News* laid out the newly accepted truth:

> Without the reserve clause the business of baseball could not be conducted. Without it, some two or three wealthier clubs in each league would whack up the great players. The players recognize that the reserve clause is an instrument for the protection of themselves and the welfare of the game in its relationship to the fan. The customer would not take kindly to an annual peddling of services by the players, and fan allegiances under such a system would collapse.

The owners withstood major challenges, both external and internal, and were able to survive with strong public acceptance of the reserve clause intact. The men who once stood firmly, willing to form a union, the Pittsburgh Pirates, made the magnates' victory clear. On August 20 Murphy got the results of his long-awaited certification vote in Pittsburgh. In light of the PRC's concessions, only three Pirates voted to certify the guild. The editors of the *Sporting News* wrote, "Long live unionism in the factory, in the mill, in American industry. But in baseball, it is dead. It was killed by its own father, the Pittsburgh club." As to the reasons why Murphy failed, the editors responded with the common wisdom about unions in postwar America: "Murphy went headlong toward defeat with the belief that he could organize ballplayers as one would organize a machine shop or a cotton mill. He failed to take cognizance of the wide gradations in skill, and the tremendous variances in pay, in the major leagues."[50] These obstacles would have to wait for another time, and for a more skilled organizer who understood how to build public support for these more complex contractual issues and how to use that support to guarantee freedom of contract and the right to negotiate maximum individual compensation.

For the time being, the owners reaped the full public relations rewards from their push for a company union. They received glowing coverage for the successful completion of a labor accord that "met the challenge of unionism and Mexican League raids by complying fully with an unprecedented player demand for an improved contract and by authorizing player representation on baseball's governing body for the first time in history."[51] The final agreement included a minimum salary of $5,000, the equivalent of $58,014 in 2013 dollars, and a pension plan. It also modified the ten-day release clause to include improved severance pay, added a per diem to cover incidental player expenses during spring training, and extended the postseason barnstorming period from ten days to thirty. Publicly this played out as a huge victory for the players; in truth it may have been an even bigger win for the owners. In the postwar economic boom their revenues were skyrocketing, so financial concessions such as these were of little consequence. The magnates had successfully survived the first major push toward unionization in more than fifty years and a significant external threat from the Mexican League by giving in on a few financial issues. The magnates escaped with their complete shop floor control intact. The public weighed in to support the kind of financial gains that many workers sought in the postwar period, but that was clearly the extent to which the players were willing to push their luck in terms of public support.

These factors combined with postwar economic conditions to make Major League Baseball more profitable than ever before. Fans, deprived of the opportunity to watch many of the game's stars in action during the war, returned to Major League stadiums in record numbers, especially as the number of night games increased. The Cleveland Indians and New York Yankees broke the "magical" two million fan barrier in annual attendance repeatedly, representing a fourfold increase over wartime attendance. Enthusiastic bidding by prospective club owners, many of whom made their fortunes in wartime industries, drove franchise values to new heights.[52]

Led by Branch Rickey and the Brooklyn Dodgers, many teams put their newfound fortunes back into their baseball operations. Rickey's actions in the years immediately following the war foretold the future of the business of baseball in the postwar era. Rickey, a baseball icon and the architect of the famed St. Louis Cardinals Minor League system, established a new standard for the way a "farm system" operated and the manner in which teams stockpiled talent like assets. By the end of the 1946 season, Rickey had built a network of twenty-two Minor League affiliates for the Brooklyn club. This gave the Dodgers a total of more than four hundred players under contract, all of whom were essentially the property of the team. The Dodgers' Minor League network provided them with the largest pool of young talent anywhere in baseball. Other teams that wanted a chance to sign players out of the Dodgers' talent stockpile were forced to deal directly with Rickey, a man who had long ago earned a reputation as the shrewdest player personnel manager in the game.

Rickey's boldest move was to bring all of this talent under one roof every spring at a surplus naval base in Vero Beach, Florida, that he dubbed Dodgertown. Here Rickey oversaw the standardized training and development of all the players in the Dodger system. He was widely regarded as one of the best pure teachers of the game and was in the unique position of being able to enjoy the financial rewards of his teaching efforts. Rickey's contract was structured in such a way that he received a 10 percent commission on all player sales. This meant, for example, that when the Dodgers received more than $1.4 million in revenue from player sales between 1945 and 1948, Rickey's share amounted to a $140,000 bonus.[53] The growth of farm systems extended management control over the baseball workforce to unprecedented levels. Management hegemony would go virtually unchallenged until 1966, when shifting societal attitudes, along with new technology and revenue streams, would finally allow the players to make a successful move toward unionization.

4

The Birth of the MLBPA

It was not until the mid-1960s that Major League Baseball players successfully formed a craft union of their own. The emergence of this union, the Major League Baseball Players Association (MLBPA), came about almost as a delayed reaction to postwar prosperity. While union members in many other industries made substantial economic gains throughout the 1950s, Major League Baseball players failed to realize similar improvement in their pay and benefits. Baseball struggled economically as an industry throughout the postwar period, even though many consider this time the game's "golden age," an era that produced some of the game's greatest moments and most memorable players.[1] Despite the high quality of play on the field, attendance fell throughout the Major and Minor Leagues. The primary response of the magnates to this drop in revenues was a reversion to a more conservative financial mind-set. They sought first to control costs, and rather than seek out the new forms of revenue now possible in the rapidly expanding postwar economy, the owners remained focused on ticket revenues as their primary source of income, a belief rooted in the traditional notion that a team needed to be just successful or promising enough to sell tickets.

Baseball was still a fairly straightforward business in 1960. Teams generated the vast majority of their revenues from ticket sales, and a team that struggled on the field was likely to struggle at the ticket office. There were two established ways to remedy this situation: a club could build public interest by acquiring proven stars from another club, or it could bring up exciting young talent from its Minor League clubs. Both of these methods generated a great deal of involuntary player movement, a problem compounded by the fact that struggling teams looked to cut costs at midseason by releasing, selling, or trading expensive veteran players in favor of the much cheaper new talent available in their vast Minor League systems. By this time most Major League clubs subscribed to Branch Rickey's system of stockpiling players and standardizing training methods. Many clubs had as many as three hundred players under contract on their affiliated Minor League teams. Thanks to the Supreme Court's continued support of the reserve clause in the 1953 *Toolson* decision, baseball's owners maintained control over the fate of every player they held under contract.[2]

Television Enters the Picture

Perhaps the greatest example of the owners' inability to exploit new revenue opportunities in the postwar era was their collective mismanagement of television revenues. Television stations needed programming, and baseball's 154-game schedule offered low-cost programming in abundance. By the late 1950s, television executives were more than eager to broadcast more games. They realized the full potential of advertising revenues from baseball's important "male head of household" demographic. Baseball's magnates, on the other hand, were slow to realize the value of their product on television. Instead of understanding the huge marketing value of having more games on television, the owners believed televised baseball might keep fans at home, instead of bringing them out to the park. Therefore, many magnates remained fearful of overexposure on television and viewed televised games as the primary cause of falling attendance. The owners, of course, wanted fans to attend games in person and spend their hard-earned money on tickets and concessions. What the magnates failed to recognize was that exposure through television might actually bring more fans out to the park. They overlooked television's potential as a means of keeping treasured middle-class fans connected to their local teams, even as these fans left the city for the suburbs throughout the two decades following World War II. These suburban families had children, lots of them. They were baseball's next generation of fans, and television could have served to keep them connected, just as radio had done for their parent's generation.

The owners also underestimated the potential of broadcast licensing fees, the growth of which could more than make up for any ticket sales lost when fans stayed home and watched the game in their family rooms. Instead, baseball management held television responsible for the huge decline in ticket revenue at the Minor League level. For years, fans in more remote areas had rabidly followed their local Minor League clubs because they lived too far from a large city to experience big league games in person. Once Major League games hit the television airwaves, fans all over the country stayed home from the Minor League parks, in large part because they could watch big league stars from the comfort of their living rooms. The bottom line was that, instead of embracing television's potential to further embed baseball in the nation's social fabric, the owners reacted in trepidation, to the expense of all who might profit from the growing popularity of the game.

Examples of this misinterpretation of television's potential abound. In 1949 baseball commissioner Happy Chandler sold the rights to the World Series and All-Star Games to Gillette for just $1 million.[3] Gillette swiftly realized what a valuable commodity it had just acquired. It turned around and sold the rights to the National Broadcasting Company (NBC) for $4 million. Chandler's mishandling of the rights sale infuriated many owners and later cost him the commissionership, but even in his absence the owners did not fare much better.[4] Total baseball rights fees rose to just $1.2 million in 1950 and were only $3.3 million by 1960. Television boomed in the 1950s, and Major League Baseball missed out. Nearly 90 percent of all American households had at least one television set by 1960, a tenfold increase over 1950. In that time, the magnates realized less than a threefold increase in real television revenues, even though the number of games on the airwaves increased dramatically.[5]

Not only did the owners fail to understand the possibilities of expanded broadcast revenue, but they also failed to understand the importance of sharing this revenue equally between clubs. Sharing broadcast revenue was an easy road to assuring competitive balance between small-market clubs like the Cleveland Indians and large-market clubs like the New York Yankees. The owners, so quick to remind the public about the reserve clause's importance in maintaining competitive balance, completely overlooked the huge advantage a large-market team enjoyed when it sold local broadcast rights.[6] The distribution of television revenue favored large-market teams like the Yankees, who were in their heyday during the 1950s, thanks in part to more than $1 million the club received in annual television revenue, the majority of which came from its exclusive local rights in the New York market.[7]

Some baseball executives believed that the only helpful thing about television was that it provided them with an easy way to make their required contributions to the players' pension fund. In the mid-1950s, a small group of players, acting on behalf of a group they called the Major League Baseball Players Association, convinced the owners to commit 60 percent of World Series and All-Star Game broadcast revenue to the pension fund established in the 1946 agreement. This arrangement was extremely important to the players, as it provided them with a guaranteed source of pension funding. The magnates favored the use of broadcast income for the pension because it allowed them to make their contribution without losing the cost-certainty that many of them valued. Allocated as it was to the pension fund, this rising broadcast revenue did little to raise player salaries. Players actually suffered a decrease in real wages between 1950 and 1965, a period in which the average player salary increased a mere $2,500. Players making the minimum bore the brunt; the minimum player salary was set at $6,000 in 1954 and was just $7,000 well into the late 1960s.[8]

The owners' missteps in regard to television rights came at precisely the wrong time for the financial health of the game. The popularity of other professional sports, especially football and basketball, grew a great deal during the postwar period. Baseball remained the most popular, both in terms of number of spectators and total revenues, but its lead was quickly disappearing. The National Football League, in particular, boomed with the help of regular television exposure. While football magnates understood the need to make their product more "TV friendly," it would be quite some time before baseball owners realized that regular television exposure, especially for the game's biggest stars, would help expand the popularity of the game and, ultimately, their pocketbooks.

A Misfiring Cannon

The players did little to help themselves in this era; they suffered from a complete lack of militancy within their ranks, as well as an absence of leadership and direction for their new organization, the MLBPA. The players' sole focus during this time was securing the pension fund. In this regard, they were more than satisfied with the 60 percent contribution from World Series and All-Star broadcast revenue promised them in 1956. With the preservation of the pension as their primary concern, the players made a disastrous move in 1959. They brought Robert Cannon, a Milwaukee municipal judge, on board as association counsel. Cannon had family ties to baseball; his father, Ray Cannon, had long been a thorn in baseball's side. In his early days, Ray Cannon had attempted to form a players' union during the 1920s. Later he was a congressional New Dealer who tried to modify the game's antitrust status.

The younger Cannon steered clear of his father's more confrontational approach. Cannon was ambitious. He used his position as the MLBPA's legal counsel to curry favor with the owners, the same men who paid his retainer out of the players' pension fund. He hoped his obsequious approach to the owners would help him parlay his position as MLBPA counsel into the commissionership of the game. The owners enjoyed Cannon's approach immensely, as it left them with little to worry about in terms of adversarial player relations.[9] Cannon even went so far as to allow the owners to add eight games to the regular season, increasing it from 154 to 162 games in 1960. The magnates wanted more games as a simple way to guarantee more season-ticket revenue, but the move was extremely unpopular with the players because it represented a 5 percent increase in workload without any corresponding increase in salaries. The players' dissatisfaction did not blow back on Cannon, because the majority of players believed he was working hard to secure the pension. The judge convinced the players that friendly, nonconfrontational relations with the owners were in the best interests of both the players and the game. In this way, especially, Cannon fit the owners' specifications for the head of the MLBPA. He not only believed in the necessity of the reserve clause, he stood ready to nourish the paternalistic relationship between owners and players at every turn. The players were so immersed in this relationship themselves that they failed to recognize that Cannon was a woefully inadequate protector of players' rights. The judge's weaknesses became even more apparent when the business of baseball underwent a series of major changes in the mid-1960s.

Three key factors brought about a shift in baseball's "business as usual" approach during the mid-1960s. The first of these was that television revenues finally began to rise. The increase was significant enough that the magnates began looking for ways to break free from their commitment to contribute 60 percent of all broadcast revenues to the players' pension fund. The owners made a significant move in this direction in 1965, when the American Broadcasting Company (ABC) paid $5.7 million for the rights to broadcast a national *Game of the Week*."[ ] These rights fees had no connection to the World Series or the All-Star Game, which meant that these funds did nothing to increase the owners' mandatory pension contribution.

The second factor changing the game was a sea change in the makeup of baseball's ownership. During the mid-1960s, large business entities or individuals with extreme wealth purchased a number of clubs with a long history of family ownership. In 1965, for example, the Columbia Broadcasting System (CBS) purchased an 80 percent stake in the New York Yankees. This type of ownership change marked a major shift at the top of baseball's power structure. These larger, wealthier ownership groups were not necessarily motivated by a sense of civic pride or an undying love of the game. As a result, the relationship between owners and their public changed as the era of family ownership with strong community ties began to draw to a close. Many fans would no longer look at their team's owner as a lovable local patriarch, and they often became more demanding in terms of the quality of the product on the field. The final departure from "business as usual," and the one that created the greatest sense of urgency for players, was the fact that the pension agreement was set to expire in April 1967. With television rights fees increasing and the ownership dynamic shifting, players grew increasingly concerned over the possibility of facing a major setback in negotiations for the new pension agreement.

A Tenacious Pitching Rotation:
Bunning, Roberts, Koufax, and Drysdale Build Momentum for the MLBPA

In the midst of this environment, two of the game's best starting pitchers, Robin Roberts and Jim Bunning, rose to prominent leadership roles in the MLBPA. Completely understanding the time-sensitive nature of the soon-to-expire pension deal, Roberts and Bunning took a serious interest in building and securing the players' pension fund. While Roberts and Bunning were hardly labor agitators, they were well equipped for the task of setting the MLBPA on a new course. Roberts was widely acknowledged as having a better mind than many of the owners for the potential of new revenue streams. By the early 1960s, he had nearly twenty years of big league service under his belt. Several times in the course of his career, his team had exploited Roberts's ability to serve as a "workhorse." He was able to withstand the physical strain of pitching many games in a relatively short period of time.[10] Since the act of throwing a baseball is not a "natural" motion for the human body, pitching workhorses such as Roberts were a rare commodity. Roberts's career even included one stretch in which he pitched three games in five days, a practice unheard-of in today's game. Roberts's experiences with the stress and strain of a lengthy Major League career made him well aware of the need to take care of players in their lives after baseball. Bunning was less experienced than Roberts but still well into a distinguished Major League career of his own.[11] The two men enjoyed the respect of their teammates both on and off the field, making them well suited for leadership positions in the MLBPA.

Bunning and Roberts believed that significant portions of these new television and licensing revenues should be set aside to help build up the pension. They were confident that, with the right union leadership, the players could tap into these opportunities to strengthen the pension fund. The timing appeared right for a move toward greater collective action. With the civil rights movement in full swing and unions making large financial gains across the nation, it seemed change and progress was the new American way. Rights consciousness was on the rise across the nation, spilling over into even more traditional institutions like Major League Baseball. The players had reason to be confident that all kinds of fans, and especially those blue-collar fans who had realized large gains on issues such as pensions and health care in recent years, would fully support a unionized push for a stronger pension.

This became especially evident in late 1965, when the Los Angeles Dodgers' star pitchers Sandy Koufax and Don Drysdale decided to stage a collective holdout prior to the 1966 season. The actions of Koufax and Drysdale are extremely instructive for the business of baseball in 1966, as well as the ways players were subconsciously readying for collective action. Their holdout demonstrated a new peak in the level of player frustration with management's desire to minimize player salaries. Koufax and Drysdale were, without question, the two most dominant starting pitchers in the National League throughout the early 1960s. The Dodgers enjoyed a great deal of success during this period, success driven by a remarkable performance of their two star pitchers. Koufax and Drysdale started nearly half of all Dodger games and were so dominant that the Dodger offense usually needed to muster only two or three runs for the team to win. This was very important to Dodger management, as it meant the Dodgers did not have to go out and sign a lot of expensive offensive talent in order for the club to succeed.

By early 1966 the two players had tired of having management dictate terms, and even play them against each other, when they negotiated new contracts. They decided to hire a Hollywood agent and negotiate collectively, in the hope of forcing the Dodgers' hand. Coming off the Dodgers' championship 1965 season, in which Koufax made $85,000 and Drysdale $80,000, the pitchers demanded $175,000 each per year, for a guaranteed term of three years. The Dodgers felt the financial demands were stratospheric and absolutely refused to budge on the idea of granting anything more than a one-year contract. Their resistance was personified in Dodger owner Walter O'Malley, who, as the longtime owner of a very profitable large-market team, was a dominant force in the game. O'Malley was not likely to cave in the face of collective action, even if playing without Koufax and Drysdale proved disastrous for the Dodgers during the 1966 season. Both sides quickly proved intractable. To the pitchers, the urgency was real. Koufax knew his body was breaking down and would likely betray him before long. He required an extensive medical regimen, including cortisone shots, before and after he pitched. Time was short for him to cash in on his stellar career.

Initial reaction to the pitchers' demands was positive. *Los Angeles Times* columnist Sid Ziff wondered if it might be time for baseball's salary structure to come tumbling down, "especially in light of all the new TV revenue that is pouring in."[12] Dodgers management included many longtime baseball executives, a few had even been schooled in the business by the "Mahatma" himself, Branch Rickey. Dodger general manager

Buzzie Bavasi was one such man, and in the early days of the holdout he used all manner of time-tested management techniques designed to win public support, especially among the traditionalists. Bavasi attempted to counter public support for Koufax and Drysdale by claiming that their holdout would only serve to create resentment among their teammates. "The club sets aside X number of dollars for the players," Bavasi explained. "If a disproportionate amount went to two men it couldn't help but stir up resentment amongst the others. There is no way in the world the club could do what they want. I couldn't look the others in the face if I acquiesced to their demands."

Bavasi had learned well at the Mahatma's knee. By encouraging the public to think about Koufax's and Drysdale's poor teammates, he played on one of the key values of the American baseball public: no one player is more valuable than his teammates' efforts make him. It mattered not that his argument was based on the questionable notion that the Dodger owners were operating on such tight margins that they could only afford to spend a relatively small, fixed amount on player salaries. Certainly, the Dodgers did not have an unlimited pool of funds from which the team could pay its stars, but Bavasi did ignore the additional revenue assured by the significant increase in attendance whenever Koufax or Drysdale pitched. Instead, the Dodger executive stuck to this claim: "We want Koufax and Drysdale, and we want them to be happy. But we can't do the impossible to satisfy them."[13] Bavasi's comments demonstrate the belief of many magnates that they could successfully sway public opinion in their favor by painting players who demanded higher salaries as selfish individuals who were acting in a manner counter to the interests of the team, or even the larger game as a whole. As early as February 28, Bavasi claimed he had made his last and final offer of "more money than two players on one team ever received."[14]

O'Malley continued to stand firm as well, in full support of his general manager. In an interview with the *Sporting News*, the magnate told the story of former Dodger manager Charlie Dressen, who, after winning back-to-back National League championships in 1952 and 1953, felt he deserved a three-year contract. O'Malley told the reporter that he politely refused, citing the club's policy of offering only one-year contracts. Dressen decided to stand on principle and resign his position. The Dodgers hired Walter Alston, who led the team to four World Series championships between 1954 and 1965.[15] O'Malley's implications were clear: no one was irreplaceable in the business of baseball, and players and managers had no choice but to accept the standard of one-year contracts that had been in existence since the establishment of the reserve clause in 1876.

By mid-March, nearly a month after the first Dodger pitchers reported to training camp, Koufax was growing increasingly frustrated with the lack of progress in the negotiations. Mounting public criticism from the Dodgers front office did not help matters. On March 16 the players' agent announced that the two pitchers had rejected the Dodgers' final offer and were looking for greener pastures. The agent announced that Koufax and Drysdale had signed a lucrative movie contract and planned to do an exhibition tour of Japan, in which they could make a great deal more money than the Dodgers would ever pay them. Moreover, their agent implied that the Dodger owners were not being truthful about their policy of never offering more than a one-year contract. The agent even asserted he had evidence to back up his claims.[16]

After this dustup, the last two weeks of March proceeded quietly, although both parties acknowledged that time was growing short before Opening Day on April 12. The current of public opinion turned sharply against the two pitchers as the calendar turned to April, and the baseball press became increasingly impatient. New York Journal American columnist Murray Robinson expressed a common criticism when he said the players' move ultimately showed huge ingratitude to a game that had already made them wealthy and famous beyond their wildest dreams.[17] Robinson's comments reflected the thinking of a traditionalist baseball public that still, for the most part, bought into the owners' view of the players. Despite the reality of stagnating player salaries, the public view held that baseball players received relatively large salaries for the opportunity to play a child's game, all while basking in the adulation of a grateful public. This was due in part to media fascination with the salaries of highly paid stars. The baseball public remained more or less unaware of the salaries paid to average players, because the magnates had long used highly paid stars to project the image of the wealthy, overpaid ballplayer. Owners remained able to count on the highest-paid stars to keep their lesser-paid counterparts in line. Baseball management knew it could depend on the highest-paid men to come out publicly in opposition to any kind of serious collective action by the players. There was little hope for a union to successfully represent all players so long as players allowed themselves to be divided by pay. Until they overcame this division, the public would continue to think first of the few highly paid star players and to give little consideration to the circumstances of the many players who made little more than the minimum salary.

Koufax's and Drysdale's holdout was finally resolved on March 30, when the Dodgers conceded enough on financial terms to reach an agreement with the two pitchers. Koufax signed a contract paying him $125,000 for the 1966 season; Drysdale received $115,000. The contracts fell well short of the players' other demands, yet they still represented something of a victory for the Dodgers' star pitchers. The new salaries represented raises of nearly 50 percent, far more than the two could have won by bargaining individually. More importantly, their ability to significantly move Dodger management off of its "best final offer" was a remarkable accomplishment. Referring to the pitchers' collective negotiating approach as an "entry," O'Malley admitted, "Baseball is an old-fashioned game with old-fashioned traditions. If we allowed this entry business to take hold it would lead to practices not possible to tolerate."[18] O'Malley's comments reflected very real fears of rising player militancy and agitation. While the magnate believed he was providing due warning to the players to stay away from collective action, he was, in fact, providing them with a roadmap. Koufax and Drysdale's combined efforts helped them dramatically improve their compensation. This outcome offered quite a contrast to the usual assumption that collective activity drove everyone "toward the middle." For the first time, star players realized that collective action could work for them as well, particularly if it won them the right to pursue maximum individual compensation. Resistance among star players was a longtime barrier to unionization, and the resolution of this holdout helped pave the way for the first successful union in the one-hundred-year history of the game.

The Koufax-Drysdale holdout received daily scrutiny in the press and provides a wealth of insight into the mind-set of baseball fans regarding everything from player salaries to contract holdouts, the use of agents, and owner greed. Letters to the editor in the *Sporting News* and the *Los Angeles Times* demonstrate the wide array of viewpoints fans held on these issues in the spring of 1966. Letters to the *Los Angeles Times* ran largely in favor of Dodger management. To some it was about loyalty: "I recollect those first years that Sandy pitched for the Dodgers, wasn't it awful? . . . Did O'Malley say 'get rid of Sandy'? No! Now Sandy feels he can dictate his own terms, like some Roman emperor telling the people he is king!" Other fans argued comparative economics: "I know people who have lived on a little tighter budget in order to buy the cheapest seat in Dodger Stadium to see them [Koufax and Drysdale]. It is certainly too bad they feel they can't afford to entertain these people for six months at a six-figure salary." Then there were those who viewed the players as public assets, not individuals entitled to pursue the highest possible salary in return for practicing their craft. "To have such talent as theirs and not use it, even for a year, is worse than having talent and losing it through injury. . . . We would like to see them go down as the greatest pitchers in baseball history, not the greediest." In the mid-1960s, many fans still clung to this view that the civic adoration great players received somehow deprived them of the right to pursue the highest price for their labor in the free market. Players badly needed public thinking to evolve on this issue if there was to be any hope for a future of the game without the restrictions of the reserve clause.

It is interesting to note that, among some of the readers who sided with Koufax and Drysdale, the efforts of the newly emerging Screen Actors Guild appear to have paved the way for the two pitchers: "Statements attributable to [Buzzie Bavasi] that 'Koufax is not worth five times as much as [Dodger outfielder] Ron Fairly' are . . . an indication of a superficial thinking. . . . It is tantamount to saying that 'Clark Gable was not five times as good an actor as John Thespian.' Clark Gable was paid five times the compensation of Mr. Thespian because Mr. Mayer recognized that Clark Gable was worth 10 times as much to the stockholders as was Mr. Thespian."[19] Fans such as these were beginning to see baseball as an entertainment industry, not a sacred national institution too pure to be sullied with the open discussion of the business side of the game. These fans displayed an understanding that player salaries would not always be based strictly on performance and that name recognition and drawing power would always be important determinants of player compensation. This was especially true for pitchers, as pitching matchups have long been a key determinant in ticket sales. A dynamic matchup between two pitching stars could easily fill all fifty-six thousand seats in Dodger stadium. A matchup of two unknowns, or "has-beens," would likely draw less than half of that number.

Letters to the *Sporting News* provided a more national perspective. One fan feared that the huge gap in players' salaries could only lead to decline in quality of play: "How can owners expect players earning $10,000 a year to give their best when one or two teammates are earning 7 to 12 times that?" Others suggested that the two were only following the lead of Walter O'Malley, whose own greed was the chief reason the Dodgers left Brooklyn in 1958. Another fan criticized the sportswriter Murray Robinson: "Does not the American Newspaper Guild represent Robinson when he has grievances with management?"[20]

After seven decades of monopolistic magnate control, many

fans supported player pay gains but remained traditionalists in their cautious view regarding tactics such as holdouts and unionization. While the thinking of some fans was shifting in a way that conceived of baseball more as an industry and less as a national institution, the majority of the baseball public had not yet embraced the ballplayer as a worker, or man entitled to improve his fate through unionization. These beliefs stemmed from a variety of sources. It was essential to most fans to see the players as individuals and teams but not as one large, face-less group. Such a view, many fans believed at this time, would no longer be possible if the players unionized. The public saw unions as bureaucratic levelers, or organizations that took the most talented and least talented and drew them all to the mid-dle, effectively stifling the competitive ingenuity and brilliance of the game. They envisioned the emergence of industrialized rationalization that would rob the game of its spark, its passion, and its spontaneity. To a large degree, this thinking represents a public attitude baseline of sorts at the moments of the MLB-PA's birth. Any successful players' union would be required to reshape this public view by helping the baseball public embrace the ways collective action would allow players to pursue some very American goals: realizing greater freedom of contract and pursuing maximum individual compensation in a highly com-petitive marketplace.

Enter the Steel Industry Organizer with the Right Kind of Mettle

Compounding management fears over rising player militancy was the MLBPA's search for a new executive director, a process that unfolded at the same time as the Koufax-Drysdale holdout. The magnates' hopes rested with the retention of Judge Can-non, who believed the primary role of the MLBPA director was to maintain friendly, positive relations between players and owners. Cannon was actually the players' first choice for the directorship as well, largely because many players, fearful of antagonizing the owners by embracing the union label, saw Cannon as a safe choice. Cannon, however, turned down the players' offer when they insisted he set up permanent association offices in New York or Chicago. Contrary to rumblings in the press that the players might look to the Teamsters and Jimmy Hoffa, the association leadership turned to their second choice, United Steelworkers economist and organizer Marvin Miller.[21] In Miller, who had a strong background in labor-management relations going back to the War Labor Relations Board, the players found just the right man. Miller ultimately helped them overcome their barriers to organization, built player solidarity by helping them better understand their common interests, and taught the association membership how collective bargaining might free them from the restrictions of the reserve clause, allowing them to leverage their specialized skills in the free market.

Miller's selection and the subsequent approval process are quite instructive regarding the state of labor consciousness among baseball players in the mid-1960s. Many owners were fearful of the prospect of an experienced labor organizer running "their" Players Association. Club management put a great deal of pressure on players to reject Miller, as his selection was subject to a vote of the entire membership. Miller knew he might be unpopular with some owners and decided to tour the various spring training sites in an effort to get to know the players and ensure a more informed voting process. Not only did Miller want to meet the players, he also wanted to gain a better measure of their mind-set. He feared that baseball players, almost all of whom lacked real-life experience in any job outside of baseball, would be difficult to organize because they had not been exposed to "real world hard knocks," or the kinds of experiences that most commonly push workers to organize.[22] Miller believed that this lack of workplace experience was one of the primary factors that made players so susceptible to management paternalism.

The owners who opposed Miller's selection saw his spring training tour as their last, and best, opportunity to keep him out. Management efforts to that end were evident from the start of Miller's travels. He began in Arizona with the "Cactus League" clubs, teams such as the Angels, Cubs, and Giants.

Early on it appeared that the players would yet again bow to the owners' wishes, as the Angels and Giants met Miller with apathetic indifference. These players were under tremendous pressure from management, and it showed.[23] Players on the Los Angeles Angels, a team owned an open opponent of the Hollywood unions, Gene Autry, wrote letters to each of the other six hundred MLBPA members, warning, "Mr. Miller is associated with labor . . . and it must be remembered that the relationship between the club owners and the players should be kept as they have been for the last seven years."[24] The Angels players' opposition to Miller made it clear that they had been taught to think of Miller as being in the same league as more notorious labor figures such as Hoffa. The Angels expressed fears that it was just a few select players "railroading" the choice of Miller and that the majority of respectable baseball men wanted little to do with him.[25] Miller struggled to gain the confidence of players training in Arizona, and the prospects for his approval looked bleak. Before he had even had the chance to travel east to Florida to meet with the "Grapefruit League" clubs, respected player representatives such as the Dodgers' Ron Fairly were saying, "I feel we have done real well without a union man, and I would like to keep our relationship with the owners like it has been."[26]

Buoyed by their early success in Arizona, the owners continued their campaign to influence and interfere with association business through a program of organized intimidation. Owners across the league pressured their managers and player representatives to sway their clubs to reject Miller. These magnates threatened players with the prospect of a much more adversarial relationship with management. Outspoken union men were often sold, traded, or sent down to the Minor Leagues, a prospect players faced with dread. These tactics were little different from the blacklisting so prevalent in baseball's early years. Under these conditions, many players of the modern era complied with the owners' wishes. These men bought the idea that they had never had it so good, even though economic statistics and comparisons of their conditions with those of workers in many other industries demonstrated otherwise.

Miller continued to work at swaying Cactus League clubs in his favor, but his prospects looked dim. Out of the 119 players and managers on the Cactus League clubs who were eligible to vote for him, only 17 voiced their approval. Longtime baseball men, such as Indians manager Birdie Tebbetts, responded to management pressure and harassed Miller with questions about his background in labor and possible ties to the Communist Party. Just one year later Tebbetts would apologize to Miller and acknowledge his value to the players, but in early March 1966 it looked like baseball's magnates would once again have their way in keeping an effective, experienced organizer at a safe distance from "their boys."

Things improved dramatically for Miller once he made it to Florida and spent time with the Grapefruit League clubs. There he benefited from the presence of more supportive player representatives such as Robin Roberts and Bob Friend.[27] Thanks to their advocacy for Miller, the players in Florida were more willing to stand up against management intimidation and specifically against Cactus League practices like allowing the team manager to take the vote. Miller received nearly 90 percent of all votes cast by MLBPA members in Florida, providing him with more than enough support, and he agreed to officially take over MLBPA leadership on July 1.

Miller knew there was much work to be done in changing MLBPA culture and building solidarity, all while helping players break free from the grasp of owner paternalism. He realized that his first task was to make the association completely independent from the magnates.[28] Baseball's owners were, of course, less than thrilled with the idea of an independent Players Association. After their campaign to reject Miller failed, they attempted a series of other measures to undermine his authority. These efforts played directly into Miller's hands. The owners' first contract offer to Miller included a variety of terms, such as a lack of accounting procedures for the executive director's expense accounts, designed to raise suspicions about Miller in the eyes of the rank and file. Miller understood the importance of remaining extremely circumspect in this regard and reacted strongly when a *Sporting News* article implied he was to receive a virtually unrestricted $50,000 annual expense account.[29] Miller rejected this contract and further distanced himself from the owners' grasp by choosing his longtime associate Richard Moss, instead of the owners' choice, former U.S. vice president Richard Nixon, as association counsel. Miller wanted to make it clear to all that he was the players' servant, not the "big labor fat cat" some owners made him out to be.

The owners, frustrated by Miller's refusal to play on their terms, responded with an attempt to deprive the MLBPA of its funding. The magnates claimed it had just been brought to their attention that the Taft-Hartley Act made it illegal for management to provide the union with funds. Since the Players Association was funded out of the players' pension fund, monies that technically came from the magnates, the owners said they had no choice but to stop funding the MLBPA in this manner. This tactic, forcing the association to generate its own sources of revenue, provided the players with a key opportunity to develop a sense of independence and initiative that was completely absent during the more paternalistic "monopoly era."

The owners made their next misstep when they decided to delay negotiations on the new pension plan. They figured that delayed negotiations, combined with a lack of funding, would generate enough frustration within its membership to send the MLBPA to an early grave. Player representatives were enraged when the owners' envoys came to a June 6 meeting at the Biltmore Hotel in New York City clearly unprepared to settle key funding questions regarding the MLBPA offices and staff. Miller, on the other hand, was quite pleased. He knew the owners' tactics would do much more to build player solidarity against the owners than any education campaign he could stage. Miller also realized that the owners' stall tactics presented him with an opportunity to pin down the owners' positions on baseball's antitrust exemption. He told the *New York Times*, "If the owners cite Taft-Hartley they are also bringing in three other things: They say they're an interstate business, they say we are a labor organization and they commit themselves to bargaining in good faith according to the law, which prohibits coming into a negotiation with a fixed position."[30] Not only was Miller trying to expose management's inflexibility, he was, in effect, starting the MLBPA's campaign against baseball's antitrust exemption and the onerous reserve clause. The Koufax-Drysdale holdout had indicated there was a great deal of work to be done in bringing the public around; Marvin Miller was ready to get down to it.

Baseball management's final tactical error came in their efforts to restructure their new television contract in a way that reduced revenue received for the World Series and All-Star Game while further increasing revenue connected to the *Game of the Week*. This was done in an effort to increase the owners' share of the TV revenue, which came from the *Game of the Week* portion of the contract, while reducing their required contribution to the pension fund, connected as it was to World Series and All-Star Game television revenues. When Miller called public attention to this effort, the owners shifted tactics and unilaterally proposed moving to a lump-sum formula for pension contributions. Such a move flew in the face of standard collective bargaining practices, and Miller expressed astonishment at baseball management's inability to understand that the days of public proclamations regarding bargaining issues were over. Miller warned baseball commissioner William "Spike" Eckert that it was illegal to unilaterally announce the amount of management's contribution to the pension to the press before any collective bargaining had taken place, adding that "the days of Judge Cannon's rubber stamp were over."[31]

Despite this series of events, many owners remained slow to embrace the new world of collective bargaining. In late July, baseball management announced they would make a flat, $4 million annual contribution to the pension fund. This was discouraging news to the players, as it broke with the 60–40 split of television revenue guaranteed under the current plan, set to expire on March 31, 1967. That was not Miller's only concern with the negotiations. He suspected the owners were already manipulating the television revenue numbers in their own favor. He was very concerned, as were the majority of the players, that they would be missing out on the boom in television revenues that was clearly on the horizon. Other sports, such as professional and college football, were already beginning to reap huge windfalls through well-negotiated television contracts. MLBPA members knew that, despite the magnates' inability to reap a windfall in negotiations with the networks thus far, broadcast revenues were steadily on the rise, and the future continued to look promising.

Miller did his research. He knew that television and radio broadcast revenue in 1946 had been a mere one-third of total player salaries. Projected television revenue for the 1967 season was $29.1 million, a number almost three times total player salaries of $11.5 million.[32] Miller argued, "The owners are looking ahead to 1969 when their new contract [with NBC] will expire. The trend in TV and radio receipts is sharply upward. What I'm concerned about is maintaining the 60–40 split. Otherwise, the owners will take further TV increases for themselves."[33] The players did not want to miss out on the television bonanza, and the MLBPA insisted the owners' proposal was inadequate. The owners' initial response was to continue to drag their feet in negotiations with the Players Association. They apparently believed that continued delays would make the players impatient and help management win a more favorable pension settlement.

In November, a new development helped break open the benefit plan negotiations. The New York State Department of Insurance, the government agency with oversight of the pension fund, informed Miller that the owners, with the approval of Judge Cannon, had essentially removed $167,440 from the fund in 1960 and had not yet paid it back.[34] Miller used this revelation of owner wrongdoing as badly needed leverage, and by December the MLBPA had successfully guaranteed owner contributions of $4.1 million for 1967 and 1968. While this broke the precedent of a strict 60–40 television revenue split, it effectively prevented the owners from attempting any further chicanery with television revenues as a way to cut back on their pension obligations, a practice Miller was fairly confident had been going on for some time. More importantly for the players, the agreement also doubled monthly pension and disability benefits, setting up a "ten-year man" to be eligible for a $500 monthly benefit after age fifty, or a $1,300 monthly benefit after age sixty-five.[35] Finally, the agreement forced the owners to reconcile their $200,000 debt to the pension fund. Players remained concerned about possibly missing out on the television bonanza, but the new benefit numbers went a long way toward swinging player attitudes in Miller's favor. The MLBPA successfully stopped the owners in their tracks, and Miller warned the magnates behind closed doors that "their present actions will make the players more militant against them."[36] Miller's early success in protecting the player's pension quickly built greater solidarity in the MLBPA's ranks, solidarity that would be tested but not broken as the MLBPA continued its ascendancy. Certainly it did not hurt, in these formative days, that the issue at stake was one well understood by the public, who largely supported the players in their quest to secure and bolster the pension fund.

Funding an Independent Players Union

Throughout the process of negotiating the pension the players dealt with an equally pressing issue: identifying a new source of independent funding for the MLBPA. This task was essential to the union's survival. As Miller put it, "When I was hired as executive Director, this new, theoretically independent organization had the financial stability of a third world nation. . . . Here's what we had: no money, no office, no staff, and no union consciousness."[37] The new executive director told the *Sporting News*, "It is interesting that the owners of the major league clubs and their attorneys found no problem involved with paying Judge Cannon directly from the pension fund, but now there are legal obstacles to the financing of the Players Association with the players' own money."[38] The rules had apparently changed now that the MLBPA was no longer a company union. Miller took quick and decisive action to bolster the association's financial health. For the previous several years, the players had contributed $2 per day, or roughly $344 per season, to the pension fund. Miller suggested that, with the players' approval, the pension fund could be made "noncontributory," and this $344 would instead be treated as union dues. The MLBPA needed roughly 80 percent of its membership to participate in this financing plan in order to raise $150,000 annually to fund its offices. The owners approved this idea, assuming the players were likely to reject this system of funding the union. The MLBPA membership proved the owners wrong in September, when all but two of its more than six hundred members voted to accept the new funding plan.

This financing plan alone was not enough. Payroll deductions for union dues could not begin until the start of the 1967 season, leaving union offices unfunded until March 1967. MLBPA leadership decided that the best short-term solution to cover this six-month financial gap was to set up product licensing agreements, a second new revenue stream readily available in the advertising-driven postwar economy. The popularity of the players with the general public was a huge asset in this regard. Despite the growing popularity of football, baseball was still the most popular spectator sport in the United States, and many players enjoyed iconic status in their hometowns, and often across the nation. Miller believed the association could leverage the sale of player images collectively, without interfering with the individual product endorsement contracts many of the big stars enjoyed. The idea was to cut deals with companies to give them promotional rights to the likenesses of all Major League Baseball players, not just a few star performers.

The one large-scale use of player likenesses in place at the time was the baseball trading card industry, which, thanks to the growing number of young fans provided by the Baby Boom, enjoyed a golden age of its own in the postwar era. By the mid-

1960s the Topps Company dominated the card industry. Topps had learned well from the business practices of the baseball magnates. The card company did not have a collective deal with the players as a group. Instead, Topps representatives signed almost every single Minor League player to a standard card contract. This contract offered relatively few financial benefits to the player. Topps counted on the players' romantic notions regarding the iconic status of baseball cards to serve as encouragement enough to sign the Topps contract. This pact gave the player $5 when he signed and promised $125 annually for every year the player was in the Major Leagues. In exchange, Topps had the sole right to sell the player's likeness on a card, either alone or with any type of confectionary product. The contract contained provisions very similar to the reserve clause, especially because Topps had the right to unilaterally renew player contracts as it saw fit. This meant, in effect, that Topps reaped millions of dollars every year in profits, in exchange for less than $100,000 per year the company paid for the exclusive rights to produce baseball trading cards.

Marvin Miller and Frank Scott, an agent who already represented some star players in their pursuit of endorsement income, knew the Topps contract was a financial disaster for most players. Collectibles such as baseball cards were a great way for the MLBPA to generate badly needed income, but the vast majority of big league players had long ago signed away their card rights. Clearly, the MLBPA needed some kind of collectible licensing agreement of its own. Miller and Scott took inspiration from an old promotion in which cards bearing the likenesses of a large number of players were placed in boxes of Wheaties. Fans who wanted to collect pictures of all their favorite stars just needed to buy enough cereal. Once these fans built their collection they could even make a few trades with their friends, just like big league magnates.

Thus inspired, Scott figured out a way around the Topps contract and negotiated the association's first licensing deal. This deal, which brought an immediate infusion of $60,000 into the association's coffers, allowed Coca-Cola to use the players' pictures inside bottle caps. Coke understood the marketing power of baseball collectibles and even offered a few incentives to those fans who could collect entire sets of bottle caps. The promotion was a success for Coca-Cola, but it was an even more important step forward for the players, as they asserted control over the promotional use of their likenesses. When the magnates tried to block the deal by claiming ownership over the team logos appearing on the players' uniforms, the players told Coke to airbrush out the team logos.[39] The licensing deal and the pension negotiations, situations generated by many owners' desire to bring the association to an early death, instead made the MLBPA much stronger. These magnates' early attempts to sabotage Miller provided him with several opportunities to prove his mettle, and his early actions in response to these challenges helped him quickly gain the confidence of the players.

The First Basic Agreement

With the players' confidence in Miller on the rise, the MLBPA entered into formal talks with Major League management regarding the industry's first-ever collectively bargained Basic Agreement in January 1967. Of primary concern to many players was the minimum salary, which still stood at $7,000, having increased little in the twenty years since the end of World War II.[40] The matter of negotiating salaries was further complicated by the lack of reliable information regarding player salaries. For years, baseball management had taken steps to maintain an environment in which players remained reluctant to discuss their salaries with one another. Such an environment encouraged and allowed team executives to misrepresent to players the salaries of similarly skilled players, both on their own club and on other clubs around the league.

One commonplace tactic was to tell a player asking for more money that he was already making almost as much as, or more than, another player of equal or better talent. Another oft-used ploy was telling a player he was among the highest-paid players on the team when in fact he was not. Stories such as those of Dodger outfielder Ron Fairly were typical. In 1966 Fairly, along with shortstop Maury Wills, was widely regarded as one of the two best "everyday players" (men who did not pitch) on the club. Dodgers general manager Buzzie Bavasi led Fairly to believe he was among the four highest-paid players on the club, telling Fairly that raising his salary would throw the club's whole salary structure "out of whack" and pose a serious threat to team chemistry. Fairly felt quite the fool later, when he learned his was actually the eighth-highest salary on the club. Experiences like Fairly's eventually made Miller's job that much easier. Players such as Fairly, who had once been willing to lend management a hand by leading opposition to a union, turned instead into loyal association men.[41]

To best address this dearth of good information on player salaries, the player representatives conducted a player salary survey on each club. The results of the survey provided the many association members with plenty of motivation. In an age when the average American worker made $8,000 annually, more than a third of all Major League Baseball players made less than $10,000.[42] The magnates' claim that big league players made piles of cash, especially in comparison with the average American, rang false with many members of the baseball public, even some traditionalists. The average salary paid to a Major League Ballplayer, inflated to a large degree by the salaries of star players such as Willie Mays and Mickey Mantle who were paid the $100,000 unofficial maximum salary, was $19,000. The median salary was $17,000, but certainly the most alarming information to MLBPA leadership was the number of players making the league minimum of $7,000.[43] Players understood that the magnates would fight any increase tooth and nail. In the words of pitcher Jim Bouton, "Don't ever think $7,000 isn't a lot of money in baseball. I've had huge arguments over a lot less."[44] Armed with this information, the MLBPA was better positioned to earn the support of the baseball public, many of whom were surprised to learn about the relatively low salaries earned by men they presumed were living lives of luxury.

Miller and the player representatives decided that the most pressing issue was the minimum salary. First, this issue would play well with the public, many of whom would be surprised to learn that they made more than a professional baseball player. Inflation figures also helped with the push for a higher minimum salary, as the consumer price index had realized a 78 percent jump since 1946, while the minimum player salary had increased only 20 percent over that same period.[45] Postwar economic conditions had done a great deal to educate the American public as to the importance of real wages. Miller sensed that these inflationary themes would play favorably with baseball's fans. His strategy quickly proved successful. Even the sports columnist Dick Young, a dyed-in-the-wool traditionalist and later a leading critic of the MLBPA, asked, "How many of the Lords of Baseball have priced groceries lately?"[46] Favorable comments such as these helped build momentum on the salary issue and showed the players they could move from the pension to other compensation-related items and remain in the good graces of the baseball public.

The MLBPA opened negotiations by pushing for a $12,000 minimum salary. When the PRC came back with a counteroffer of $8,500, Miller decided to open the scope of bargaining to every conceivable issue. While many players remained focused solely on pension and minimum salary, Miller worked to emphasize the importance of other issues, such as arbitration of grievances, official recognition of the MLBPA as the sole collective bargaining representative of the players, and the modification of the reserve rule.[47] With his leadership of the MLBPA still in its formative stages, Miller knew that successful negotiations would do a great deal to build players' confidence in their association. He asked players to make a list of every issue they could think of, from the condition of outfield warning tracks to having operable hair dryers in the clubhouses.[48] Miller wanted to demonstrate that their association could be about a great deal more than salary and pensions, and the players responded favorably over time.

One major obstacle to successful bargaining came in the person of Bowie Kuhn, baseball management's counsel of choice. Kuhn was a career baseball man, having served for many years as a staff attorney for the National League. He had initially won the magnates' favor by successfully handling a 1965 lawsuit brought against the National League by the city of Milwaukee, after the Braves fled Milwaukee for Atlanta. Kuhn was similar to Judge Cannon in his firm belief that the magnates' interests were his own interests. He believed that by advancing the magnates' interests he could advance his own career. Toward that end, Kuhn saw himself as baseball's point man in breaking the new Players Association before it got off the ground. He started negotiations on the basic agreement with the same stall tactics the owners had employed during the benefit plan negotiations. Like other magnates before him, Kuhn underestimated how much these delays would fail to serve his intended purpose and instead serve to strengthen player solidarity.

Kuhn opened the negotiations by claiming that the owners were there only to listen to the players' proposals, not to participate in any sort of negotiations. This infuriated the players and quickly pushed them closer to the stronger collective mindset Miller knew they needed. Instead of acting brashly, Miller responded cautiously. In doing so, he demonstrated the importance of waiting out the owners and building public support around issues that were easier for the general public to understand, such as minimum salary. The owners, hampered to a certain degree by their own disunity and confusion, responded by continuing to stall.

Facing a continued lack of progress in June, Joe Cronin, the American League president and chair of the Player Relations Committee, went to the *Sporting News* in an effort to apply public pressure to the MLBPA. Cronin was a forty-year baseball man. His roots in the game went all the way back to a successful playing and managing career that began in 1926. His ties to the magnates were strengthened through marriage, as his wife was the daughter of Clark Griffith, patriarch of one of baseball's oldest families. According to Cronin, "Miller is an industrial labor technician who is intellectual, shrewd, and very capable, but he elected to blow up the issue of the minimum salary and make an assumption of bad faith on our part. To the contrary, good will means everything to us in our relations with the players and we have their interests in mind at this time, just as we have in the past."[49]

Cronin's statement reflected a key element of management's negotiation strategy. Time and again, management representatives like Cronin attempted to portray Miller as an outsider who failed to understand the inner workings of the game. The PRC argued that if negotiations were slow, it must be due to Miller's unfamiliarity with the game. Any and all delays in negotiations, according to the owners, were due to Miller's general rigidity and inflexibility stemming from his background in industrial relations. The owners believed they could count on the traditionalists within the baseball public to respond to this campaign, a belief that proved well founded. There were more than a few reporters willing to help the owners' cause by scoffing at the notion of unionized players making financial demands. Among them was Bob Addie of the *Washington Post*, who wrote, "If the modern ballplayer has his way, he will soon be chauffeured to the game in an air conditioned limousine, have the services of a valet and be eligible for a substantial pension at the age of 21." In response to the players' request for a revised reserve clause, Addie referred to the clause as a "yoke of gold."[50] Addie's remarks reflect the exact sentiment that baseball management hoped to elicit from the baseball public: that ballplayers should be overjoyed with their current working conditions.

In addition to building a public relations campaign, the owners were stalling for time, at least in part because they were ill prepared to respond to the wide variety of requests that came from the MLBPA. Foremost among these issues was the scheduling of double headers, or two games in one day, following a night game. Scheduling practices such as these, in which a player left the ballpark after midnight only to return later that same morning for a fourteen-hour workday, took a tremendous toll on the players. Travel requirements compounded these scheduling issues. It was not uncommon for players to put in a full day of work, get on a cross-country overnight flight, and try to get a few hours of sleep at a hotel before reporting for the next game. Additionally, many players called for an immediate return to the 154-game season.[51] To Marvin Miller, the schedule offered a chance to demonstrate to players the importance of including "shop floor" issues in the collective bargaining process. The magnates, of course, thought any kind of formal player input on the scheduling process was ill conceived. Joe Cronin argued that the scheduling process was already much too complex to add "minor" player considerations into the mix. He trotted out the magnates' typical line, arguing that kindly, paternalistic management practices, such as resting older players when a day game followed a night game, already provided the players enough protection from the strains of the schedule.

Beyond securing the players a say on scheduling issues, Miller badly wanted to win the right to grievance arbitration. He understood that such an arbitration process could easily be expanded, in the near future, to include issues such as the reserve clause and salary negotiation. Miller also believed the right to arbitration would help make the players more assertive on behalf of their own interests, and ultimately make them better union men. Arbitration was a threatening concept, but more threatening still to the magnates was the MLBPA's request for a collective review of the reserve clause. Kuhn and Cronin responded to this request with the time-tested arguments that the reserve clause protected the player more than the owner and that the game would quickly meet its demise without the reserve clause in place. This demise would be likely, management argued, because competitive balance would disappear as the wealthiest clubs purchased all of the most talented players. It is to their credit that the magnates continued to successfully use this line of reasoning, because the facts in evidence proved otherwise. At the time Kuhn and Cronin made their pitch, the New York Yankees, by far the wealthiest team in the game, had won thirteen of the last seventeen American League pennants.[52]

Kuhn and Cronin carried on this public relations campaign, reinforcing the notion that there had never before been a time when the players had it so good. In reality, the two were hard at work in an effort to cover the growing dissension and disunity in the owners' ranks, caused in large part by the complexity of the players' demands. In the face of all these specific player demands, the magnates finally decided that they needed a professional labor man on board, and in the spring of 1967 they turned to John Gaherin. All sides welcomed Gaherin, who had just finished a stint as president and chief negotiator for the New York Newspaper Publishers Association. *New York Times* baseball writer Leonard Koppett expressed hope that "the context for tougher, longer and perhaps more productive bargaining has now been created, disconnected from the emotional explosives of players and owners facing each other across a table too often."[53]

Many of those experienced in the world of 1960s labor relations could see that, even with Gaherin on their side, the baseball magnates were overmatched in their efforts to deal with Miller and his legal counsel, Richard Moss. Both men were polished products of industrial labor relations in the steel industry, arguably the biggest playing field in the arena of organized labor during the 1950s and 1960s. As Bruce Johnston, a former chief negotiator for U.S. Steel, put it, "These [Miller and Moss] were people trained in that system, then turned loose on an industry that was, in terms of labor relations, naïve and illiterate. The owners were a loose amalgam of highly individualistic entrepreneurs, who are the worst people in the world to deal with labor. . . . Most of them have never worked inside structures where cooperation with other strong personalities is required. They were thus very poor in cooperating in the face of unified opposition. The baseball industry presented open borders to a Panzer division."[54]

Just a little more than a year into his tenure with the MLBPA, Miller consistently demonstrated this insider knowledge and experience. He stayed true to the common wisdom of labor in the postwar era by insisting on collective bargaining, rather than turning to the state to intervene on the players' behalf, as the best path to improving the players' circumstances. The MLBPA director told *Los Angeles Times* labor editor Harry Bernstein, "We are prepared to function as a union, since it is the only thing we can do. . . . If an issue becomes big enough and important enough, perhaps the players would all say they would not return to their contracts."[55] In the short time since he had assumed leadership of the MLBPA in the spring of 1966, Miller had moved from his early comments that strikes had no place in baseball to instilling fear in the owners' hearts by hinting at the possibility of a work stoppage. Miller wanted the owners to know that the MLBPA remained determined to stay the course and realize significant improvement in pay and working conditions, and the players had established enough common ground with the media and fans that the MLBPA might be willing to push its luck in the court of public opinion.

It was not long before John Gaherin figured out the frustrations of bargaining on behalf of baseball's magnates. Technically, he represented the seven-member Player Relations Committee, but the reality was quite different. Baseball's real power brokers were men like longtime Dodger owner Walter O'Malley, and these men felt free to disrupt the bargaining process whenever they saw fit. As a result of these disruptions, negotiations dragged on into the fall of 1967, and while Miller and Gaherin were able to hammer out some of the financial details, including a $10,000 minimum salary and $12 per day in spring training meal money, grievance arbitration became the chief sticking point in finalizing baseball's first-ever Basic Agreement. The players hoped for resolution of this issue at the magnates' winter meetings, but the owners continued to stall, their frustration over the grievance impasse becoming increasingly apparent.

The owners decided not to meet with the players in December, and Atlanta Braves vice president Paul Richards responded strongly when Marvin Miller publicly criticized the owners for breaking their promise to meet with the players. "Somebody's lying and I don't think it's the owners. If this guy [Miller] continues with these tactics we'll just have to get in the gutter with

him, I guess."[56] Arbitration was simply too much for many owners to agree to, despite Gaherin's assurances that it was inevitably
something they would be forced to accept. Baseball management
remained tightly wrapped in the privileged mind-set afforded by
their antitrust exemption. Gussie Busch, the crusty old brewing
scion and owner of the St. Louis Cardinals, cried, "No, no, no,
no! Did you hear me say no?" Dodger owner Walter O'Malley
was even more direct with his feelings, telling Gaherin to "tell
that Jewish boy [Miller] to go back to Brooklyn!"[57]

Despite management's bluster, Miller remained patient, demonstrated his ability to keep the players unified, and won a major
victory for the players the following March in the form of Major
League Baseball's first ever Basic Agreement. The agreement,
nearly a year in the making, included a 66 percent improvement in the minimum player salary, raising it to $10,000. It
also included improvements in provisions for meal money and
travel accommodations, moving expenses for players who were
traded or sold, a formal arbitration process for player grievances,
and the formation of a joint committee to study the length of the
season and the reserve rule.[58] It had not taken the players long to
gain an appreciation for the importance of maintaining a strong
bargaining position through patience and common purpose.

Marvin Miller's first two years of leadership allowed the MLBPA
to establish a beachhead for unionization in the management-
dominated world of Major League Baseball. Miller demonstrated
the resourcefulness needed to make the association financially
independent. He brought in the bargaining expertise required
to bring the magnates to the table. Finally, Miller had the organizational and strategic savvy needed to build public support
for the union and a strong collective consciousness among
the vast majority of Major League Baseball players, men his-
torically proven to be difficult to organize. From their new
beachhead, Miller and the MLBPA continued their quest for
further gains in salary, pension, shop-floor control, and the
freedom of contract that would only come with the elimination of the reserve clause.

5

The Players Grow a Backbone

Following the successful negotiation of the 1968 Basic Agreement, the MLBPA entered a critical period in its development. As they had done so successfully in 1946, the magnates would surely attempt once again to use the players' satisfaction with the newfound gains to diffuse growing player militancy. After all, earlier attempts at collective action often foundered as a result of player satisfaction with gains even smaller than those made in the 1968 Basic Agreement. In the late 1960s, however, the MLBPA leadership skillfully avoided this hazard. Marvin Miller and the player representatives successfully seized this opportunity for continued progress. They took full advantage of the players' developing rights consciousness and kept their membership focused on the association's primary goals, foremost of which were the complete elimination of the reserve clause and the opportunity for a player to pursue the full value of his services on the free market.

In the short term, however, MLBPA efforts to modify the reserve clause were put on hold by yet another threat to the pension plan. Negotiations over the first Basic Agreement became so protracted that it was only two months after the Basic Agreement was finalized that negotiations on the new pension agreement began. The magnates, flush with cash from a new television contract and franchise expansion fees, believed the concessions they made in the 1968 Basic Agreement were more than adequate and strongly opposed any further increases in pension funding. On the other side of the table, the players were determined to secure their gains against the dual threat of league expansion and growing inflation. The resulting clash between players and magnates tested wills on both sides and resulted in intense scrutiny and active debate among the baseball public. Like many other people in positions of authority in the late 1960s, many longtime baseball men believed the players were bent on destroying the old order and were likely to take the entire game down with it. In the face of rhetoric that, at times, lumped them in with other cultural revolutionaries of the day, the players now needed to redouble their efforts to maintain public support if they expected to push past the initials gains made on the pension and minimum salary.

Baseball's Own "Revolution of 1968": Securing the Pension at All Costs

The players knew the magnates would not part with their new financial gains easily, and so the MLBPA went on the offensive early. The MLBPA's executive committee, comprising the player representatives from each club, issued a "Statement of Policy" on July 8, 1968, more than eight full months prior to the time when the existing pension and benefits agreement was set to expire. The players took great pains to lay out the extensive historical background that set a clear precedent for their request. In short, they believed they were entitled to a significant increase in the owners' pension contribution, funds the players felt could be easily drawn from baseball's new $50 million national television contract.

The players charged the owners with a number of bad-faith practices surrounding this contract, including meeting secretly with NBC against the clear wishes of the Players Association. From the start of their new television negotiations, it was evident that the owners wanted the new television deal structured in such a way as to leave the players without any claim to their rightful share of broadcast revenue. The players further accused the owners of settling for much less than they would have received had they waited and opened the contract up to competitive bidding between all three major networks. These issues aside, the players were alarmed because, "the Association has been informed [by the owners] that the Clubs recognize no interest of the players in the new N.B.C. contract and, in fact, there has been no communication whatsoever with the Players Association concerning any aspect of that contract which was entered into almost a year ago. It seems evident that storm warnings have been raised by the owners, and the danger of a bitter contest has been presented." This reflects the players' largest concern regarding the upcoming negotiations. They knew one of the owners' primary goals during this set of talks was to eliminate any and all player claims to a share of commercial broadcast revenue. In this booming media age, the players understood the rising value of the commercial use of their images. Unlike many other players' rights, this right was not relinquished in the standard player contract. Miller and the MLBPA leadership made it abundantly clear to the membership that this principle, ownership of the rights to their images, was at the center of everything the players were working for in the upcoming negotiations.[1]

The players' statement also shows increased savvy as to the ways of collective bargaining. This is first evident in the players' attempts to establish a bargaining timetable. The owners, the players knew, would request to defer negotiations until the upcoming off-season. Such a request would leave only three and a half months for the negotiation of a new pension agreement. The MLBPA wanted the owners to enter negotiations early, hoping to avoid the negative public fallout sure to accompany protracted pension talks. Lengthy negotiations threatened to interfere with the start of the 1969 season, and the owners believed that, with public opinion on their side, they would be able to use any delays in the bargaining process to cast the players in a negative public light. The owners, the players also knew, preferred to negotiate during the off-season because it would make it more difficult for the players to maintain unity, as most players would be spread out across the country at that time, having returned to their hometowns for the winter. Miller and the association's leadership wanted to be on the record early with their request to begin productive negotiations as soon as possible, especially in an effort to keep public opinion from sliding too far in the owners' favor as the 1969 season drew near.

Aside from timely negotiations, the players had a number of other concerns. They knew that the owners' plans to add four new franchises for the 1969 season would further complicate negotiations.[2] Such an expansion plan represented a 20 percent increase in the Major League workforce and a corresponding increase in the number of men eligible for the pension. Players were apprehensive regarding the impact of the upcoming expansion on existing pension benefits, and they were especially wary of the strain put on the pension by adding beneficiaries without securing additional funding.

Ultimately, the players' statement returned to their primary concern: their rights in regard to broadcast revenue, particularly as a funding source for the pension: "The Clubs must recognize that the players not only have a vital interest in seeing that the best possible arrangements are made, but also have clear property rights in that which is being sold. The players sincerely believe, as they are often told by Club owners, that the goals of the parties are intertwined and that we all must work together to enhance the best interests of baseball." The MLBPA concluded this statement by declaring its intention to work for progress in the upcoming negotiations, saying, "The players regard the Benefit Plan to be of crucial importance in their total relationship with their Clubs. Therefore they consider completion of an Agreement on a new Benefit Plan to be vital before individual player contracts can be considered for 1969."[3] This left little doubt as to their position. They wanted a prompt start to negotiations, despite a fair amount of outcry that midseason negotiations would keep them from properly focusing on their on-field performance. The MLBPA made it absolutely clear that the players belonged at the bargaining table when it came time to negotiate broadcasting contracts and make decisions about the use of the resulting revenue. Finally, their refusal to consider new contracts was a de facto strike threat. This was by far the MLBPA's most aggressive move yet, as it made it clear that the owners risked endangering the scheduled start of the 1969 season if they once again dragged their heels.

As expected, league expansion plans immediately complicated the 1969 pension negotiations. Plans to expand each league by two new teams threatened to add more than one hundred new beneficiaries to the pension rolls. The players wanted to make certain that the addition of these new beneficiaries would not dilute the hard-won benefits secured in the 1967 agreement. Toward that end, the MLBPA began the talks by calling for a substantial increase in owner pension contributions, from the existing amount of $4.1 million to $5.9 million. The players also pushed for a reduction in the service requirement to four years, largely in response to research by Miller's office that showed that less than 40 percent of all players earned five years of service credit.[4] This bold opening position was indicative of the players' more aggressive posture. These men were developing a knack for the collective bargaining process.

The owners, on the other hand, were struggling to a certain degree to put together a united front and thus were ill prepared to respond to the players' demands. The magnates' earlier failed attempts to break the Players Association, coupled with expansion concerns and an intense debate over possible rule changes designed to boost the offense, made it especially difficult for the owners to foster the kind of harmony they needed in a standoff with the MLBPA. The magnates' discord did little to help an already contentious negotiation process. They attempted to cover up their disarray by opening negotiations with a "hardnosed position including a claim that the players have no rights in the radio-TV area, [and] never had any rights," Miller told the MLBPA executive committee. "They [the PRC] are not even willing to admit, as a starting point, that the contribution of the clubs under the present Plan [$205,000 a year by each of the twenty clubs] should be expanded to $205,000 a year by each of the 24 Clubs, despite the expansion of the number of Clubs to 24."[5]

Miller feared that this particular position, which ignored the basic mathematics of expansion, meant that extremely antagonistic negotiations lay ahead.

The owners' hard-line stance, while risking the alienation of the players, was well received by the baseball public. Fans and the media, many of whom initially supported many of the players' demands for a better minimum salary and the right to organize, grew increasingly wary of the players' union. This shift in attitudes became apparent as early as August 1968, well before the new pension negotiations heated up. An editorial in the *Sporting News* noted that the newspaper "has looked with favor on the Major League Baseball Players Association because there are many matters that the performers can solve only through joint action. However, we are beginning to have second thoughts regarding the organization now that it is beginning to make noises like a hardnosed labor union." The editorial went on to criticize Miller for his attempts to begin pension negotiations in mid-August even though there was "more than enough time to reach a settlement." It concluded by calling Miller "a past master at impugning the motives of the owners," taking him to task for criticizing the magnates' stall tactics. The final line of the editorial marked a clear shift in public perception: "Come on, Marvin, you know better than that—and so do the players, who already enjoy the most lucrative pension plan in the world."[6]

In two short years, the MLBPA had gained enough through the 1967 pension and benefits plan and the freshly minted 1968 Basic Agreement that the baseball press believed players ought to now be satisfied with their place in the world. Writers from across the nation echoed this sentiment in December 1968, when pension negotiations finally began in earnest. Such a shift in sentiment was consistent with public opinion following Robert Murphy's attempts to form the American Baseball Guild in 1946. After years of mistreatment, it appeared the owners could make a few minor concessions and win back the hearts and minds of the baseball public, who would ultimately be drawn back to their traditionalist roots. Whatever honeymoon the MLBPA once enjoyed with the public was over. The players needed to work hard to maintain public support through the difficult period ahead, especially as the issues, such as the dissolution of benefits due to expansion, became more complex and more difficult to explain to the baseball public.

Throughout the winter of 1969, whenever the owners balked at a meaningful increase in their pension contributions, Miller reminded the players of the importance of solidarity: *"The progress we make will come about only as a result of the players showing support for their negotiating committee. We are confident that enough time remains for an equitable agreement without a crisis, but this result can be achieved only if the Owners are convinced of the players' determination to obtain a fair Benefit Plan Agreement before signing 1969 salary contracts."*[7] Miller and the MLBPA executive committee believed a collective holdout was the most effective tactic at the players' disposal. The primary intent of the holdout threat was to pressure owners to reach an agreement on the pension prior to the start of the 1969 season, since any unsigned player would stay out of spring training camp until he was under contract.

The prospect of missed training time provided the primary leverage for such a holdout. Players who missed training time were often less productive and had a greater risk of injury during the first months of the season. The threat of holdouts also had an important secondary purpose. MLBPA leaders believed that any player who played through the season without a contract was essentially a free agent at the end of that season. Miller felt that player solidarity behind a holdout would leave the owners with no choice but to increase their pension contribution, rather than deal with the prospect of widespread free agency at the end of the 1969 season. Despite their public confidence in the legality of the reserve clause, many owners were nervous about the rule's ability to stand up to a serious legal challenge in the changing political and business climate of the late 1960s.

The baseball press, in keeping with rising traditionalist sentiment, labeled Miller's action a strike threat, but the executive director did not see it as such. "We are not in a situation here where a group of players are saying to the owners, 'if you don't give us everything we want, then down you go,'" Miller explained. "We have not issued an ultimatum. We want to sit down and negotiate, and we've got plenty of time."[8] Miller tried to use expansion in the same way he had used the minimum salary issue during the 1968 Basic Agreement negotiations. To Miller, expansion was a concrete issue involving simple numerical data that the general public could understand. He reminded the public that expansion required an additional $600,000 to $700,000 in contributions from the owners simply to maintain current pension benefit levels. Miller pointed out that the magnates were set to receive a $4 million increase in national television revenue, 40 percent (or $1.6 million) of which were funds traditionally set aside to help fund the pension. Further, Miller argued, this amount did not include the rising amount of local broadcast revenue many clubs received. Miller wanted the public to understand that the magnates, despite their protestations to the contrary, had more than enough renewable new revenue to cover the larger pension contributions. All the magnates needed to do, according to Miller, was simply honor the twelve-year precedent of the 60–40 split.

Miller was right on point. Broadcast revenue proved to be the most hotly contested issue in these negotiations. The owners' basic argument was that revenue is revenue. They believed there was nothing special about television money that required sharing it with the players. The MLBPA felt otherwise and extended the argument laid out in its statement of policy: players owned the rights to the commercial use of their images, and such use extended beyond trading cards and bottle caps to television broadcasts. The players believed the standard contract gave the owners the right to use footage of the players for publicity purposes but not commercial purposes. The MLBPA maintained that money from the television contract came from the commercial use of the footage, and therefore the players were entitled to a share of that money.[9] Maintaining the players' rights to broadcast revenue, therefore, was an ongoing MLBPA priority throughout the negotiations.[10]

Strike One? Standing Up to Management Pressure

In short order, the players demonstrated that they were far from the tentative group that, just two years earlier, had been so very cautious about hiring a "union man" to head their association. Players now understood the importance of collective action and proved more than willing to throw their weight behind Miller's publicly stated positions. In early December 1968 the MLBPA's executive committee issued yet another preemptive strike in its efforts to get negotiations underway. The players' representatives issued a press release in order to serve clear public notice that the players were ready to deal with whatever program of intimidation the owners had in store.

> Some of the clubs, but not all, have engaged in a program of pressuring players in an attempt to have them sign contracts. Young players have been told to sign now or play in the minors next year. Others, who are close to vesting in the pension plan, have been told they will never get the necessary five years of service unless they sign. Veterans have been told that baseball has a long memory and that if they refuse to sign now they should forget about staying in baseball after their careers have ended. Immediate financial needs of still other players have been shamelessly exploited. . . . The club owners negotiating representatives have been engaging in delaying tactics. They refused to begin benefit plan negotiations until late October and, to date, have refused to make any substantive offer or respond in any meaningful manner to the extensive proposals made by the association. Furthermore, they have insisted that a necessary condition to any new benefit plan agreement must be a surrender by the players of their interests and legal rights with regard to radio and television broadcasting.[11]

Fueled by Miller's successes and a societal climate filled with collective action, labor consciousness within the MLBPA's ranks was unmistakably on the rise. They boldly called out the magnates for their persistent use of intimidation practices, a campaign that had been in place since the founding of the Brotherhood of Professional Baseball Players in 1887. The MLBPA membership wanted owners to know that the tactics they had used in the past would not save them now.

Players understood the need for support from the fans and press and hoped their position would resonate with many blue-collar fans who experienced the same management pressures in their places of work. In an effort to demonstrate solidarity and show support for Miller and the MLBPA leadership, more than one hundred players publicly attached their names to the association's press release. Perhaps most significantly, this list of names included many of the game's elite players. Don Drysdale, Willie Mays, Al Kaline, Bob Gibson, and many other star players went public with their support for the MLBPA's position.

The participation of these stars was critical for two reasons. First, these men had the most to lose by holding out, as any holdout would cut into their salaries, the highest in the game. Second, and perhaps more importantly, they put the magnates on notice that they would not be successful in any attempts to turn high-profile players against their lesser-paid counterparts, as had happened so often in the past. For more than eighty years, dating back to the Brotherhood War of 1890, magnates had curried favor with star players by offering them big raises or preferential treatment. In exchange, the stars publicly sided with the owners. The baseball public's hearts, and wallets, almost always followed suit. If the stars were happy, the public assumed, all must be right in the business of baseball.

This change in player attitudes did not go unnoticed in the baseball press. Joseph Durso of the *New York Times* noted, "Miller, a one-time economist for the United Steelworkers of America, has been calling the signals for the major league baseball players association [*sic*] for two years. During that time, the players have grown more militant in phrasing their views on minimum pay, pensions, travel allowances, night games, and the length of the season."[12] The MLBPA successfully put management on notice that the days of turning to the likes of Mike Kelly, Ty Cobb, or Rip Sewell to squash players' collective action had ended. For their part, the magnates responded by declaring their frustration with the public exposure generated by the players' statement. Player Relations Committee representative Warren Giles complained, "These charges do not make the climate any better for an amicable settlement. . . . I don't think we'll settle this thing with press releases."[13]

Management rhetoric went up a notch the following day, December 6, as several magnates sought to turn public opinion against Miller and the "rabble rousers" on the MLBPA executive committee. San Diego Padres president Buzzie Bavasi, in yet another attempt to paint Miller as a labor leftist and baseball outsider, said, "It sounds like somebody's about to call a steel strike." Another outspoken Miller critic, Atlanta Braves executive Paul Richards, claimed, "Miller speaks mainly for a few rabble-rousers and greedy ballplayers. As for the players who want to leave, I say to them: good luck, we could replace them with Triple A minor leaguers and keep all the TV money, and be better off." Richards's sentiments remained typical of magnates who believed, in their "long view" of the business of baseball, that all players were ultimately replaceable. This belief had a strong basis in truth, but what Richards failed to realize was that the immediacy of life in the new media age diluted such truths. Miller had a strong understanding of this new reality, noting, "If Richards thinks the networks will pay that kind of money [upwards of $16 million annually] for minor leaguers, he has another think coming."[14] Miller understood TV's need for large volumes of exciting, immediately relevant content. Nobody could produce that content better than Major League Baseball, but only the great stars of the game could generate the kind of national interest that drew large numbers of fans to the national *Game of the Week*. In order to draw high ratings, for example, such broadcasts needed to give a Pirates fan in Pittsburgh a reason to watch an exciting young star playing for an American League club like the Angels in California. If Miller's thinking was on target, the networks would surely bring pressure on baseball management to make sure that national stars such as Carl Yastremski and Willie Mays were on the field for Opening Day. In responding to management criticism, Miller always stopped short of using the word "strike," but his implication was clear enough. For their part, the baseball press, fascinated by the prospect of an actual strike disrupting the regular season, needed little encouragement to decry the possibility of a work stoppage interrupting the national pastime. The players and owners appeared deadlocked, and with the start of spring training only three months away, the possibility of a strike seemed quite real.

The players' growing awareness of the importance of protecting their rights was unmistakable in their public comments throughout the winter of 1969. MLBPA executive committee member Jim Bunning believed the magnates were telling the players, "You have no right to something [broadcast revenue] you have been getting for 12 years."[15] Bunning could be expected to advocate for Miller's rights-based argument, as he was a longtime MLBPA man. It is perhaps more significant how many younger players began to embrace the importance of MLBPA solidarity. Beloved twenty-six-year-old Red Sox pitcher Jim Lonborg, the 1967 Cy Young Award winner and Stanford graduate well known for his intellectual and cultural interests outside the game, was a prime example of the new generation. "There are revolutions all over the world today," Lonborg claimed. "I think it's because of improved communications. Kids today are asking more questions. Questions about basic rights. Ballplayers are asking questions, questions that we think have to be determined now. If they aren't it will just be more difficult for ballplayers in the future." Houston Astros first baseman Rusty Staub was less loquacious but just as sure about what was rightfully his: "We've told them [the owners] that we'll share and share alike. If that's not the fairest thing, I don't know what is. Without us the owners are nothing. Without them, we're nothing. If that's not a 50–50 proposition, what is?"[16] Staub sought to address growing criticism that players greedily sought to extort the owners, without whom the players "would be nothing." He believed this relationship ought to be reframed in ways that asserted the players' equal share in the enterprise. This shift in player attitudes was widely noted and drew a fair amount of criticism from the more stalwart defenders of the baseball order, who were shocked that players could be "asking for more" in the wake of so many significant gains.

The uproar over the pension negotiations was the final straw for baseball's commissioner, the former Air Force general Spike Eckert. The owners took out many of their frustrations on Eckert, who was already in a tenuous position in the wake of his decision to continue games, as scheduled, in the days following the assassination of Robert Kennedy. The consensus view of the baseball press was that Eckert was ill equipped for the job from the start. The commissioner, many writers felt, also had the misfortune of serving at a time when the Lords of Baseball would rather do without a commissioner altogether. The *New York Times'* Leonard Koppett wrote, "The men who run baseball with such absolute power—the owners of the major league clubs—would have preferred no commissioner at all, but they could not face the public-relations consequences of abolishing the office that stood for baseball's integrity."[17]

The owners' search for Eckert's replacement rapidly became contentious. Early discussion centered on the need for restructuring and focused on choosing the right man to oversee the process of leading baseball in a new direction. The demands of the media age and growing competition from other professional sports leagues, the National Football League in particular, led to calls for a new "young Turk," such as the former CBS executive and current Yankees president Mike Burke, to take the reins.[18] Baseball's magnates, especially powerful old-timers like Horace Stoneham of the Giants and Walter O'Malley of the Dodgers, would never back such a move, a situation that became increasingly clear as the selection process moved forward. Many of the National League owners wanted Giants vice president Chub Feeney, while the American League owners pressed hard for Burke.

When neither man could earn the required votes, Walter O'Malley once again steered the owners in the direction he desired.

O'Malley recommended that National League counsel Bowie Kuhn, a man already well seasoned in negotiations with the MLBPA, take the reins as interim commissioner for one year and lead a group studying the possible restructuring of the game. Kuhn's selection at this juncture meant that, yet again, baseball's magnates turned inward, to "an immensely respected figure within the baseball community."[19] With Kuhn's selection, the magnates followed Walter O'Malley's lead down baseball's traditionalist path, instead of embracing the game's future in the new media era. Kuhn's selection also assured a more antagonistic relationship between management and the Players Association. Bowie Kuhn, the man who once saw it as his responsibility to break the Players Association, now headed up a committee tasked with planning baseball's future course.

The search for a commissioner delayed the magnates' response to the players' proposal. When the magnates finally responded, it was clear the hard-liners now ran the Player Relations Committee. As such, it was not surprising that the PRC's new offer failed to solicit satisfaction from the players. The owners proposed to increase their contribution by $1 million, raising it to $5.1 million. While on the surface this looked like a 25 percent increase, the players quickly expressed their displeasure. The magnates' proposal barely covered the new demands on the fund created by expansion, not to mention the growing obligations the fund would incur as the number of eligible players grew each year. This amount was well short of the players' request, but it was far from the biggest sticking point in the owners' proposal. The magnates' offer included language denying any specific tie between television revenue and the pension fund. The owners made this position abundantly clear: "When the players claim, as they do, the right to share in national television and radio revenue, they are claiming a property right they do not now have, nor ever had." To this statement the owners added, "Radio and television revenue is the same as any and all other revenue on which the clubs must rely on to pay players' salaries as well as the literally hundreds of employees essential to the operation of a major league club, maintain operations, and pay other benefits."[20] This was the owners' principal argument in the rights-based debate regarding the function of broadcast revenue. After more than a decade of devoting broadcast revenue almost exclusively to the players' pension fund, the owners now wanted to divorce the funding from this purpose. In the minds of the fiercest MLBPA loyalists, this was a move akin to the U.S. government's decision to push the Sioux off of their reservations following the discovery of gold.

Miller responded immediately. Calling the statement "fraudulent, inadequate, and outrageous," he told the press, "I don't understand how they can say that. For more than 10 years [1956–67] there were written agreements that stipulated a certain percentage of World Series radio-television receipts would go to the pension fund. The current agreement, which is for a flat sum, says in just so many words that this figure is tied to the television percentages used in the past."[21] Miller and the MLBPA would not budge on this issue and hoped that the magnates' refusal to honor a traditional agreement might swing public support back to the players. As the calendar turned to 1969, it appeared that the start of the upcoming season was in jeopardy.

The Baseball Press Learns the New Rules of the Game

In his autobiography, *Hardball*, Bowie Kuhn lamented the favorable treatment he believed Miller and the players constantly received from the baseball press. Kuhn wrote of Miller,

> His ability to cultivate the press was perhaps his greatest talent. He had some built-in advantages. Many writers, of course, were union people and no strangers to confrontations with management; so he found a naturally sympathetic ear. Most of the press also had no inherent sympathy for millionaire owners with elitist personalities. Miller's egalitarian pose was an effective counterpoint to the ownership. Miller was ever ready to give the press

the kind of controversial, often exaggerated, stories that made news while his counterparts were rightfully hobbled by management policies requiring more attention to accuracy and less stirring up of public controversy.[22]

Kuhn was frustrated with the support the MLBPA received in the *New York Times,* but across the rest of the nation the baseball press was far from supportive of Miller and the association membership. Public reaction to the perceived threat of a strike was largely negative, and the press placed the lion's share of the blame squarely on the players. Some writers, such as *Los Angeles Times* columnist John Hall, were incredulous that baseball players could possibly strike over an issue as "minor" as owner contributions to the pension plan. Hall's columns embraced the traditionalist notion that baseball players were simply grownups being paid exorbitant amounts of money to play a child's game. To men like Hall, it was unnecessary to consider the substantial profits players generated for the owners. He let his fears about the game's future run rampant and invoked the specter of an inglorious end to the national pastime: "It is doubtful if suicide can be accomplished after all these years, but it's not impossible and the grand sportsmen who wear the uniforms and labor in the grim, roofless (apologies to Houston) factories insist they couldn't care less." Like many sportswriters before him, Hall claimed the voice of moral authority. He believed he spoke on behalf of the vast majority of baseball fans when he said, "If anything, the reaction to the latest proposed player revolt borders on disgust. And count me in please. *It's not that anybody is opposed to a guy making what he's worth or taking what he can get. It's merely that as living goes, baseball professionals are already living better than most. Much better.*"[23]

It is unreasonable to expect that Hall could accurately foresee the future of the game, but he clearly lacked the vision needed to foresee the multimillion-dollar contract a player would actually receive when he "got all he was worth." The columnist, and many others like him, was swayed by the tales of men like the

Angels owner and former Hollywood Western star Gene Autry, who intimated that the players' demands would all but put baseball out of business. Writing that Autry had told him, "I can still climb back on my horse and earn enough to pay the rent without the players," Hall added that "the Angel owner . . . became an owner for a very simple, romantic, and outdated reason. He loves the game of baseball."[24] Hall's comments were consistent with those of many of his peers in the baseball press, who believed the players had gained enough in the two and a half years since Marvin Miller took over the MLBPA leadership. If men like Hall were unwilling to accept that players were entitled to something as simple and traditional as a fair share of broadcast revenue, they would be even tougher to convince that the time had come to eliminate the reserve clause and give the players the basic right of freedom of contract.

Other writers soundly rejected the players' argument that they were rightfully entitled to a share of broadcast revenues. The *Sporting News* argued that "the owners do the investing. They take the financial risks and they rightfully refuse to permit the players to dictate from what source the pension money must be paid."[25] Like Hall's comments, this editorial implied that players had little or no right to demand their rightful share of the proceeds derived from the use of their images, even though players had not approved such use of their images in the standard player contract. In this view, baseball players were already so fortunate they should not also expect to have their contract rights protected like "regular workers." The owners' supporters had seen and heard enough, and now they pushed back.

Other writers also happily lent their voices to the magnates' cause, demonstrating real concerns over the magnates' financial woes. *Chicago Tribune* baseball writer Edward Prell wrote, "This confrontation [is] mainly built up by the players' desire to fatten the already rich pension program, as management seeks to persuade Marvin Miller, the players' leader, to put on the brakes."[26] Prell's comments were characteristic of writers' calls to arms in support of the magnates. Most baseball writers argued that the pension was already much larger than it should be, and therefore any demands to increase the pension were absurd. In the view of these scribes, rash action like a strike threat by the players, who just a few years earlier had been a largely complacent bunch, was clearly the work of Marvin Miller. Miller rapidly became the scapegoat of choice for any possible interruption in play. This new outlook meant that, in just two and a half years, many members of the press had gone from caution, to mild praise, to condemnation in their treatment of the man now seen by many as the villainous leader of the Players Association.

All of this meant that Miller and the MLBPA leadership faced a new challenge, seriously adverse public opinion, as they attempted to stay the course and keep their promise to hold out en masse in the absence of a favorable pension and benefits settlement. Bob Oates of the *Los Angeles Times* wrote, "If major league baseball's first strike begins as threatened nine days from now, the sporting world may soon be renaming the National Pastime, calling it, instead, the National Disaster." Oates argued that many clubs, including the California Angels, bordered on bankruptcy and that the collapse of baseball franchises would ultimately stick taxpaying fans with huge financial losses. He turned to Jim Lonborg to answer on behalf of the players, questioning the Boston pitcher's assertion that the players had a right to organize. Lonborg responded, "It certainly is [a right], if the owners all band together on a financial matter the players certainly have the same right. All but two of us today are standing firm. We're not being disrespectful to the owners. This is a question of the players' self-respect. If we lose this time, the owners have got us. This is the big test." Oates, like his colleague Hall, claimed to speak on behalf of the majority of the baseball public. He told Lonborg, "Nonetheless, a majority of the public believes that the owners already are paying you a good living for a few hours of work each day and that the players are greedy to ask for more." Lonborg replied, "I think it is unfair to consider any person pampered or greedy if he is just trying to prepare for his future. We're not trying to get more

Cadillacs and palaces today. We're thinking about groceries 25 years from today."[27]

The exchange between Lonborg and Oates exemplifies the contrast between traditionalists in the baseball press and the members of the MLBPA executive committee, men beginning to demonstrate a great deal more understanding of the nuances of collective action. Writers such as Prell, Hall, Oates, and the *New York Daily News'* Dick Young expressed continued astonishment that players dared to ask for more. These men consistently reminded readers that baseball's pension paid some of the best benefits found in any pension in any industry. Lonborg, on the other hand, knew he and his fellow players needed to move the public toward thinking in terms of the average player. Lonborg knew the players were fighting an image war against the public view of the life of a jet-setting, star baseball player generated by media puff pieces portraying the glamorous lives of stars like Mickey Mantle and Don Drysdale.

Lonborg made sure to point out that 60 percent of all Major League ballplayers would never serve long enough to qualify for any part of the current pension plan. The pitcher contended that there were no guarantees that inflation would not completely erode the benefits the players had worked hard to secure two years earlier. Oates attempted to take Lonborg to task over the financial burden new pension demands placed on the magnates, but Lonborg would have none of it. He argued that television was changing the face of sports and that the new television contract brought in more than two and a half times the total player salary outlay of all twenty-four big league clubs. The interview concluded with Lonborg downplaying the possibility of an actual strike but making a firm statement in regard to the players' position: "I hope nobody signs until this is over. The only strength we have is collective. This is the crossroads year in baseball. Only by sticking together can we keep our self-respect."[28]

Hall, Prell, Oates, and *Los Angeles Times* columnist Charles Maher all argued economics in response to MLBPA reasoning, but Players Association critic Dick Young's rhetoric sought its

basis in the "average fan's" emotional reaction to baseball players being out on strike. According to Young,

> There is no public sympathy for this strike, or boycott, or what-
> ever it is. . . . So I doubt Joe Schnook [Young's fictional fan] would
> feel very guilty about walking through a picket line formed by
> Willie Mayes, and Carl Yastremski, and Denny McClain, and I
> doubt very much there would ever be a picket line without those
> eminent labor pioneers. If there were it would be the first picket
> line being asked for autographs by the people walking through
> it. One reason Joe Schnook is pretty fed up with the baseball
> boycott, or whatever it is, he reads enough of that carp every day
> in politics or industry and he has always looked to baseball as
> some kind of escape.[29]

Young, who had spoken favorably of the players' push for a higher
minimum salary in 1966, now felt the MLBPA had made all of
the gains to which baseball players were entitled. He believed
that recognition of the reality that Major League Baseball was
indeed a business would seriously diminish the average fan's
appetite for the game. Writers such as Young did not always
portray the owners as saints, but they did believe the magnates
were entitled to a modicum of collusive behavior, particularly
when the interests of the game were at stake. The players, in
this view, were the fortunate few who played a game for a living. These privileged men, therefore, must respect the role of the
owner as the entrepreneur and ultimate authority on all financial matters. Times may have been changing in the late 1960s,
but traditionalist writers like Young were not buying the players' rights-based argument. They remained confident that most
fans still wished to think of baseball as just a game and wanted
to remain somewhat naïve regarding the business of baseball.

Prell kept up a similar line of criticism in the *Chicago Tribune*.
The columnist turned to figures from baseball's storied past to
help support his conviction that the MLBPA was simply taking
things too far. Prell interviewed six longtime baseball men, most
of them with Chicago ties. All of these men expressed concern

that the players' demands would only serve to antagonize the owners, much to the detriment of the game. Former Chicago Cubs manager "Sweet Lou" Boudreau, whose own playing career dated back to the 1930s, said, "I don't like to see them getting so greedy as to possibly upset the owners—especially the older ones, like Phil Wrigley [Cubs], Horace Stoneham [Giants], and Tom Yawkey [Red Sox]. They have done everything within reason for the players. It would be a sad day for the players if men of this type quit baseball." Prell tried to strum the nostalgic heartstrings of Chicago-area fans, reinforcing the notion of baseball clubs as players and owners united to fight the good fight on behalf of their loyal local fan base. Another of Prell's interviewees was Mr. X, who, Prell assured his readers, was a longtime baseball man, still in the game after fifty years. Mr. X told Prell, "Miller can outmaneuver himself and the players. Sure baseball is a big business. But it's also a big sport. When it no longer has the flavor of a sport you can have it. Some of the owners might just chuck it all. Then where would the players be? Many of the clubs lose money. . . . If a team has a bad year, did you ever hear of a player offering to return part of his salary?" Prell finished his column with remarks from former All-Star White Sox pitcher Billy Pierce, who summed up the sentiments of many of those clinging to the belief that Major League Baseball was mainly a game. Pierce said, "It would hurt me deeply if the relationship [between players and owners] suffered. 'Strike' is a word I don't think belongs in the baseball vocabulary unless you're a pitcher."[30] Prell's work offers a clear illustration of how deeply entrenched the traditionalist viewpoint remained and how far the players still needed to go in their efforts to win the favor of the baseball public.

Baseball's first real strike threat loomed, and many of the men responsible for covering the game feared nothing short of the game's collapse. The mere possibility of a players' strike shattered their romantic notion of baseball as an American institution. The constancy of baseball was something to which they clung tightly, especially amid the upheaval of American life in the late 1960s. These writers, like the many traditionalist fans they wrote for, needed the reassurance of spring training and the coming of a new season. Marvin Miller and the MLBPA, they felt, stood firmly in the way of what they needed so badly.

Resolution in the Nick of Time

Miller and the player representatives worked steadily to keep the MLBPA membership resolute in the face of this public criticism. The players overwhelmingly rejected the owners' first offer on January 17, voting 461–6 against the magnates' proposal. The association took several steps to try and regain public support in the wake of their rejection of the magnates' offer. Star players like Henry Aaron, Ron Santo, and Frank Robinson restated their public support of the union's position.[31] The MLBPA condemned what it believed was a smear campaign being run by the owners, in an effort to turn the public against the players and bring about the players' union's demise. The statement charged, "They [the owners] still refuse to understand that Baseball belongs not only to the Owners and the players, but also to the fans—they seem quite willing to sacrifice fan interest if, in the process, they can 'teach the players a lesson.' . . . The Players Association will continue to strive for peace in Baseball, but will not do so at the cost of conceding the players' rights and surrendering players' dignity."[32] The players sensed the shifting tide of public opinion and hoped this type of rhetoric, combined with the open support from some of baseball's greatest players, might help win back the kind of fan support they had enjoyed in 1966.

The players' holdout threat swiftly shaped up to be the first major test of MLBPA unity. Many young stars, eager to cash in on the increased bargaining power from their recent success, were in a hurry to sign new, more lucrative contracts rather than risk holding out and eventually playing the 1969 season at their previous salary. This made it all the more difficult for the MLBPA leadership to keep players in line. Things looked especially promising for the owners when player solidarity began to erode with the start of spring training in mid-February. The owners preyed on this as much as possible, publicly questioning the resolve of the players and implying that the MLBPA membership was not receiving accurate information from their leadership. Miller worked to stem such speculation, saying, "Of the 402 players who authorized us last month to use their names publicly in support of our stand, 391 have not signed and have not reported." Miller "attacked as 'misleading and deceptive' figures sent to the players by the clubs in a 'propaganda document' and cited recent statements by the owners as evidence they were not bargaining in good faith but were intent on testing the players' unity." Miller claimed the owners were attempting to "increase friction in the hope of destroying the players' association."[33]

Despite Miller's efforts to maintain solidarity, several veteran star players signed contracts. Some teams saw as many as two-thirds of their returning players report to camp in preparation for the 1969 season.[34] The owners felt they were making headway, even privately claiming they had Miller "by the balls." As February passed, and the time for spring training approached, the Lords of Baseball and their representatives unleashed a torrent of criticism toward Miller. Atlanta Braves vice president Paul Richards helped lead the charge. Richards said, "I have always been for the players, but when they come up with a four-flushing, mustachioed union organizer by the name of Marvin Miller . . . I don't know." In a straightforward appeal to America's "silent majority," Richards went on to say, "The whole country will suffer unless we learn to respect authority." The Braves executive attempted to frame the struggle by making the players out to be subversives intent on destroying the underpinnings of the Great American Society. Richards closed his comments by playing the oft-used owner poverty card. "I think the owners should make some money. They're giving something to this business. How would you like to run a business where you might lose $700,000 a year?"[35]

Throughout this period, the magnates continued to enjoy strong support from many prominent members of the baseball press. By February 19, *Chicago Tribune* baseball writer Richard

Dozer was officially fed up with the players. Leading off his column with "somewhere in this country or the Caribbean there must be a great baseball player who will . . . ," Dozer launched into a laundry list of his grievances with the players. Dozer's column is a classic appeal to all those who, in the midst of the turmoil of the late 1960s, wanted so desperately to hang on to their romantic notions of the game. He called for players to be grateful to the owners for their paternalism. He rejected the idea that Marvin Miller had brought any value to the game, and he made scapegoats out of the Players Association leadership. Finally, Dozer demanded the start of the baseball season as if it was an inalienable right guaranteed by God and John Locke and insisted that players demonstrate obsequiousness to the fans and owners. Dozer, John Hall, Bob Oates, Edward Prell, and Dick Young were spokesmen for the last generation of traditionalist baseball writers who clung desperately to the romantic purity of the game. They believed their readers felt the same way. These men wrote for an audience they felt was incapable of loving the game while simultaneously embracing baseball as a business. The work of these writers during the 1969 pension holdout would later prove to be a high-water mark for traditionalist resistance to the MLBPA.

In this very moment, when it appeared the owners were regaining the upper hand, player militancy and solidarity grew, in part in response to widespread criticism in the press. As players worked to counter the efforts of the traditionalist baseball press they, like the Brotherhood members of the 1890s, turned to the image of slavery. In early February Miller told the *Sporting News*, "Labor relations-wise the owners have not yet reached the 19th century. This business of owning people is the worst form of slavery I've seen. At one time I thought slavery was abolished; but not in baseball." Miller reinforced the MLBPA's rights-based argument while firing a few new shots at the magnates' paternalistic practices. "Right now the owners are trying to get rid of the Association as an effective voice. . . . What it comes down to is this: The owners are like an old father who can't seem to understand that his young boy has turned out to be a man. They resent the resurgence and have mounted a major attack on the players."[36]

As time passed without a meaningful response by the owners, Miller ratcheted up his rhetoric in an effort to both build public support and pressure the owners for some kind of meaningful response that might help move negotiations forward. This strategy was rewarded in short order. On February 20 Miller received a memo from the Player Relations Committee outlining a much-improved proposal from the owners. The magnates indicated a willingness to increase their pension contribution to $5.3 million and agreed to almost all of the players' demands on issues ranging from disability and dental benefits to early retirement options. On the biggest issue, the players' insistence on an established connection between television revenue and pension funding, the owners "proposed to the Players Association that the issue regarding the relationship between the Clubs' contributions and national radio-TV revenues be resolved by a status quo agreement which would preserve all rights and obligations of the parties as they existed immediately after execution of their previous Benefit Plan Funding Agreement in January 1967."[37] The association had already indicated that this position would be acceptable in the event the owners increased their contribution to the pension. The PRC's more favorable proposal, made in the face of growing public pressure to broker a deal that would allow the season to start on time, helped successfully reopen negotiations.

This turn of events marked a huge shift in favor of the MLBPA as its membership looked to the future. The Players Association benefited from its members' willingness to stay the course in the face of the owners' criticism as well as receiving some unexpected assistance from one of baseball's new sources of emerging revenue. As it turned out, the association held on long enough for outside help to arrive from two separate sources. The first of these was federal mediators. The second source of help was the television networks, which were growing nervous about the prospective loss of programming due to games cancelled by an MLBPA walkout. By mid-February Interim Commissioner Bowie Kuhn was under a great deal of pressure from the networks to broker a deal with the players. Kuhn, now acting in what he believed were the best interests of the game, made himself an active part of the negotiation process. In very short order, the magnates went from the cat-bird seat to having terms dictated by the external pressures of their coveted new revenue streams.

When the players failed to fall apart at the start of camp as the magnates predicted, many members of the baseball press sat up and took notice. *New York Daily News* columnist Phil Pepe appreciated the strength of player solidarity, writing that "players in that category [stars like Willie Mays and Mickey Mantle] do not have to worry about a few extra bucks [in the pension plan]. . . . It is to their credit that they are willing to risk their 1969 salaries [all in the $70,000–$100,000 range] to help the little guy."[38] Pepe acknowledged what had to be one of the magnates' greatest fears, their inability to co-opt star players and turn them against their lower-paid brethren. This new support for the union from some of the game's most revered stars made the 1969 pension holdout a major turning point for the MLBPA. It was much easier for the players to generate public support with a united front, as fans were much less likely to turn against a players' union backed by their greatest heroes. In the face of this pressure from growing player solidarity, the owners, who by now were also fearful of the possibility that unsigned players might be able to test the reserve clause at the end of the 1969 season, moved off of their hard-line stance and returned to negotiations with significantly more generosity in their hearts.[39]

The PRC and MLBPA reached final agreement on the 1969 pension and benefits plan in late February. The clubs agreed to annual pension contributions of $5.45 million, a 32 percent increase over the $4.1 million the owners had contributed in each of the previous two seasons. The agreement lowered the service requirement to four years, allowed for early retirement at age forty-five if a player so desired, and increased retirement benefits by nearly 20 percent. The agreement also expanded widow's benefits and added a dental plan. Most importantly for the players, the agreement stated, "The execution of this Agreement shall not be deemed to change any rights or obligations of the Clubs or the players with respect to the funding of the Plan . . . or with respect to radio and television, as such rights and obligations existed immediately after the execution of the Agreement Re Major League Baseball Players Benefit Plan of January 1, 1967."[40] The players accepted a much smaller pension contribution; their original demand was $5.9 million, in exchange for official acknowledgement of their rights to the commercial sale of their likenesses.

In the wake of this settlement, Miller shared his thoughts regarding the strength of the players' collective consciousness: "Something better could have come out of it if we had been given something close to unanimous support. The players held ranks remarkably well. You can't believe what pressure some of the players were under."[41] Miller wanted to praise those who stayed the course, while providing clear notice to men like Tom Seaver and Jerry Grote, who had broken ranks. His message was unmistakable: the players must follow his lead in matters pertaining to collective bargaining, and player solidarity was an absolute necessity when it came to winning the best possible settlement from the owners.

This episode taught the players several valuable lessons. MLBPA members learned the importance of bargaining pressure generated by new outside revenue streams such as television. More importantly, achieving a successful outcome after a near breakdown in union solidarity did a great deal to reinforce the value of patience and unity. Television's intervention reinforced the MLBPA members' belief that the players' on-field efforts were the primary source of club revenue and that they could not be easily replaced. Without the players' very specialized labor, the owners could not offer what the baseball public demanded: the highest possible level of competitive baseball. In this case, television's essential responsiveness to public opinion further tied the MLBPA's fate to its level of public support.

Finally, by moving to settle in order to avoid having a large number of potential free agents without new contracts, the owners clearly demonstrated just how important it was to them to protect the reserve clause.[42] Interim Commissioner Bowie Kuhn, fearful of having his first Opening Day fizzle, got a great deal of credit as an effective peacemaker.[43] This praise served only to encourage Kuhn, a man already inclined to believe that a commissioner who got directly involved in negotiations was serving the "best interests of the game." Over time, Kuhn developed what the historian Robert Burk calls "commissioneritis, the belief that despite owing his job to management, the commissioner somehow exercised a dispassionate, even-handed patriarchy over all of baseball's constituencies." The 1969 pension holdout crisis was the first of a number of times that Kuhn, who sought to serve the game in the same manner as Judge Landis, interfered in player-management negotiations to the detriment of the game.[44]

A Second Basic Agreement

By the time the pension negotiations were settled, there were less than ten months left before the 1968 Basic Agreement was set to expire, so Miller and the MLBPA set their sights on preparing to negotiate a second Basic Agreement. Many of the financial issues at stake, including an increase in the minimum salary and a longer period for severance pay, were agreed upon with relative ease by the union and the PRC. The largest stumbling block proved to be the makeup of baseball's arbitration panel. The owners knew the reserve clause was the next big issue the players wanted to tackle, and the makeup of the arbitration panel would clearly be a deciding factor in the clause's fate. Miller and the players obviously wanted to reconfigure the arbitration process in a manner that would allow for more-favorable rulings on the interpretation of the reserve clause. This meant the removal of the commissioner from the three-member arbitration panel. The players had good reason to be optimistic on this point, as John Gaherin advised the PRC that they could afford to allow for some flexibility on this issue. Kuhn, who was now baseball's full-fledged commissioner, his "interim" tag having by now been removed, balked at his potential removal from this panel. He knew such an action would limit his power and prevent him from playing a significant role in maintaining baseball's traditionalist order.

Kuhn's wishes in this case would not be granted when the MLBPA and PRC finally reached agreement in early June 1970. Players were pleased that the terms of the new Basic Agreement contributed to a significant jump in salaries. The minimum player salary was increased 20 percent, to $12,000. More importantly, the commissioner was removed from the three-member arbitration panel in favor of an independent professional arbiter. This development cleared the way for the MLBPA to address the reserve clause solely through arbitration and collective bargaining, without any help from Congress or the courts.

Those developments, however, would have to wait for the longer term. In the short term, the introduction of an outside arbitrator quickly proved financially valuable to the players. While salaries themselves were not yet open to arbitration, the players' salaries increased when they won grievances calling for increased post-season compensation. Management added an additional round of playoffs after the 1969 expansion, essentially adding 3 percent to many players' workload, without any accompanying increase in pay. Arbitrators recognized this and made the appropriate adjustments in player salaries.

Other factors helped push salaries even higher. After years of low offensive production, baseball management changed several rules in the late 1960s in order to boost offense. The magnates hoped more offense would draw more fans out to the sparkling new stadiums that accompanied the 1960s expansion boom.[45] Higher TV revenue, increased attendance, and expansion fees also played a role in boosting player salaries. The owners were understandably quite pleased with their new revenue streams but also alarmed at what they saw as an explosive trend in labor costs.[46] So while the new decade began with the relatively peaceful settlement of a new Basic Agreement, the baseball labor front was far from calm. The magnates had grave concerns over the direction of player salaries, and, thanks to arbitration, the reserve clause was more vulnerable than ever. Most importantly, in December 1969, Marvin Miller found a man willing to challenge the reserve clause all the way to the Supreme Court: a determined St. Louis outfielder named Curt Flood.

6

Magnates' Worst Fears Confirmed

With their pensions duly protected and their newfound financial gains safely in the bank, the MLBPA finally moved forward with the very battle that had precipitated the Brotherhood War eighty years earlier. Major League Baseball players prepared for a serious challenge to the reserve clause. The first step had already been taken by making the establishment of a reserve rule study group a priority during negotiations over the Basic Agreement in 1968. By 1969 the magnates knew full well that this challenge to the reserve rule was on its way and, as by that time could be expected, were publicly dismissive of the MLBPA's agenda.

Recent union successes had made the magnates more than a little nervous about losing the reserve clause, which had long been the crown jewel of a standard player contract that preserved the owners' monopoly over the baseball labor market. The Supreme Court and Congress had upheld its legality, and baseball traditionalists accepted it as essential to the survival of the game. Many fans and writers still treasured the roster continuity and sense of community ownership that they believed depended on the reserve clause. On behalf of the owners' Player Relations Committee, the chief negotiator, John Gaherin, wrote, "As the future of the reserve clause is central to the future of organized baseball itself, this Committee believes it to be vitally important that all clubs participate in this initial meeting [to discuss the players' challenge to the reserve clause]."[1] The owners' concerns were more than justified, because the players quickly found the ideal candidate to push their cause.

The Right Man for the Job

The Players Association did not have to wait long to find the perfect test case for a legal challenge to the reserve clause. The St. Louis Cardinals, disappointed at the outcome of the 1969 season, traded star outfielder Curt Flood to the Philadelphia Phillies in exchange for Richie Allen, a power-hitting first baseman. Flood was a bright, respected, thirteen-year veteran, a man many believed to be one of the premier outfielders of the era. It was also not insignificant, in this time of national upheaval over racial equality, that Flood was black, born in Houston, Texas, and raised in Oakland, California. While he was not a militant activist in sympathy with the Black Panthers, Flood was certainly well aware of the gains and frustrations of the civil rights movement. Flood's was a life shaped by the hands of bigotry and segregation. He played two years in the Minor Leagues in the Deep South, where the only available housing was a college dormitory restricted to African Americans. Time and again, Flood was refused service in restaurants and other businesses. Even after he rose to prominence as a Major League Baseball player, armed vigilantes kept Flood and his family from moving into a home in Martinez, California, in 1964. Adding complexity to Flood's public image was his well-known work as a painter of portraits, including a highly regarded portrait of Martin Luther King Jr., whom Flood met on several occasions prior to the civil rights leader's assassination in April 1968.[2]

Because of experiences like these, Flood had a rights consciousness much more deeply cultivated than that of the average baseball player. He was dismayed at the prospect of being forced to leave St. Louis for Philadelphia. The outfielder did not want to leave a successful Cardinal franchise to play for the Phillies, a lackluster team that played in one of the league's most antiquated stadiums. Flood was a beloved favorite of Cardinals' fans, and he feared he would be unwelcome in Philadelphia, where the fans had a reputation as a raucous and even racist bunch. Flood quickly came to see the Cardinals' attempt to trade him as a violation of his civil rights, especially the Thirteenth Amendment's protection from involuntary servitude. Most significantly, Flood opposed the trade because he believed he was being treated not as a man but as a piece of property. The outfielder believed he was being wronged, in the same way his enslaved ancestors had been wronged for more than three hundred years. In the weeks following the trade, Flood began to feel strongly that he was not just another asset of the St. Louis Cardinals, to be bought or sold at management's whim.

Flood first consulted with a local St. Louis attorney before taking his concerns about the trade to the MLBPA's executive director, Marvin Miller. Miller was intrigued by the possibilities of Flood's case but wanted to make sure Flood understood the potential risks. Miller engaged Flood in several lengthy discussions regarding the pros and cons of a legal challenge. Primary among Miller's concerns was the distinct possibility that protracted legal action could, effectively, end Flood's career. Following these conversations, Miller and Flood took the situation before the MLBPA's executive committee. The player representatives ultimately decided to support Flood's cause and help provide him with legal representation. In exchange, Flood agreed he would not accept any legal settlement that did not include permanent modification of the reserve clause in the players' favor.[3] Miller was excited about the possibilities of Flood's case, saying, "For three years we've been trying to change it [the reserve clause]. The owners won't lift a finger to change a comma. They sit and listen and reject every idea. . . . They're in the 19th Century and don't want to leave."[4]

Flood built his legal challenge on the idea that the Cardinals were violating interstate commerce law in an attempt to deny him employment. In language inspired by the Thirteenth Amendment, the civil rights movement, and baseball players' long-standing complaints about their contractual conditions being akin to slavery, Flood publicly insisted he was not a piece of property to be bought, traded, or sold. In an effort to resolve the matter without resorting to legal action, the outfielder appealed to Commissioner Bowie Kuhn: "I believe I have the right to consider offers from other clubs before making any decisions. I, therefore, request that you make known to all clubs my feelings in this matter, and advise them of my availability for the 1970 season."[5]

Kuhn, who had been in the commissioner's office for only sixteen months, believed that Flood's arguments based on property and involuntary servitude did not apply, since Flood willingly surrendered those rights when he entered into his first Major League contract with the Cincinnati Reds in 1956. Kuhn's reply also effectively demonstrated to Flood what might happen if he chose to push for arbitration on the matter. Kuhn had the deciding vote on the three-member arbitration panel, as the commissioner would remain on the panel until the new Basic Agreement took effect. In the face of Kuhn's denial, Flood, who was at the peak of his playing ability and could ill afford to miss out on the chance to practice his craft for an entire season, realized he had no choice but to move forward and challenge the reserve clause in the courts.

The MLBPA leadership subjected Flood to careful screening before agreeing to support his legal case, and Flood assured the association he understood the potential risks and sacrifices. The MLBPA, as always, also had concerns about how Flood's challenge would play out in the court of public opinion. Player representatives were sensitive to the societal turmoil surrounding the ongoing civil rights movement and were concerned that Flood might be making this move as his own way of demonstrating solidarity with more militant civil rights groups. After a discussion of the civil rights movement and Black Power, Dodger catcher Tom Haller asked Flood, "Are you doing this simply because you're black and you feel baseball has been discriminatory?" Flood's reply did a great deal to win the support of the player representatives. "I'd be lying if I told you as a black man in baseball I hadn't gone through worse times than my white teammates. I'll also say that, yes, I think the change in black consciousness in recent years has made me more sensitive to injustice in every area of my life. But I want you to know that what I'm doing here, I'm doing as a ballplayer, a major league ballplayer, and I think it's absolutely terrible that we have stood by and watched this situation go on for so many years and never pulled together to do anything about it."[6]

The player representatives knew it was time for a change in the reserve clause. They also knew enough about the conservative factions within the baseball public that they remained cautious about closely associating their cause with civil rights militancy. After all, it had been just over a year since Tommie Smith and John Carlos were stripped of their medals for raising gloved fists at the Mexico City Olympics, and Lew Alcindor was publicly maligned for sitting out the Olympics in protest. As much as Flood and other players were inspired by the various social movements of their time, the player representatives wanted assurances that their challenge to the reserve clause would not forever be associated with Curt Flood, standing on the steps of a federal courthouse, raising his fist in solidarity with the Black Power movement. Aware of the power of potentially strong public backlash, the MLBPA demonstrated considerable caution about alienating its base of public support in this increasingly divisive public atmosphere.

Miller knew Flood needed top-notch legal counsel and secured the representation of the steelworkers' former general counsel Arthur Goldberg. Goldberg's selection demonstrates the significance of Flood's case to the MLBPA. Few attorneys of this time had the resume and legal acumen to match Goldberg's. He had a lifetime love affair with baseball, starting with his job as a Wrigley Field coffee vendor at age twelve. Goldberg graduated from Northwestern University's law school in 1930 and put together a long and distinguished career as a labor lawyer before being appointed secretary of labor by President Kennedy in 1961. Twenty months later, Kennedy appointed Goldberg to the U.S. Supreme Court, where he served as an associate justice for three years, until Lyndon Johnson asked him to serve as the U.S. ambassador to the United Nations. Goldberg accepted the post in the hope that he could help shape U.S. policy in Vietnam, but he and Johnson clashed, and Goldberg resigned in 1968. The attorney agreed to take Flood's case pro bono, because he felt it would be "a public service to upset a series of unconscionable rulings that should have been overturned by the courts long ago."[7] As Flood's legal challenge moved forward, Goldberg's presence assured the outfielder the best possible representation.

In many ways Flood, the consummate gentleman and star center fielder, and Goldberg, the former Supreme Court justice, were a "dream team" for the players' assault on the reserve clause. There is no small irony in this, however, because Flood was not actually the type of player who felt the greatest impact of the reserve rule. That position was reserved for the career Minor Leaguer. Many of these players were talented enough to play somewhere in the Major Leagues but spent their careers "in the bushes," usually because their parent club had an established star already playing their position at the big league level. The ten-year Minor League veteran Bob Gilhooley, detailed their plight in a letter to the editor of the *Chicago Tribune*:

> What escape is there for such a player? . . . Leaving means leaving baseball entirely. And baseball owners have continued to operate under this shelter, leaving the ballplayer with absolutely no bargaining power and no recourse whatever but to comply and rot in a course directed by the owner . . . Do not expect the superstars to flock to Flood's side. They will not endanger their position with management. It is time for the imbalance between the players' rights and the owners' power is rectified. For every Yastremski and Santo there are one hundred Gilhooleys. And the Gilhooleys are whom this suit is for. Thanks a million, Curt.[8]

The reserve clause stakes may have been high for Major Leaguers such as Flood, but it was Minor Leaguers such as Gilhooley, who felt trapped in their organization, who had the best arguments regarding involuntary servitude and the Thirteenth Amendment.

In the legal world of the late 1960s, it was starkly evident that the 1922 antitrust ruling was something of an anomaly, and Goldberg hoped the court's more recent interpretations of interstate commerce stood in Flood's favor. Flood made his thoughts on the issue clear to reporters in the wake of filing his suit: "From the moment a player leaves the amateur ranks of high school, college, or sandlot baseball, the player must play for the team which first acquires him. . . . The reserve system is a practice constituting and resulting in peonage and involuntary servitude."[9] Flood's suit asked for $25,000 in damages, as well as an injunction allowing him to sign a contract with the club of his choice for the 1970 season. In the event that an injunction was not granted, Flood's suit asked for $1 million in total damages, based on the assumption that lengthy legal proceedings would essentially end his playing career.

Flood and Goldberg built their legal argument on five basic premises. They argued that baseball should now be subject to antitrust laws, as its broadcast revenue, which represented well over 50 percent of total club revenues, was clearly an interstate activity. They further argued that interstate travel and communications were essential to the staging of baseball games, that baseball teams colluded to suppress salaries, and that the reserve clause imposed involuntary servitude. The suit included additional allegations that demonstrated an increasingly sophisticated view of the business of baseball. For example, it contended that Major League baseball was rife with practices, such as the exclusive sale of Anheuser-Busch beer at Cardinal home games, designed to hide club revenues and suppress player salaries. Practices such as these increased revenue for the brewery, which owned the baseball club, but decreased Cardinals' revenues available for increased player salaries.[10] Flood and Goldberg were prepared to show the courts, and the baseball public, the hidden workings of the business of baseball.

The Court of Public Opinion

Right from the beginning of Flood's challenge, widespread public debate ensued over both the reserve clause and the larger
issue of baseball's antitrust status. The initial media reaction
was mixed, ranging from arguments that the reserve clause was
essential to the game to support for Flood and his argument that
the reserve system amounted to involuntary servitude. Papers
such as the *New York Times* seemed to relish the upcoming battle. The *Times* ran a series of articles intended to inform its
readership of the case's legal background, as well as the importance of the reserve clause to the business of baseball. Some
papers acknowledged that, given the direction of antitrust law
over the prior two decades, a serious challenge to the reserve
clause was long overdue. Finally, there were publications, such
as the *Chicago Tribune,* that took a more traditionalist view and
were outspoken in their criticism of Flood. These papers condemned Flood; in their view he was yet another ballplayer who
clearly failed to realize just how good he had it. They sided with
the magnates and argued that the end of the reserve clause would
effectively mean the end of professional baseball. Regardless of
the point of view, four years of MLBPA activism had made the
press much more sophisticated regarding the business of the
game. Flood's case received the full attention of a burgeoning
sports media that was well attuned to the business nuances of
professional sports.

In response to the wave of media attention surrounding Flood's
case, in mid-January the magnates sent two of the Major League's
great patriarchs, league presidents Charles "Chub" Feeney and
Joe Cronin, to defend the traditionalist view of the game. Showing fresh wounds from the 1969 pension battle, Feeney and
Cronin pulled no punches. They "believed the game would simply cease to exist" if the reserve clause were abolished, as it was
"absolutely necessary to the successful operation of baseball."
Ignoring the prevailing agreement in legal circles that baseball's
antitrust exemption was increasingly an anomaly, Feeney and

Cronin emphasized the fact that the Supreme Court had held up the legality of the reserve clause on three separate occasions. The two men declared their "complete confidence that the rules of professional baseball, which have been central to the success of the game over many decades and which have permitted players such as Curt Flood to reap rich personal rewards, will withstand this new attack."

Prominently displaying their nearly lifelong ties to the game, Cronin and Feeney trotted out all of the tried and true arguments regarding the centrality of the reserve clause to the success of the game. Among them was the notion that a free market for baseball players could only result in a few wealthy clubs controlling the vast majority of the available on-field talent, an argument that continued to ignore the dominance a handful of clubs enjoyed with the reserve clause in place. The magnates further argued that the ability to negotiate with other clubs would make a player less loyal to his current club and would call into question the integrity of the game, as players might be susceptible to playing poorly in exchange for a rich contract from the opposition down the road. Finally, Cronin and Feeney believed that affording a player any say regarding his playing situation would disrupt the natural flow of player transactions, the sales and trades critical to maintaining competitive balance, and the successful operation of the game.[11]

Baseball is by nature a tradition-bound game, and one can understand why the magnates turned to many of the same arguments that had carried them through previous trade wars and legal challenges. Flood's situation was different, a fact the magnates would come to understand quite clearly as the next decade unfolded. Flood enjoyed the full support of baseball's first effective players' union. He had the legal counsel of a former union leader and Supreme Court justice, Arthur Goldberg. The owners also failed to grasp that, in this era of newly emerging electronic media, many of their previous tactics would become ineffective. Their oft-used "competitive balance" argument rang false, especially when the perennial success of clubs like the Yankees, who won fifteen American League pennants between 1947 and 1964, was taken into account. Increasingly, large groups within the baseball public were recognized the changing nature of the business and were more likely to question the owners' pleas of poverty, especially after the magnates proved capable of meeting increasing financial demands from the players at every turn and because new stadiums were springing up across the country.

Miller immediately took Cronin and Feeney to task in the press. The MLBPA leader took exception with the league presidents for criticizing the MLBPA executive committee's support for Flood: "[Cronin and Feeney] attacked the players association as being in bad faith for supporting Curt Flood. Both Mr. Cronin and Mr. Feeney know better, and it is unfortunate that they have permitted their public relations advisers to use them for the purpose of making libelous public accusations." The owners had criticized the MLBPA for not making its "best efforts" to see that all the terms of the 1968 Basic Agreement were carried out, including those related to the reserve rule. Miller countered, "The players association took the view that the reserve clause was illegal and that it could not agree to use its best efforts to see that illegal provisions were enforced."[12] Miller wanted to set the reserve clause aside as an "illegal provision" in the eyes of the public. He hoped this move would exonerate the players from the stain of being promise breakers as well as shift public dialogue regarding the legality of the reserve clause.

Not surprisingly, the magnates countered by continuing their campaign to place a fair share of the blame on Miller for all of baseball's recent ills. The game's grand statesman, Dodger owner Walter O'Malley, took advantage of a mid-February interview with Los Angeles Times baseball reporter Ross Newhan to make sure the public knew whom it could fault for its disenchantment with the game. O'Malley argued that the Dodgers, as one of baseball's premier franchises, actually had a great deal to gain from the elimination of the reserve clause. He knew better, of course, and attempted to reinforce Cronin and Feeney's arguments that the game would collapse without the rule. The Dodger patriarch then shared his thoughts on Marvin Miller:

> I'm sure that Mr. Miller is a capable man who thinks he's working for the best interests of his clients. I can only say that I'm disappointed in the methods he's used. He's created an aura of negativism that has harmed the image of the sport. Last year, for example, it was the threat of a strike. This year it's the threat of litigation. The cumulative effect is that baseball is always in a negative position without substantial reason. I mean I seriously doubt that any player during the last few years has been treated callously by an owner. Really, their benefit plan is unparalleled and their salaries are quite good. If Mr. Miller would use his office to build up baseball, to help improve its image, then there would be much more money to siphon off to his players.[13]

First, it was no accident that O'Malley chose to make himself available for an extensive interview in the midst of the *Flood* proceedings. As one of baseball's most senior owners, O'Malley wanted to seize this opportunity to reinforce the magnates' positions on the key issues. It is ironic that O'Malley based his argument on gains the players won through the collective bargaining efforts of the MLBPA, under the leadership of his nemesis, Marvin Miller. O'Malley could not be expected to acknowledge that at least some of baseball's woes stemmed from decades of monopolistic practices, as well as the inability of his contemporaries to respond creatively to the changing landscape of the professional sports business. It is somewhat ironic that the Dodgers patriarch implied that the players would receive their fair share of new revenues when owners consistently battled to maintain complete control over new revenue streams. On the whole, it is a telling sign that a standard-bearer like O'Malley missed his mark when he attempted to discredit Miller in the eyes of a baseball public growing increasingly unsure of the veracity of the magnates' standard company line.

It was, indeed, good news for the players that the baseball public was developing a more sophisticated understanding of the business of baseball. The more perceptive public, on the whole, was much less willing to take the magnates at their word than it had been just five or six years earlier. Veteran syndicated sports columnists such as the *Los Angeles Times*' Jim Murray made this readily apparent to the owners. In a column published just two days after Cronin and Feeney made their comments, Murray wrote, "The 'reserve clause,' the last vestige of slavery in America, binds the player to the club in perpetuity. He can be traded . . . but only at the whim of the slaveowner . . . otherwise known as the general manager. . . . All it [baseball] can save is itself. I would try to keep that Flood between its banks.[14] Murray, by 1970, was a seasoned columnist so widely respected that he had been named "America's Best Sportswriter" fourteen times. In this case he effectively turned the owners' "they don't realize how good they have it" argument right back on them. His disdain for the owners' inability to make the necessary modifications to their sacred cow provides a clear example of the sea change occurring among sportswriters, who held a great deal of sway in shaping public opinion.

This shift in public perception was perhaps most evident in the way that many former MLBPA critics lent their voices in support of the players. *Chicago Tribune* columnist Richard Dozer, an especially outspoken critic of the MLBPA during the pension holdout, wrote a column supporting the need for change. While Dozer was far from openly sympathetic with Flood, he did agree with Marvin Miller that there was a serious need to study the existing reserve rule and make some modifications. Dozer's shift was a big win for the players, and Miller continued to work carefully to sway writers like Dozer to the players' camp. "There has been a tendency to oversimplify the problem as if there were only two alternatives," Dozer wrote. "The present set of rules or no rules at all."[15] Miller, entering his fourth year at the MLBPA's helm, knew well enough that major changes in the structure of the game would take time; hence his cautious tack with traditionalists like Dozer. In the days leading up to Flood's trial, Miller worked to remind the baseball press that the

MLBPA sought only to open a conversation with the magnates regarding the restrictions of the clause.

Flood v. Kuhn Goes to Court

Legal proceedings got underway in early February, when trial judge Irving Ben Cooper agreed to hear arguments regarding Flood's request for an injunction. Goldberg wanted to reinforce the "reserve clause as slavery" argument by attacking head-on the notion that a highly paid athlete could indeed be subject to involuntary servitude. Goldberg also reasserted his position that Flood's case pushed for modification, not rejection, of the reserve rule, and "is not designed to cripple or harass baseball. He desires to be treated as a free man. The chamber of horrors about the end of baseball if antitrust applies is dispelled by reference to other activities. Football, boxing, and theaters have similar situations and they seem to do alright under antitrust." National League attorneys argued against the injunction, primarily on the grounds that an injunction would provide the Flood with the same result he hoped to win at the end of a full trial, the right to negotiate a contract with the club of his choosing. They contended that an injunction should only be used to maintain the status quo. Goldberg and Flood indicated they would be thrilled with such a result, as it would mean Flood could return to the Cardinals for the 1970 season.

Even in these early proceedings, there was plenty of evidence that Judge Cooper was a proud member of the traditionalist camp. He peppered his language with baseball references, demonstrating just how deeply baseball culture ran throughout American society. The judge called a "seventh-inning stretch," instead of a recess, after hearing Goldberg's argument. Cooper concluded proceedings by likening himself to an umpire: "Now you have thrown the ball to me and I hope I do not muff it."[16] Cooper's language indicated a familiarity with the game that hinted he might have a sympathetic ear for the time-tested arguments of the National League's attorneys. His lighthearted approach demonstrated a personal view of baseball more as game and pastime and less as a serious business subject to regulation in the courts. As Flood's suit moved forward, the judge's apparent viewpoint did not bode well for the three-time All-Star, or his brethren in the MLBPA.

On March 4, after hearing testimony from a wide variety of witnesses, ranging from the league presidents to the disgruntled former magnate Bill Veeck to play-by-play man Joe Garagiola, Cooper denied Flood's request for an injunction. In his ruling, Cooper favored the National League attorneys' arguments. The judge agreed that an injunction would provide Flood with the same benefits he sought to gain from a full trial. The decision showed Cooper's caution in moving away from established precedents: "For years professional baseball players have chafed under the restrictions of the reserve system: a long line of litigation so attests. Many of their grievances appear justified. Yet, regretfully, as the Supreme Court stated in Radovich, we are not writing on a clean slate.[17] Recognizing the equity of plaintiff's claims, we must also recognize the existing, well-established, and controlling precedents against his position." Cooper did say that he was "impressed with Flood's argument that the rule of reason should govern, and that baseball, like boxing and football, should be included under federal anti-trust law. . . . But in light of the consistent and clear holdings of the Supreme Court that baseball is not subject to the federal anti-trust laws no matter how illogical such holdings may appear to some by reason of subsequent events, the final outcome of this litigation is doubtful to say the least. Indeed, plaintiff has a formidable hurdle to leap to achieve ultimate success."[18] Cooper appeared inclined to grant baseball the same legal "hall pass" the game had used for nearly fifty years. Baseball was so completely ingrained in American culture that many Americans had difficulty seeing it as unworthy of the special status granted to it in the 1922 anti-trust ruling, even in the face of rulings holding other professional sports to higher antitrust standards.

In the meantime, Flood was under a great deal of public pressure to play for the Phillies while legal proceedings moved forward, but the outfielder knew such a move would render his legal challenge moot. "The failure to obtain a restraining order means I've lost my one chance to play ball for this year. I can only hope that after a full hearing on the merits that my position will have been vindicated and that my career will not have been ended by the time lost pursuing what I believe to be right."[19] Goldberg indicated that he and Flood would weigh their immediate options but made it clear that successful negotiations regarding modification of the reserve clause were the surest way to get Flood to drop his suit. Flood wanted to play in 1970 and hoped that the threat of a lawsuit would bring about changes in the reserve rule, especially changes that might benefit ten-year veterans such as him. By March 1970, however, it was apparent that such modifications would not be in place in time for the 1970 season.

The magnates were pleased with Cooper's ruling but did not have long to sit back and enjoy it. The owners' wishes to simply move forward were further disrupted in early March by Richie Allen, who attempted to use all of the publicity surrounding Flood's hearing to pressure the Cardinals for a higher salary. Cardinals owner Gussie Busch was fed up, telling reporters, "I can tell you point blank, we ain't going to give in. He's [Allen] going to play at our figure or he's not going to play for the Cardinals."[20] As always, Busch proved to be the most quotable of the reactionary magnates. His indignation at Allen's attempts to negotiate a higher salary, as well as future Hall of Fame pitcher Steve Carlton's efforts to improve his $31,000 salary, made clear the deeply ingrained nature of the privileged paternalistic mindset held by some owners.[21]

What Busch and magnates like him failed to recognize was that the players were no longer willing to meekly follow management's lead. Former Dodger pitcher Sandy Koufax's comments on Flood's case indicated the players' new willingness to make public their objections to management paternalism. Koufax described player-management negotiations as "a fun thing for the general manager. He talks to the player and it's fun as long as the general manager wants to play that game. Whenever he gets to the point where he's tired of that game, he says 'ok that's it,' and you either sign or get out."[22] Ten years earlier, a star of Koufax's magnitude would undoubtedly have cautiously protected the game's long-standing business practices. Now, even though he still worked in baseball as a broadcaster and counted on the game for his income, Koufax took a public stand in favor of increased players' rights. As was the case with his public holdout in 1966, Koufax demonstrated the growing realization among star players that their celebrity status offered them a modicum of protection from owner retaliation. Koufax was among the first of the top tier of baseball men to realize that a players' union could improve the lot of all players, not just those getting by on the minimum salary or fighting their way out of the Minor Leagues. His joint holdout with Don Drysdale helped him understand the way in which star players could pry open the owners' wallets through collective strength.

Flood's trial was set to begin in May, and Miller took advantage of the lull in legal action to continue his public campaign against owner paternalism. The MLBPA executive director told reporters that the players' struggle against the reserve clause boiled down to their search for basic human dignity. "The rules and regulations that people call the reserve clause cover every aspect of the player-owner relationship. They make a dignified relationship between player and owner, or employer and employee, difficult to achieve." After providing examples, such as regulations regarding the length of a player's hair or curfews limiting players' social opportunities on the road, Miller argued that owner paternalism was "built into the system—and they [owners' abuses] rise to the surface in 100 different ways. It's inherent in the situation. Some people, when they have people under their thumb, abuse their power. In the final analysis—if you can't disagree with your employer and be able to tell him you are going to work elsewhere, dignity is impossible."

By underscoring the complete lack of freedom of movement in the standard player's contract, Miller once again proved masterful in framing the players' struggles in a manner more appealing to the average workingman. The MLBPA leader challenged the notion that the high salaries paid to a few stars, such as Flood's $90,000 annual salary, made these restrictions and paternalistic practices acceptable. "There is principle involved. To assume that everything is OK if the price is right is a system I don't buy. I think there are more important things in this world than money." This did not mean Miller was ready to concede that player salaries had risen to an acceptable level. He argued that when you "measure the progress of salaries against other sports or the entertainment field, baseball lags. Salaries today are a smaller part of total baseball revenue than they were 10 years ago, 20 years ago, 30 years ago."[23] Such comments frustrated the magnates, who after years of exemption from antitrust regulation had grown accustomed to paying their players as little as possible, regardless of how much total revenue they earned.

Miller's ability to frame issues in terms of principle and decency frustrated the owners, especially when some members of the public refused to accept the magnates' depiction of Miller as a labor agitator extraordinaire. Commissioner Bowie Kuhn made his, and the owners', sentiments regarding Miller abundantly clear: "Essentially, it seemed to me, Miller had a deep hatred and suspicion of the American right and American capitalism. And what could be more the prototype of what he hated than professional baseball, with its rich, lordly owners and its players shackled by the reserve system."[24] The players had quite a different view of Miller by 1970. In a time of widespread societal change, many players saw Miller as a uniquely talented, progressive reformer who could free baseball from its hidebound past. Miller successfully portrayed Commissioner Kuhn as the greatest barrier to successful resolution of the game's problems, with the magnates playing key supporting roles. Kuhn did little to help this image. Seeking to increase his credibility as the great protector of the game, the commissioner cast himself as the next Judge Landis.[25] This only made the MLBPA's public relations efforts easier, especially when it came to painting Kuhn as mired in the game's paternalistic past. While some older fans may have responded positively to Kuhn's efforts to slow progress, many younger fans were put off by his lack of outward willingness to help move the game forward into the modern age.

Flood v. Kuhn Goes to Trial

Testimony from Flood and Miller filled the first day of Flood's trial. Proceedings continued with testimony from Hank Greenberg and Jackie Robinson, two men well known for their contributions to the game. Greenberg had a long and distinguished playing career, followed by an eighteen-year period in which he was a club official, general manager, and ultimately a team owner. This long and varied background made his testimony essential to Flood's case. Greenberg argued that the "reserve clause is obsolete, antiquated, and definitely needs change." The Hall of Famer called for more-harmonious relations between players and owners and expressed his hopes that the owners might voluntarily make some of the needed changes in the best interests of the game. In response to the argument that baseball franchises would lose much of their value without the reserve clause, Greenberg said, "I'd be happy to invest in a club tomorrow if there were no reserve clause. The owners should have some control over the players, but it should be limited." Greenberg's comments carried the weight of a lifetime in the game. Robinson, the man who had broken the game's infamous color barrier twenty-four years earlier, framed his criticism in much broader strokes: "Anything that is one sided is wrong in America. The reserve clause is one sided in favor of the owners and should be modified to give the player some control over his destiny. . . . If the reserve clause is not modified you will have a serious strike by the players." Robinson's presence symbolized the ways the game could change for the better, and his reference to a possible players' strike implied his support for the players to move as they best saw fit. If Robinson's was the voice of progress, then the path of progress required serious modification to the reserve rule.[26] Once again, fans and writers hoping to see baseball move forward surely took note.

Goldberg wrapped up Flood's case by calling on executives from the National Basketball Association and National Hockey League, both of whom described their league's contractual system as much less restrictive than baseball's.[27]

The magnates' attorneys opened their side of the proceedings by continuing their efforts to group Flood's case in with previous decisions. They filed a motion for dismissal, based on the grounds that Flood and Goldberg had brought no new evidence showing that conditions were any different in 1970 than they were when the Supreme Court ruled on the *Toolson* case in 1953. Cooper denied the motion, forcing the magnates to move forward with their case.

Bowie Kuhn was the first witness for the defense, and he opened by condemning the MLBPA for pursuing changes in the reserve clause through legal action instead of collective bargaining. The commissioner thus set the tone for the defense, which based much of its argument on the notion that players had other means to effect changes in the reserve system. Kuhn argued that the clause was necessary to preserve the integrity of the game, which would be called into question if a player was in negotiations with his current club's opponents. In doing so, Kuhn ignored the prospect that free agency might encourage such a player to play even harder in an attempt to enhance his negotiating position for the upcoming season. Additionally, Kuhn testified that the clause was necessary to maintain competitive balance. He said most clubs could ill afford the bidding wars that would certainly ensue if the reserve clause was struck down and the players were granted free agency. The commissioner held fast to his belief that "the totality of the players are better off in the present system."[28] Like his predecessors, Kuhn insisted that the chaotic period leading up to the 1890 Brotherhood War offered clear evidence of the reserve system's necessity, demonstrating to the public a management mind-set still somewhat rooted in the manner of thinking of the Gilded Age. After retiring as commissioner in the early 1980s, Kuhn would say that he knew modification of the reserve clause was a necessary inevitability, but during the Flood trial the commissioner never wavered from the almost century-old path of his forbearers.

A series of other high-ranking baseball officials followed Kuhn, led by Charles "Chub" Feeney, who testified that the millions spent each year on player development created widespread owner poverty. Feeney argued that player-club negotiations were far from the one-sided affairs the players presented and that baseball was unique in its need for the reserve clause because basketball and football had quality college programs to develop their talent, while baseball, which relied on a Minor League system stocked with players largely signed right out of high school, had no such luxury. Baseball clubs, therefore, needed legislation that allowed them to hold on to their players, especially since it was so expensive to develop new players.[29] Several additional magnates followed Feeney, all insisting that the reserve clause was the only reason they believed baseball was a safe investment.[30] The magnates' chief negotiator, John Gaherin, testified next and restated Kuhn's assertion that any necessary modifications should be made through the collective bargaining process.[31] Little did Kuhn and Gaherin know that, by publicly relegating the issue to collective bargaining, they were playing right into the hands of Marvin Miller.

The defense concluded its portion of the case with the economist John Clark, who attempted to shore up the owners' claims of poverty.[32] Flood's rebuttal witnesses included Miller and ended with the colorful former magnate Bill Veeck, a longtime critic of established baseball men like Feeney and O'Malley. Veeck offered several alternatives to the current reserve system. The first of these was a contract similar to the motion picture industry's, in which a team could hold a player for seven years, after which time the player would become a free agent. Veeck's second choice was a system similar to football's, in which a player could play out the last, or "option," year of his contract and then sign with a new club. Veeck argued that the clause should be modified, because "everyone, at least once in their business career, should be able to determine his own future—not be held in perpetuity." His emphasis on freedom of contract and personal liberty helped drive home the primary message players hoped to deliver over the course of the *Flood* proceedings. Veeck concluded his direct testimony by disagreeing with the magnates' contention that free agency could only result in just a few wealthy clubs snapping up all of the most talented players. Veeck insisted, therefore, that the modification of the reserve clause would not discourage him from investing in a Major League ball club.[33]

Veeck was the trial's final witness, and after closing arguments the case was turned over to Cooper. One of the trial's closest observers, Leonard Koppett, who wrote for both the *New York Times* and the *Sporting News*, weighed in on the likely impact of the trial on the game. Koppett argued there was no reason to believe that baseball would not remain healthy, even thrive, regardless of the outcome. He took both sides to task for misleading the public, ultimately to the detriment of the game. After criticizing Flood's camp for using the word "slavery . . . strictly as an emotion word," he added, "the baseball arrangements are one sided enough, and the players' lack of choice clear enough, without dragging in a deliberately inflammatory term." Koppett then turned his attention to the magnates.

> But two phrases employed by the defense were even more misleading, because they were subtler and had the appearance of responsibility. These were, "baseball is unique" and "baseball as we know it." To the extent that baseball is "unique" . . . in practical terms the uniqueness baseball claims centers on its "player development costs," which other professional sports don't face to the same degree. But it is perfectly reasonable to consider player development the equivalent of raw materials and manufacturing in ordinary business: if the product is a major league baseball game, the stuff that goes into it is the finding and training of thousands of minor league players.[34]

Koppett set these remarks in context by discussing all of the significant changes in the game that had come about during the previous fifty years. He brought up everything from franchise relocation to changing roster sizes to the legalization of the spitball, all in an effort to show there was really no such thing as "baseball as we know it." In the end, his point was that baseball could adjust as needed and maintain its prominent position in American life. The emergence of writers like Koppett meant the magnates could no longer play by the old rules or expect to win disputes such as Flood's based on the arguments of the past. In the wake of the *Federal League, Gardella,* and *Toolson* rulings, which established and upheld baseball's antitrust exemption, there was little outcry in the baseball press. It was clear, in the days following the conclusion of Flood's trial, that there were plenty of voices in the baseball press who rejected the owners' argument for exceptionalism and held them to the same standards as other businesses. The emergence of these new sentiments marked a major shift in the discourse surrounding baseball's antitrust status and showed that significant changes were on the horizon, perhaps even regardless of the outcome in Flood's case.

Judge Cooper issued his decision two months later. He essentially ruled by not ruling, writing that it would remain up to the Supreme Court to decide whether to overturn baseball's antitrust exemption. Cooper wrote, "Prior to the trial, we gained the impression that there was a view, held by many, that baseball's reserve clause had occasioned rampant abuse and that it should be abolished. We are struck by the fact, however, that the testimony at trial failed to support that criticism; we find no general or widespread disregard of the extremely important position the player occupies." Kuhn, for the time being, declared victory, announcing, "I am particularly pleased that the court has recognized the need for a reserve system and has recognized further that baseball has not disregarded the important position the player occupies." The commissioner went on to say, "I share Judge Cooper's conclusion that any changes necessary in the reserve system can be achieved by bargaining." Miller, on the other hand, made efforts to assure the media that this was the expected outcome of the first trial: "I think everyone knew it would be difficult for a district court to overrule the Supreme Court. . . . There will be an almost immediate appeal to the Federal Circuit Court of Appeals."[35]

Media reaction in the wake of the decision was somewhat subdued. Charles Maher of the *Los Angeles Times* expressed sentiments similar to those of quite a few other reporters when he argued for modification in line with professional football's option clause. Such a change would allow baseball players with five or six years of big league experience to play out an "option season," after which they could sign with the club of their choosing. The player's original club would receive some kind of fair compensation—money, a draft pick or picks, or even another player—from the player's new club. Maher sought to put public pressure on the owners to make the needed changes, arguing, "Bowie Kuhn has said he thinks differences over player control can be resolved through negotiations. But I doubt the club owners are prepared now to make any real concessions to the players. With a court decision in their favor the owners will be bargaining from a position of strength. If Flood doesn't get any satisfaction in the courts at the appellate levels, he probably won't get any at all."[36]

Six months later, on the eve of spring training, Flood was still newsworthy and Jim Murray weighed in on the baseball labor situation.

> The reserve clause enables a marginal operator to stumble on, say, a Johnny Bench, because a scout gets lucky and, then, three years later a franchise owner like Charlie Finley offers $2 million, why shouldn't he get it instead of a bunch of shareholders? Or if he doesn't want to move to Oakland, why should he have to? If the reserve clause is indeed Flooded out, the game may get washed away, too. But, even if it isn't, it would seem to behoove the game to shore up its levees and provide that 1) no player should be traded without his consent; and 2) no player shall be sold for cash without his participation. If it's unwilling to do this, Baseball better get the Ark ready.[37]

Murray took a leading role in the public push for major changes in the business of baseball, carrying forward the arguments advanced by writers like Leonard Koppett at the time of the trial. Murray remained openly critical of the magnates, questioning their use of "tradition" as a primary reason for resisting change in the baseball labor situation. He understood the dramatic changes in the game, ranging from expansion to skyrocketing television revenues, that had occurred over the course of the previous two decades. Murray hoped the Supreme Court would acknowledge these changes if it agreed to hear Flood's case and revisit the *Toolson* decision made twenty years earlier.

Flood attempted a playing comeback in 1971, agreeing to a $110,000 contract with the Washington Senators. His return to baseball was short lived, however, when it became clear, early on, that advancing age and his year away from baseball had deteriorated his skills. Flood hung up his cleats but became no less important to organized baseball. In October the Supreme Court agreed to hear his appeal. A *New York Times* piece anticipated a groundbreaking decision. "Justice Holmes' view of baseball, as a sport rather than commerce, has come under increasing criticism as the years have passed and baseball has become an increasingly lucrative and unsentimental business. This attitude was underscored in recent Senate Judiciary Subcommittee hearings that looked into the business practices of professional sports." Even in the face of such shifting public sentiment, the magnates stuck to their claims that baseball remained unique and that the elimination of the reserve rule could only lead to chaos.[38] Comments such as those made by Minnesota Twins owner Calvin Griffith were typical of small-market magnates: "The reserve clause is the salvation of our sport. Without it, we can't protect our own players; there will be no competition. Elimination of the reserve clause would destroy our balance." Griffith, in many ways the model of a small-market magnate who was used to getting by on much smaller revenue streams, even argued that the modification of the reserve clause would require players to forgo their pensions.[39]

An interesting subplot in the antitrust drama emerged later that winter, when owner Bob Short packed up the Washington Senators, the club he had just recently purchased in a highly leveraged deal, and headed for the booming Sunbelt market of Texas. The move required the approval of two-thirds of the magnates, many of whom were more than happy to oversee the expansion of the game in the nation's fastest-growing region. Washington DC, however, was now without a Major League franchise for the first time in seventy-one years, and several congressmen worked hastily to remedy the situation. Their saber rattling included a threat to revoke baseball's antitrust exemption if the owners did not immediately act to place a new franchise in the Washington DC area. Some feigned shock over Congress's threatened involvement, but, as veteran *Washington Post* sports columnist Shirley Povich pointed out, this was merely one more episode of political interplay between the federal government and Major League Baseball.[40]

Venerated *New York Times* columnist Red Smith weighed in as well. In reference to the abundance of player trades at the winter meetings, Smith wrote, "The men who own baseball swapped bodies as if the slave trade was going out of style, which, indeed, may be the case. . . . The decision in the [Curt Flood] case may set up restraints on the flesh peddlers. Even if the Court does not uphold the 13th Amendment, Congress just might get the notion that baseball has been above the law too long, and do something about it." Smith continued, "Ordinarily they [members of Congress] haven't the stomach to challenge anything as popular as baseball, but the climate is changing. The arrogant self-interest of the men who own baseball and their cynical disregard for the communities whose support they solicit has worn perilously thin."[41] Ultimately, Congress's threats failed to gain momentum, but the uproar over the Senators' departure did a great deal to elevate the debate over baseball's antitrust exemption and fuel the fires of the greatest critics of owner hypocrisy.

Arthur Goldberg used the eighteen-month interlude between trials to refine and redirect his arguments in favor of the revocation of the reserve clause. He believed recent Major League expansion made the business of baseball more interstate in nature than ever before. Moreover, Goldberg argued that the recent moves of the Senators to Texas, where they became the Rangers, and the Los Angeles Angels to Anaheim demonstrated just how willing the magnates were to abandon the communities they once called home. Goldberg believed this trend indicated baseball was no longer run like the "national treasure" that the Supreme Court had deemed worthy of an antitrust exemption in the past. If owners expected fans to be adaptable enough to embrace this kind of franchise relocation, how could they think fans would be so adverse to the rapid player relocations that would come about with free agency? Flood's attorney was quick to point out that these moves marked a clear shift from twenty years earlier, the last time the Supreme Court had revisited the reserve clause in the *Toolson* decision.[42] Goldberg was not alone. Many members of the sporting press took notice of the changing nature of club ownership. Gone were the days, for example, when the Wrigley family owned the Cubs primarily to generate publicity and goodwill in the Windy City. The new trend, as observed by many, was toward club ownership by corporations and wealthy syndicates. This change was largely driven by the rapid expansion of television revenue. These revenues lessened owner dependence on ticket revenue and brought an infusion of funds that helped drive up player salaries and, more significantly, franchise values. As Leonard Koppett argued, higher franchise costs and potentially rising values often meant that owners, such as the Rangers' Bob Short, borrowed significant sums in order to make their initial purchase. Servicing such debt put a great deal of pressure on club resources and exposed baseball to the vagaries of the larger national economy. According to Goldberg, the new dependence on television revenues made Major League Baseball, without question, interstate commerce.

Flood v. Kuhn Makes It All the Way to the Top

The Supreme Court finally heard arguments on March 20, 1972. Goldberg, as expected, advanced his argument that the court must overturn the antitrust ruling because baseball had truly become interstate commerce. Major League attorneys argued that, since the MLBPA was financing the case, this dispute was really more about labor law than about the rights of one individual player. Therefore, the magnates' attorneys argued, the court should turn things back to the association and magnates to resolve through collective bargaining. This tack had always been part of the owners' strategy in the case, but, in their final arguments before the court, league attorneys took additional steps to even further tie the resolution of player-owner differences on the reserve clause to the collective bargaining process. This was a development welcomed by Marvin Miller. He knew that once the owners fully committed to handling the reserve system through the bargaining process, the players stood to finally make some headway against the reserve clause. Even in the event that the Supreme Court rejected Flood's appeal, the magnates' commitment to subjecting the reserve system to the bargaining process was a huge victory for the MLBPA. Bowie Kuhn would later argue that it was his intent all along to push the reserve clause issue toward the bargaining table, but if that was indeed the case, Kuhn played right into the hands of the MLBPA leadership.[43]

The court delivered its opinion three months later, ruling five to three that it remained Congress's responsibility to enact legislation overturning baseball's antitrust exemption. Acknowledging the obvious inconsistency in baseball receiving an exemption from antitrust laws while professional basketball and football did not, Justice Harry Blackmun wrote, "We continue to be loath, 50 years after *Federal Baseball* and almost two decades after *Toolson*, to overturn those cases judicially when Congress, by its positive inaction, has allowed those decisions to stand for so long."[44]

As was the case with Judge Cooper's handling of the original trial, baseball's hold on the national psyche remained in evidence, both throughout the proceedings and in Blackmun's opinion. The justice opened his opinion with a paean to baseball titled "The Game." This section of the opinion was intended to provide a bit of background to baseball's past labor difficulties, but it also included Blackmun's own reverential recounting of the game's storied past. The justice even included a list of more than seventy noteworthy baseball personalities, almost as a way of proving his dedication and loyalty to the national pastime. It was more than evident that the judges in the majority had difficulty looking past baseball's unique place in the nation's cultural tradition. Jim Murray offered this assessment of Blackmun's approach: "It was like coming into court on a slavery case and having the court hand down the lyrics to Old Black Joe or Sewanee River."[45] As had often been the case, this particular Supreme Court ruling connected more strongly to the notions of America's past than the realities of its present.

It was fitting that the civil rights advocate Thurgood Marshall wrote the dissenting opinion. Marshall stood in clear disagreement with the majority's lack of willingness to bring baseball's antitrust status in line with that of other professional sports. "The importance of the antitrust laws to every citizen must not be minimized. They are as important to baseball players as they are to football players, lawyers, doctors, or members of any other class of workers. Baseball players cannot be denied the benefits of competition merely because club owners view other economic interests as being more important, unless Congress says so."[46] Marshall, joined in dissent by William Brennan, represented a new national perspective, shaped by people with their eyes open to the possibilities of equal rights for all. They saw baseball as a business, not an exceptional American institution deserving of freedom from antitrust laws, the very measures designed to protect the rights of individuals struggling to hold their own in the face of corporate power. "Americans love baseball as they love all sports. Perhaps we become so enamored of athletics that we assume that they are foremost in the minds of legislators as well as fans. We must not forget, however, that there are only some 600 major league baseball players. Whatever muscle they might have been able to muster by combining forces with other athletes has been greatly impaired by the manner in which this Court has isolated them. It is this Court that has made them impotent, and this Court should correct its error." Marshall was, in his own way, implying that baseball players had no choice but to form a strong craft guild. It was understandable to Marshall that baseball players would explore all such avenues in their efforts to protect their rights in the face of baseball's monopoly power. Marshall's voice, like Jackie Robinson's, spoke strongly to more progressive members of the baseball public who wanted to see the business of the game move into the modern age.

Braves vice president Paul Richards again stepped forward to offer a response on behalf of some of the more intractable owners. Richards called the decision "probably the best thing that ever happened to the player. Without it [the reserve clause] players would be shuttled around, the average baseball player would be penalized in salary and they'd lose the fringe benefits they gain from identity with certain cities."[47] Richards's argument was familiar but was based on a few key tenets now being called into question. The first of these was the notion that funds available for player salaries were extremely limited and therefore a star free-agent player could only get rich at the expense of his brethren. Richards's second tenet was the suggestion that players could accrue fringe benefits such as endorsements and the like only at the local level. Management representatives such as Richards failed to see the national advertising potential of a star player, who, with free agency, might establish a strong public identity in as many as three or four major markets during the course of his career. Once again, more-traditionalist owners failed to recognize emerging marketing opportunities in the evolving economic landscape, as new forms of media reshaped the public's relationship with the game.

Texas Rangers owner Bob Short, the underfunded magnate who fled Washington DC for the Dallas market, joined Richards in praising the decision. The arguments of Richards and Short were, by this time, worn quite thin, and they fell with a clang on ears now more closely tuned to the business of baseball. More progressive members of the public were tiring of the same old arguments from the magnates, especially in the face of the players' public position of flexibility and their willingness to negotiate a modified version of the clause that would allow a player some freedom after he had honored his team's investment in his development. This shift in fan and media sentiment was critical to the players; they badly needed public support behind the notion of free agency if baseball was to remain profitable following the modification of the reserve system.

Strategy in the Wake of the *Flood* Decision

Miller understood that the court's decision required a new plan for action against the reserve clause. He knew the magnates had painted themselves into a corner by insisting that collective bargaining was the best possible way to resolve player-management differences on this section of the standard player contract. The recent changes in the makeup of the grievance arbitration panel, which replaced the commissioner of baseball with an independent arbitrator, could help the players successfully plead their case. Miller told the press, "We will continue in our efforts to remedy the inequities in baseball's present reserve system through collective bargaining. In addition, we feel confident that the Congress will accept the Court's clear invitation to act in this matter and we will be cooperating fully with the Congress to achieve that result." Miller knew he had Congress's ear, especially with a large number of congressmen in a lather about franchise relocation. Moreover, as contemporary legal scholars pointed out, Congress proved increasingly willing to keep the other major professional sports leagues within the boundaries of antitrust laws.[48]

Several players commented on the decision as well. Chicago Cubs pitcher Milt Pappas offered this assessment:

The ruling doesn't make a lot of difference and the players were not looking to make utter chaos which complete elimination of the reserve clause would do. However, some owners have an idea now how the players feel. What we are still going to seek at the meeting table is an agreement that will give veteran players some freedom in negotiating. After a certain time with a club, say five years or eight years, a player should be able to sit down and negotiate on whether he can get more money if he's worth it, or be free to bargain with another club.[49]

This position resonated with the baseball media. The very next day, the *New York Times'* Arthur Daley wrote in support of modifying the reserve clause to allow for free agency after a set period of service.[50] Charles Maher of the *Los Angeles Times* also chimed in: "Why deny a man occupational mobility simply because he is well paid?"[51] The players welcomed this shift in sentiment. They may not have won in the courts, but their efforts were making a difference in winning badly needed media support as they pushed toward free agency.

The *Flood* decision was a short-term setback for the players but proved valuable in many other ways that became evident over time. The case stirred up a great deal of dialogue on the reserve clause, providing a superb opportunity for the baseball public to learn more about the players' frustrations with management. The owners made several mistakes in their handling of the decision. Their repetition of the same tired arguments in favor of the clause wore the media's patience thin. This was especially apparent as professional football grew dramatically in popularity, all while giving its players greater freedom of contract.[52] The owners' mishandled public relations efforts helped bring about a shift in public opinion, most clearly evidenced by the work of key opinion makers like Red Smith and Jim Murray, who threw their wholehearted support behind the players' cause.[53] The MLBPA welcomed this support, especially as it marked a significant shift from the public outcry that followed the 1969 pension holdout. The owners' inability to maintain public support was far from their only problem. Their insistence on resolution through collective bargaining pinned them to the negotiating table, where they would ultimately find themselves outmaneuvered by Marvin Miller and the MLBPA executive committee.

7

"Strike" Gets a Whole New Meaning

By the time the Supreme Court ruled on *Flood v. Kuhn*, Major League Baseball had successfully navigated its way through its second Basic Agreement and suffered through its first work stoppage. The first of these events, the 1970 Basic Agreement, set the stage for the second, the 1972 players' strike. The terms of the 1970 Basic Agreement contributed to a significant jump in player salaries, a development that served to raise understandable concerns among the magnates. The owners' resistance to further player gains grew quickly, and both sides readied for battle as the 1972 season approached.

A number of aspects of the 1970 Basic Agreement contributed to what many owners believed was an alarming jump in player pay. First, the minimum player salary got a 20 percent boost, to $12,000. Much more significantly, the commissioner of baseball was removed from the three-member arbitration panel in favor of an independent professional arbiter. The MLBPA and its executive director, Marvin Miller, were excited by this development. For the first time in the game's history, an independent third party would hear player grievances. The players no longer needed to look to Congress or the courts in their efforts to curtail management control. In the short term, the introduction of this outside arbiter proved financially valuable to the players. While salaries themselves were not yet open to arbitration, the new panel made several rulings that contributed to the growth of salaries. For example, the players won grievances allowing for increased compensation in exchange for the additional rounds of divisional playoffs caused by the 1969 expansion. This ruling, by itself, generated additional pay for players on the four teams that participated in postseason play at that point.

Additional factors not related to the Basic Agreement helped push salaries even higher. The first of these factors, in the late 1960s, was the previously mentioned set of rule changes that baseball management made with the intent of boosting offense and drawing more fans out to their sparkling new stadiums. As the magnates well understood, higher offensive production drew more fans but also boosted salaries for star offensive perform-ers.[1] Higher television broadcast revenue, increased attendance, and the expansion fees paid by new clubs such as the Padres and Expos also played a role in increasing player salaries. The owners were quite pleased with their new revenue streams but concerned about what they saw as an explosive trend in labor costs.[2]

The Magnates Dig In

As the negotiations for the new 1972 Basic Agreement approached, the owners publicly expressed their desire to staunch this bleed-ing and regain the tight control over labor costs that they had enjoyed prior to 1966. They were led in these efforts by a group of six or seven hawkish, hard-line owners, including the likes of August "Gussie" Busch IV. Busch was scion of the Anheuser-Busch brewing fortune and the owner of the St. Louis Cardinals. He summed up the uncompromising owners' position best: "I can't understand it. The player contracts are at their best, the pension plan is the finest, and the fringe benefits are better than ever. Yet the players think that we [the owners] are a bunch of stupid asses."[3] As baseball's owners continued to break into var-ious factions, Busch represented those magnates most closely connected to the traditional methods employed by baseball man-agement since nearly the beginnings of the game's history. This group of owners, which also included Cincinnati's Francis Dale and Baltimore's Jerry Hoffberger, was determined to make few, if any, concessions to the players in the 1972 negotiations. For their part, the MLBPA membership wanted a significant increase in the management contribution to the pension fund, which the players feared was being eaten away by expansion and inflation. Moreover, the players wanted to take the next step forward in their assault on the reserve clause, specifically by winning the right to salary arbitration for all players who met a basic service requirement. Salary arbitration was an important step toward increased compensation, as well as an attack on the salary limits imposed by the reserve system. These were key issues for the players' small talent guild, which increasingly understood the power of the free market, in their pursuit of maximum financial compensation.

The players flirted with a strike in the 1969 benefit plan negotiations but never seriously moved forward with the idea of an actual work stoppage. A lot had changed since 1969. The players' militancy, combined with the hard-line stance of owners like Busch and Hoffberger, made a strike a very real possibility. This was evident from the moment it became clear that the two parties remained far apart on key issues related to the pension. The owners were alarmed about what they thought were skyrocketing payroll and pension expenses, and their sense of panic gave unwarranted influence to the hard-liners who refused to budge in pension negotiations with the players. Going into the 1972 season, player pay and benefits amounted to roughly 40 percent of operating costs. This share was far lower than in other major industries, but labor costs as a percentage of operating costs was not the main issue. Many magnates felt they needed to hold the line, if for no other reason than to reassert some level of control over the players in the bargaining process. In their view, rising pension and payroll costs symbolized a loss of power, perhaps even an end to the more paternalistic traditionalist era.[4]

Both the players and the owners knew that money from television broadcast rights was the game's most promising new revenue stream. When the owners tried to keep the amount of revenue brought in by the new television contract under wraps, Marvin Miller went on the offensive. The MLBPA polled the players and learned that 99 percent of them favored keeping a strong tie between broadcast revenue and pension contributions. As a result, the MLBPA pushed for a 17 percent increase in the owner contribution agreed to in 1969, an amount equal to $6.5 million annually.[5] Miller and the players believed this amount was in line with gains made in other industries and was necessary for the pension and benefits plan to keep up with the rising cost of living. The magnates clearly felt otherwise. They showed up to a February 25 bargaining session with what amounted to no new offer. The PRC flatly refused to make any increase in the owners' pension contribution over the $5.45 million agreed to three years earlier. This shock came just five weeks before the agreement was set to expire and, for the first time in his six years at the helm of the MLBPA, Miller openly acknowledged the possibility of a players' strike to the press, explaining, "If the agreement expires there's no obligation to work as a group."[6] This was no small development; many members of the baseball public viewed an organized player walkout as the "nuclear option." Fans and the media had a difficult time imagining what the future of the game would look like in a world where strikes and lockouts could interrupt the seasonal coming and going of the national pastime. As had been the case since the Brotherhood first shook up the business of baseball in the 1890s, many feared a players' strike would only serve to permanently cripple and ultimately destroy Major League Baseball.

Two weeks later, the owners had not budged. In fact, they reduced their offer by roughly $250,000. The players decided it was time for them to draw a hard line of their own. After meeting with Marvin Miller, the Chicago White Sox became the first team to authorize a possible strike, with a vote of 31–0. Miller told the Associated Press that the owners' move to reduce their offer was "deliberately trying to provoke a players' strike—That's the only way you can explain that kind of negotiating behavior."[7] The crisis escalated in the following week, even though Commissioner Kuhn continued to express his optimism that the situation was no more serious than in the 1969 negotiations.

Kuhn believed a strike was far from imminent, a sentiment that rankled Miller to no end. "Nothing could be more factually removed from the truth than that view," Miller contended. "I don't know where he gets his information. To me it sounds like an attempt to mislead the players. It's a joke except it isn't funny." Various management representatives responded by proclaiming their allegiance to the tougher stance assumed by owners such as Busch. Edmund Fitzgerald, chairman of the Milwaukee Brewers' executive committee, told reporters, "If they vote for a strike, everything ends. That's it. It's the end of the ballgame. All they will be entitled to is plane fare home, and I hope they have a nice summer."[8] Fitzgerald's comments were typical of those owners seeking to place responsibility for the conflict in the players' laps.

As the third week of March passed, the conflict took on a more defined shape. Busch helped lead the charge for the owners who seemed most determined to break the union. He claimed the rapid growth of pensions and salaries was proving disastrous for the industry. He claimed that few clubs were actually making any money and that the players had grown so greedy "I wouldn't give a damn if the players went out. I'd vote to let them take a walk. . . . I am afraid that with the constantly increasing player demands, plus the attempt to rule out the reserve clause, it's getting impossible to operate reasonably."[9] Angels general manager Harry Dalton pled poverty as well, saying, "The profit margin is almost negligible. . . . In bad years you can take a real beating."[10] Pleas such as these gained traction with a baseball public increasingly conscious of rising player salaries but still unaware of the enormous impact of new revenue streams, such as television broadcast rights. Owners understood the power of these themes; they knew if they continually simplified the industry and pinned increased player salaries to rising ticket and concession costs, public sentiment would turn against the players. Owners convinced fans, for example, that a ballpark beer now cost one dollar more because the left fielder had demanded a big raise in the off-season. Owners wanted fans to believe that these rising prices had little to do with supply and demand projections made by team management, which were wholly independent of team labor costs.

Busch's comments were part of a massive ownership campaign to regain the upper hand in the battle for public opinion, especially after losing so much ground over the course of the *Flood* proceedings. It hurt the owners, though, that Busch was not particularly well suited for this task. The brewing and baseball magnate continued to tread in waters dangerously close to a failure to bargain in good faith in the eyes of the National Labor Relations Board. Their public relations failings, however, did little to soften the owners' resistance to increased pension contributions. On March 22 the owners voted 24–0 against offering any kind of increased funding to the Players Pension and Benefits Fund. The owners agreed to pay what amounted to cost-of-living increases to maintain the current levels of health insurance. They refused to budge on any increase in the amount of pension benefits, despite widespread public fears of inflation and the MLBPA's claims that a 17 percent increase was necessary to keep up with the rising cost of living. As Busch proclaimed, "We voted unanimously to take a stand, we're not going to give another god-damn cent."[11] Many members of the baseball press took Busch at his word. There was some speculation that the owners would be willing to budge slightly on increased benefits in order to avert a strike. For the most part, however, the press remained overwhelmingly concerned about the possibility of the game's first-ever work stoppage. Coverage of a potential strike was virtually nonstop, with plenty of fans and writers weighing in on both sides of the debate.

As the March 31 deadline approached, more and more strike votes rolled in. Most teams voiced unanimous support for the strike; very few teams had more than one or two dissenting votes. One notable dissident was the star Dodger first baseman and player representative Wes Parker. He risked the ire of his compatriots and voted no, explaining, "It's just that I don't want to strike against the Dodgers or against baseball."[12] For the time being, Parker's voice was a reminder that even with all the recent changes, many baseball men remained traditionalists at heart. In the long term, Parker's dissent, and Miller's ability to keep Parker involved in the Players Association, would later prove just how far the MLBPA had come as a democratic organization working to represent and include all players.

Many people, even those close to the game, entered the final days of March convinced baseball would avoid its first-ever work stoppage. *New York Times* columnist Arthur Daley was among them: "Marvin Miller, the professional unionist who directs the players' union, has jostled the complacent ballplayers into threatening a strike that could begin tomorrow. Virtually no one close to the situation, however, believes that there will be a strike because such a strike would counter every principle of logic." Daley went on to detail the basic differences between the players and the owners and then, in a quote that would be picked up off the wire services by papers across the nation, wrote, "The owners and the players are well-matched antagonists. Both are so greedy and self serving that neither group can evoke much sympathetic support in the outside world. The owners are the Establishment and it's fashionable to attack the vested interests. The players are the slaves on Massa's plantation despite the fact that the average salary is between $31,000 and $32,000 per season with 22 of these peons getting more than $100,000 a year. Downtrodden masses? Not quite."[13] It was significant that many writers who had once sided with the MLBPA, such as Daley, now felt the players had gained enough. These writers believed baseball could ill afford any work stoppage and held both parties, the players and the magnates, responsible for the potential death of the national pastime. This was not exactly the total public relations victory the owners were hoping for, but it did mark something of a setback for the players, especially in light of the positive way in which many fans and writers had responded to their point of view during the *Flood* proceedings.

Daley's colleague at the *New York Times*, Red Smith, was much more critical of the magnates. Smith's column on March 30 questioned many of the owners' financial practices. Smith called on the magnates to be more forthcoming with their financial information if they expected greater public sympathy. He wondered why franchise values kept going through the roof if baseball clubs faced such huge losses. The writer questioned why Bob Short would be allowed to run the Senators deep into debt and then be rewarded "with exclusive rights to the Dallas-Fort Worth area, possibly the richest virgin territory on the continent."[14] It would be a long time before baseball teams offered anything close to the financial transparency called for by Smith.

All of the team votes had been tallied by late March, with the final count at 663–10 in favor of allowing the team representatives to call a strike.[15] Mets pitcher Tom Seaver, who just a few years earlier broke ranks during the 1969 pension holdout, summed up the position of many players: "He [Miller] has had faith in us, now we must have faith in him."[16] John Gaherin assured the owners that the strike vote was merely saber rattling: "A strike vote never impresses me. It's just an extension of the collective bargaining procedure. If a labor leader can't get a strike vote in a tense period of negotiations he isn't even in the ball game."[17] The owners followed Gaherin's lead and dug their heels in further. Many of them felt Miller was bluffing. There were even a few magnates who believed that, even if the MLBPA called for a strike, the players would not follow the order.[18] Most of the magnates remained tight-lipped, but Gussie Busch could not help himself, repeating his favorite mantra: "We're not going to give them another goddamn cent. If they want to strike, let 'em."[19] Miller tried to make peace prior to the deadline, to no avail. He even attempted, in a final meeting before the March 31 deadline, to persuade the players not to strike. The MLBPA's executive director feared his organization lacked the strong base and the funding needed to withstand a lengthy strike. Miller believed that "if they [the players] struck and couldn't sustain it, the blow to the still young Association could prove disastrous."[20] When the player representatives met with Miller on the day before the deadline, forty-seven of the forty-eight representatives voted in favor of a walkout. In six years, Miller had gone from working hard just to gain the players' acceptance to leading a labor organization that was nearly unanimous in its desire to strike, even in the face of tremendous risk.

It seemed many owners would prove intractable in the event of a strike, a situation that alarmed much of the baseball public. The editor in chief of the *Sporting News*, C. C. Johnson Spink, wrote, "This time, it is certain there are enough owners with Busch's backbone to hold the line and resist the striking players, especially since this time most fans are on the owners' side."[21] Of course, there was plenty of commentary from the owners supporting Spink's concerns; an April 6 press release from Cincinnati Reds vice president Bob Howsam typified their response. Howsam told the press the strike was solely Miller's fault and bristled at the fact that Miller called him a liar in reply. Howsam was happy to be counted among those who placed the strike squarely at Miller's feet:

> I believe a strike has been in his mind ever since he became associated with the players' union. . . . If he wants to influence and guide the players, let him impress upon them the need for better cooperation in autograph sessions, personal appearances, hospital visits. Let him [Miller] help baseball, not hinder it. . . . Baseball is not the steel industry, and he can't use the tactics of a steel negotiator. His approach to this unique situation which we now face can only start the decline of a great game which has meant so much to so many for over a century.[22]

Howsam had plenty of company. Detroit Tigers general manager Jim Campbell said of Miller, "I just plain and simple disagree with him. I don't think he knows his posterior from center field."[23] These comments, once again, reflect the management view that baseball's exceptional nature meant clubs did not need to think of their players as a traditional labor force. Men like Howsam were clearly threatened by the idea of dealing with a legitimate union that was more than willing to carry out a strike threat. On the whole, the magnates' public assault on the players' union, and its executive director, reached unprecedented levels in the weeks leading up to the 1972 strike. It was wise of Howsam to play on the image of baseball players as public servants, even community assets. He touched a nerve with many fans by implying that ballplayers were more than just wageworkers exercising their right to strike. It seemed that fans might sympathize with the players' need for greater freedom of contract but viewed their decision to use a strike to reach that goal as a total violation of the public trust. American communities needed their baseball-playing heroes to lift spirits, inspire the young, offer comfort to the infirm, even help remind Americans of their rich cultural traditions. In this way, many fans saw a players' strike as akin to the kind of betrayal typified by a police officer or firefighter who considered going on strike.

Other magnates found their own ways to question the players' integrity. Dodger owner Walter O'Malley tried to turn the tables on the players' argument that they needed to maximize gains over the course of what was, on average, a short Major League career. O'Malley used the players' short tenure as a means to question their long-term commitment to the institution of baseball: "My only complaint today is that the owners must negotiate with people who are not fully committed to the industry. Steelworkers, teamsters, and other labor unions are tough, but they are not trying to kill the industry in which they will earn their living for the rest of their lives. Since ballplayers are only around for a few years, they don't have this feeling of responsibility."[24] O'Malley's message was clear. The owners were the only party in this dispute with a long-term interest in preserving the national treasure that was Major League Baseball. Comments like these surely played well with many traditionalists, frustrated as they were in a time when constant upheaval affected beloved American institutions such as baseball.

Public Support for the Establishment

The magnates' public relations efforts did not go unrewarded. They enjoyed plenty of support in the press, from both new voices and old. Their longtime friend, the *New York Daily News'* Dick Young, placed the blame squarely at the feet of Marvin Miller: "Marvin Miller is a smoothie. Ballplayers are no match for him. He has a steel-trap mind wrapped in a butter melting voice. He runs the players through a high pressure spray the way a car goes through a car-wash, and that's how they come out, brain washed." Young argued that most players did not actually want to strike; it was simply a matter of Miller's powers of persuasion turning the players into a group of sheep, willing to vote 663–10 in favor of a strike. Young played up letters from fans, such as the one he got from John Disponzio, a fan in Jamaica, Queens, who complained, "The crybabies we have in sports are not to be believed. I make much less than $10,000 a year, two weeks vacation, and I pay for my own family's doctor and dentist bills. They're going on strike? I'm going on strike, from them."[25] Comments like Disponzio's fueled the fire of the writers in Young's camp. They demonstrated the disillusionment of many fans who had long seen ballplayers as their working-class brethren. Ballplayers were supposed to know when they had it good and understand that, by calling a strike, they were asking the fans to pay the greatest price, which was life without the national pastime. Writers like Young believed that once players severed this connection, they could never regain the trust and loyalty of the baseball public. In past years, Young could be counted on as one of the strong public voices opposed to the MLBPA. In 1972 he had plenty of fans and fellow journalists in his corner.

Growing fan opposition to the players' strike encouraged the magnates. As the *Christian Science Monitor's* Ed Rummill wrote, "As the seasons unfolded, a genuine smugness gripped the big league ballplayer. He became increasingly aware that he could do no wrong—that no matter what the club owners or the demanding press might think of him, the fan was always on his side—would always come to his defense. Well, we have some news for today's ballplayer. The fan—and we are speaking of the average, the majority—no longer is willing to go to bat for him." Rummill revealed the results of his own informal fan survey taken during spring training games in Florida. The quotations Rummill collected are telling. Comments ranged from the old standards, like "Let them [strike]. Who cares? They get no sympathy from me. Why not? Because they're the best paid, and at the same time most pampered, group of men in the working world. If you want to call what they do working." To more specific comments, such as, "I'm a long time fan . . . so I've seen a lot. I was a card carrier [in a union] for many years, so I'm familiar with that side of it. And the minute they signed Marvin Miller up, you knew there'd be trouble up ahead. Any boob can see that a man in his position must keep demanding more money to justify his salary. If he stops, the players don't need him anymore." Rummill concluded with accusations that many players believed it was more than fair for the average fan to bear the brunt of increased pension and health benefits in the form of higher ticket prices. "The players think the fans should come to the rescue. They would be surprised at how little the fans are concerned over their problems. The way the world is turning these days, the fans have problems of their own . . . far more serious and justified than the money demands of a group of men who are already among the best paid in America."[26] Such articles helped strengthen management resolve. They reinforced the notion that the players alone, not the owners, were on the verge of shattering the fans' sacred trust.

Fans all over the country claimed the strike threat was truly the final straw. The sports editor of the *St. Louis Globe Dispatch* openly solicited fan letters regarding a possible strike. The response was overwhelming. The letters he received criticizing the players outnumbered those expressing support twenty to one. One fan even submitted poetic thoughts on the subject, beginning his letter with, "They charged me four bucks for my seat; I rooted through the game. And then the scales fell from my eyes, I knew them all by name. For greed was playing second base, Cupidity was at first. At third base was Ingratitude and shortstop was the worst."[27] This fan's response was more refined in its composition than most. In the days leading up to the 1972 strike, however, its theme was far from rare. Much more frequently than ever before, fans threatened to stay away from the game as their own protest against what they saw as the transformation of baseball from sacred pastime to contentious business.

Many fans resented being treated as pawns and reconsidered the iconic status they had accorded to their ball-playing heroes of yesteryear. They were understandably apprehensive about the new role the game might play in their lives. Whether the traditionalist view of the game was realistic or not, baseball bound families and communities together. Every year, from April until September, baseball provided a daily ritual, even a rhythm to life, for its faithful. Even during the cold winter months, fans were warmed by talk of the local team's prospects for the upcoming season. More so than any other labor clash, the 1972 strike proved to be the greatest crisis yet for the fans of the game. In the minds of many, this was a situation made all the more serious by the booming popularity of professional football and basketball. These sports were well suited for television, and their professional leagues more than doubled in size between 1960 and 1972. In the face of this perceived threat, baseball fans echoed the fears of sportswriters and owners, who believed a work stoppage would permanently diminish the game's status as a national icon. It was difficult for fans to watch an institution they held sacred for its traditions and constancy facing such a threat.

Fan dismay with player attitudes was driven, in large part, by a sense that players had lost touch with the realities of everyday living. According to baseball fan Howard Carvajal, "The baseball strike may be the necessary step to properly educate the athletes to life in the 'real world'. When the salary of the marginal player exceeds the median income of all Americans, when the meal money is $18.50 a day, when the minimum pension exceeds the median social security check (for which the recipient must work a lifetime), there needs to be a reordering of priorities. Let the players get a job and work for a living without the artificial atmosphere of hero worship." Overall response to the *Sporting News* poll ran ten to one against the players. Most fan comments ran in the same vein as Carvajal's.[28] An informal poll by WGN radio in Chicago found that, out of two hundred callers, fully 90 percent sided with the owners and placed full blame on the players for baseball's labor woes.

Criticism poured in from all sides. The *Washington Post's* Shirley Povich commented, "This was a thumping vote against Motherhood, Apple Pie, Eagle Scouts, Little Match Girls, and the American Dream. . . . Athletes for the first time cannot count on the backing of a one time adoring public." To veteran columnists such as Povich, the owners' play was clear. "The team owners also appear to be determined to make the most of their novel position as the abused parties in a baseball dispute. They would like to use it to dismantle Marvin Miller as the players' professional negotiator and spokesman, and the cactus under the saddle of the club owners."[29] Povich questioned the strength of the magnates' self-proclaimed united front, but there was no mistaking the fact that the owners recognized this was their best, and perhaps last, opportunity to break the players' union.

The March 31 strike deadline came and went. Baseball fans woke up on April 1, 1972, to find that a baseball work stoppage was reality, not an April Fool's joke. Many writers, even those with a sympathetic record toward the players' cause, were openly critical of the MLBPA. Dave Anderson of the *New York Times* celebrated Roy Campanella's belief that "to play major league baseball you had to be a man, but you had to have a little boy in you too." Anderson now believed that was no longer the case: "From the 1966 day when the players hired Miller, a strike was inevitable. With his labor background with the United Steelworkers, he couldn't fulfill his mission without influencing a strike. And the players have gone along firmly, like the steelworkers Miller once guided. To play baseball now, you've got to have the shop steward in you, not the little boy."[30] Anderson's transformation of the player image from little boy to shop steward is perhaps one of the best examples of the way in which the strike harmed the public image of the average Major League Baseball player.

A number of other columnists who were once sympathetic to

the union took note as well. Arthur Daley, who called Miller "the players' chief string puller," observed, "A refusal by the owners to yield to Miller could prolong the strike beyond opening day and into the season. The damage this would do to an already frayed baseball image is beyond calculation. . . . Ever since the strike threat began materializing, many critical words have been written . . . about the greed of the ballplayers. They won virtually no support or sympathy from the working stiffs who help pay for their fancy salaries and pension plans."[31] This response was decidedly different from the outcry surrounding the 1969 pension holdout. Baseball writers assumed that the vast majority of fans, while not necessarily supporting the owners, were clearly opposed to any sort of players' strike. The outpouring of negative fan reaction showed that the MLBPA's days of appealing to the fans on bread-and-butter issues were over. The gains that had served the players so well—on issues like minimum salary and pension security—now stood firmly in the way of public acceptance of the strike. Miller and the players' representatives needed to develop a new approach to regaining public support in their conflicts with the owners.

Fans evidently felt that the players had gained enough. They were no longer swayed by the argument that players needed to maximize salary and pension benefits during the brief period when they played in the Major Leagues. They appeared unmoved by arguments related to a player's right to pursue maximum compensation in the free market. Fans still compared player salaries with those of the average worker and seemed unwilling to consider the highly specialized value of a baseball player's skill set. According to Ray Sons of the *Chicago Daily News*, "The difference is the strikers. When they 'work' it is for about five hours a day, roughly seven months a year. Most of their working day is spent standing around, waiting for a ball to be hit their way, or sitting around waiting for a turn at bat."[32] The players had their work cut out for them as they sought to convince the public they had a right to pursue the greatest possible price the market would bear in exchange for their highly specialized and unique talents.

Sons's comments reflect the views of the many fans that base-ball players were first and foremost working-class guys lucky enough to be involved in physical labor for which they were highly paid. This view held that, as working-class men, these players should rejoice in the fact that their actual physical labor was minimal. This early 1970s view of a ballplayer also failed to take into account the other, nonlaboring aspects of playing the game: the constant travel, the intense public scrutiny, and the fact that ballplayers worked twenty-five or twenty-six days a month, instead of the twenty or twenty-one days of the aver-age worker. The fans' view is also highly informative of what the public saw as organized labor's primary role at this point in time. Organized labor was intended to protect workers, whether skilled or unskilled, from the overwhelming power of big busi-ness and the vagaries of the marketplace. In the spring of 1972, the public was not ready to accept the notion that highly special-ized and skilled workers, such as baseball players, might need to tap into the power of collective action just as much as an auto-worker or truck driver.

The Players Seek Middle Ground

In the face of this substantial public backlash, the players began serious efforts to bargain their way toward a middle ground with the owners. The magnates, bolstered by the continued outpouring of public support, maintained their widely proclaimed solidarity. Pirates general manager Joe Brown told the *Los Angeles Times*, "I doubt very much that the owners will back down from their present stand. Never in my years in baseball have I seen them so solidified on any issue."[33] Miller did his best to win back public support by demonstrating that the players were more than flex-ible on several key issues. He argued that the $800,000 needed to provide the cost-of-living increases was at the owners' finger-tips, in the form of a surplus in the existing pension fund. He pointed out that the players were willing to make a number of concessions, including accepting a one-year agreement instead of the four-year pact on which they had originally insisted. All the owners needed to do, according to Miller, was agree to increase their health care contribution in order to cover rising costs and agree to sink the surplus amount back into the pension fund in order to cover increases in cost of living. Miller also told reporters that things could be settled quickly if the owners simply got their act together and agreed to the players' compromise.[34]

The press zeroed in on money as the key issue separating the players and owners in the early days of the strike, so Miller countered by recasting the showdown in terms similar to those used so successfully in the MLBPA's earlier campaigns, explaining, "Money is not the issue. The real issue is the owners' attempt to punish the players for having the audacity not to settle and for having the audacity not to crawl."[35] Miller went further in his efforts to paint the magnates as men bent on breaking the back of organized labor. He told the *Sporting News* that the owners were "out to break the Association" when the strike "could be solved with a 10 cent phone call."[36] Miller was clearly attempting to win back the support of fans, especially those from blue-collar backgrounds, who had sided with the players during earlier disputes.

For the time being, however, this argument had little effect on the baseball media, which continued to insist it was fed up with player greed. There was some appreciation for Miller's role in shaping a strong union, although writers no longer portrayed Miller as a man fighting alongside David against Goliath. In a column questioning Miller's role as villain, Bob Sudyk of the *Cleveland Press* wrote, "Labor boss Miller is too much of a match for the owners and they know it. Now more than ever with the players' strike on. He is an expert tactician in marshaling his players' forces and keeping the owners negotiator John Gaherin off balance. Almost daily, Miller is grabbing the headlines with compromise proposals, placing Gaherin in the position of turning down all conciliatory gestures."[37] Sudyk's words were complimentary, but most members of the baseball public were more than happy to acknowledge Miller's skill and strategy while continuing to blame him and the MLBPA membership for this unwanted interruption of the nation's pastime.

During the strike's early days, speculation focused on whether the players and owners would be able to sort out their differences in time for Opening Day on April 6. The key point of contention was whether there was an $817,000 surplus in the pension fund and the proper role of such a surplus. The players asked that the surplus simply be added to the pension fund, thereby providing the increase in benefits that they felt was necessary to fight off the effects of inflation. The players argued that the surplus, along with a contribution of $11,000 from each club, was enough to shore up the pension benefits' purchasing power. The owners first claimed that the surplus did not exist and then commissioned an outside actuarial study for the purpose of ascertaining the existence of such funds. Miller and the player representatives believed this was just another management stall tactic and were outraged: "That's just a smokescreen. The fact is, they [the owners] have given him [John Gaherin] no authority to bargain. They're most concerned now with face. They've said they're not going to give us a damn cent."[38] Miller had in hand an actuarial report from an independent consultant, previously authorized by the owners, clearly showing the surplus existed.[39] He hoped the magnates' failure to move forward with good-faith negotiations might help swing public opinion back in the players' favor.

The players took additional steps to win back public support by offering a compromise proposal. They responded with an offer to drop the request for an additional $11,000 contribution from each club. The MLBPA indicated that it was enough for the owners to simply roll the $817,000 surplus into the existing fund. The PRC rejected the players' offer almost immediately, without even a cursory consultation with the sixteen clubs not represented on the committee. In the wake of this speedy rejection, Gaherin told the press he feared the strike might be a lengthy one. Miller reiterated his beliefs that the real goal of the owners was not to save operating costs but to punish the players: "The owners were, and are, intent on making the players eat dirt. . . . The owners are taking full responsibility for prolonging the strike right into the season. I think the owners have miscalculated grievously."[40]

Miller was correct in predicting that the PRC's strategy would begin to swing some public sentiment toward the players' side, even if it came only from tried-and-true friends such as Red Smith. Smith's first column during the strike, dated April 5, played up the players' willingness to compromise on key issues, such as accepting a one-year agreement instead of a four-year agreement. Smith pointed out that the players had offered to pay back any losses incurred by the use of the surplus, a move designed to take the risk out of using the surplus to help fund the pension. Of the PRC's rejection of the players' most recent offer, Smith wrote, "It was as though the subcommittee was saying to the owners' group as a whole: 'We're fighting the good fight. If you reverse us it will make boobs of us all.'"[41] Smith's support was welcome, though not surprising, in the early days of the strike.

Miller further tried to win support for the players by demonizing a few select characters on the PRC. He charged Baltimore's Hoffberger, whom he singled out as the man behind management's quick rejection of the players' counteroffer, with holding improper meetings with players and leading the owners around like dogs on a leash. Miller evidently felt that, if he was going to be singled out as the puppet master of the Players Association, the public should know who was pulling the owners' strings.[42] Miller had more invective for the owners when they promised to start negotiating again, but only if the players returned to the playing field. "You don't end a strike that's caused by their failing to negotiate by saying 'let's negotiate.' That's the rankest of amateurism." Player representatives, such as the Astros' Larry Dierker, did their best to promote player unity and reinforce the idea that bread-and-butter issues were still central to the players' interests. "When you read about baseball," Dierker noted, "you read about Hank Aaron . . . signing for $100,000. What you don't read about is Bob Stinson who spent eight years in the minors and now is making $13,000 a year. He's the one really trying to get something out of this pension. And he deserves it."[43]

One week into the walkout, the positions of each side were clearly delineated in an NBC *Today Show* interview with Milwaukee Brewers general manager Frank Lane. Lane, who was taking his turn as management's national voice, made a series of claims designed to win public support for the owners. In an effort to curry favor with the public by steering clear of blasting the players, Lane effectively blamed the entire strike on Miller's machinations. He charged the MLBPA's executive director with telling half-truths, fixing strike votes, and pressuring the players to "play ducks and drakes" with their careers. He further portrayed the players as essentially naïve souls "who strive through sweat and blood and tears to get up in the major leagues and the duration of a major league player's career is about five years, and naturally they want to get as much as they can in that short period of time, so they're fair game for somebody to suggest to them that they're entitled to more money, but it has to be proven to them that they are." Lane said the magnates had no objection to the players choosing "skillful financial advisors," but Miller, "a great purveyor of half truths," did not fit the bill.[44] This pattern of attacking Miller but not the players was driven by the owners' desire to do as little public damage to the game as possible. The magnates knew they could ill afford to turn fans completely against the players and then expect fans to flock back to the ballpark when the strike ended. It was, therefore, very important to the owners to ensure the public continued thinking of Miller as an outsider, a no-good interloper set on destroying the national pastime.

Miller had prepared assiduously to deal with an attack like Lane's. He prepared a set of handwritten notes regarding his thoughts on the interview. These notes offer great insight into his approach at the peak of tensions regarding the 1972 strike. Miller noted the "David and Goliath" nature of the ballplayers' struggle in the face of the club owners, whom he described as "24 multi-millionaires." Miller feared there was "no honorable way out for the players," who, in his view, "had already proved on several occasions that money was not the primary issue." Miller believed the players' request for a 17 percent increase in order to keep up with the rising cost of living was only reasonable, especially as the pension plans negotiated by so many other unions provided guaranteed cost-of-living increases. He believed player solidarity, especially if it could be maintained in the face of continued public outcry, would play out well for the union over the course of the strike.

Miller's mounting frustration with the owners' inability to understand the new realities of collective bargaining in baseball was especially evident when he wrote of Lane, "he is symptomatic of what is wrong with baseball—has learned literally nothing in the past five years." Miller felt that "today's players are different—collective bargaining—will not accept law of the land." Six years into his tenure as the MLBPA's executive director, Miller knew what he had created. Baseball's players were now bound tightly together in a strong, disciplined craft union. In Miller's view, the magnates, especially those similar in mind-set to Lane, believed club owners should be able to "move players like one once shipped merchandise." Miller was further frustrated by Lane's insinuation that the players had demanded "over and above what the owners could afford" financially, especially when, at the time of Lane's interview, the players had agreed to the owners' financial terms. He wrote that Lane's tactics were "typical" because the owners "couldn't make a case on the merits," so they resorted to "cowardly & shameful character assassination." Miller closed his notes on Lane's interview with thoughts on where the players might have to turn "if these multi-millionaires can succeed in starving the players into succumbing." His list of possible options included Congress, federal regulation, the Supreme Court, and Miller's longtime ally, public opinion.[45]

Opening Day came and went, and the daily loss of revenue began to take its toll on owner unity. The players, by now well versed in the importance of solidarity, recognized this and stood determined to maintain a united front to the public. The owners, on the other hand, quickly began to fracture as a result of the mounting financial losses brought about by the strike. Big-market teams, such as the Los Angeles Dodgers, suffered the largest financial losses at the turnstiles. Small-market teams living closer to the margin, such as the Minnesota Twins, feared a prolonged strike would run them out of business. Negotiation committee hard-liners, such as Busch and Hoffberger, had a difficult time maintaining their momentum in the face of resistance from both small- and large-market clubs. When John Gaherin's outside actuarial consultant suggested that Miller's plan to fund improved health benefits with pension reserves might actually work, many of the more moderate owners, like Ewing Kauffman of the Royals and P. K. Wrigley of the Cubs, began to push for a settlement. The pension issue was resolved, with help from federal mediators, on April 10. The owners agreed to pay the full cost of the increased health care benefits, using $500,000 of the pension surplus to fund the additional benefits.

Things appeared to be headed down the path to settlement when a few of the more intransigent owners tried to save face by throwing in a new demand intended to show that they, not the players, ultimately held the upper hand. These magnates demanded that doubleheaders be scheduled to make up games lost due to the strike in order to preserve the integrity of the entire 162-game regular season. Many of these doubleheaders would be run as "day-night doubleheaders," in which the stadium is cleared between games so that the club can sell separate admissions to each game. Under this plan, the clubs would be able to collect all of their lost ticket revenue. The players, on the other hand, would not regain any of the pay they had lost during the strike. Miller responded, "There is no back pay issue involved here. The players are on strike, they've lost pay and that's it. They accept that. If the owners want to pick up the schedule from here there's no issue."[46] The owners believed they could turn a small success—forcing the players to accept less than half of what they'd originally sought in pension gains—into a huge conquest by forcing the players to play a full season for a partial salary. The players' acceptance of such conditions would amount to assuming full blame for the strike and would accomplish the owners' goal of breaking the union. MLBPA members knew they could never accept such terms, as accepting full blame for the strike would only add credibility to the owners' ongoing public attacks on the union.

Settlement at Last

The small group of more conservative owners, men such as Busch who had done so much to distance themselves from the players, finally gave in to the pressure from small-market clubs about to buckle under the financial strain of the strike. The owners, now with significant divisions in their ranks, agreed to start the season without rescheduling any of the missed games. On April 13 the two sides met in Chicago and reached an agreement that essentially reflected Miller's proposals of late March. Management agreed to use $500,000 of the pension surplus to help pay for improved health benefits. Players lost a total of about $600,000 in salary; the owners suffered more than $5 million in lost revenue.[47] On the whole, most involved parties were glad to get back to playing the game on the field. The strike resulted in an uneven schedule in which some teams played more games than others. Pennant races were determined strictly on won-loss percentage, a method that gave the Detroit Tigers the American League East title over the Boston Red Sox, even though the Red Sox won more games over the course of the season.

The real significance of the strike was the owners' failed attempt to "break the union." Instead the magnates developed deep divisions within their ranks and provided a valuable lesson to the players regarding the importance of solidarity and the irreplaceable nature of their specialized skill sets. Men like Dick Young and C. C. Johnson Spink, longtime management supporters, called for greater owner unity in the future. They decried the owners' inability to keep the upper hand, even at a time when public opinion was largely in their favor. "We recommend Teddy Roosevelt's advice, 'Speak softly and carry a big stick,'" Spink wrote. "The owners didn't speak softly and although they carried the big stick of public opinion, they let it turn into a hollow reed in their hands."[48] Other sportswriters believed that the owners had failed because the strike made player unity so strong. As a result, Marvin Miller was at this point possibly the most powerful man in baseball.[49]

Fans demonstrated their distaste for the strike with a slow return to the ballpark. Even the Dodgers, who were less affected than most clubs, drew a total of only eighty thousand fans for their first three home games. This number was well below average, and even "mellow" Dodger fans, such as R. O. Gau of Torrance, were happy to share their reasons for staying home. "The baseball players' strike is history," Gau wrote in a letter to the editor in the *Los Angeles Times*. "However, many fans are and will continue to be disturbed about the greediness and the selfishness of the players. . . . I support the owners, and the owners must have good attendance to stay in business. As a permanent personal protest against the players, I will never again purchase any products endorsed by an active major league baseball player."[50] Fans in other cities were less subtle in demonstrating their displeasure. There were numerous reports of fans throwing oranges and other debris at players during the opening weeks of the season. In almost every city, players were, at a minimum, subjected to a chorus of boos from the fans who showed up at the parks.[51] They had won the battle in seeing their way through the strike, but the players had some important groundwork to do if they hoped to win the war for the support of the baseball public.

1973: Right Back At It

The 1972 pension deal was only a one-year agreement, and the 1970 Basic Agreement was due to expire before the start of the 1973 season, so the fall of 1972 brought with it the start of renewed negotiations between players and owners. Players turned their attention squarely to making gains through arbitration, on both the reserve clause and salaries. Notes from an MLBPA strategy session Marvin Miller held with Dick Moss and player representatives such as Joe Torre indicate that the reserve rule was a top priority for the players in the upcoming negotiations. The men discussed the possible modification of the rule to provide more options for "ten year men," especially as it related to the approval of trades and the pursuit of better contract terms with other clubs.[52]

In late November the owners rolled out their first response to the MLBPA's moves on the reserve clause. The owners proposed a version of limited free agency in which "five-year men," who made less than $30,000 per season, and "eight-year men," who made less than $40,000 per season, would be eligible to pursue better salaries with other clubs. Ten-year men would not be automatically eligible for free agency but would gain the right to veto trades.[53] This proposal was designed to show the owners' interest in helping the journeyman player, who was trapped from pursuing more playing time and a higher salary by the reserve system. The magnates hoped this would appear to be a reasonable and fair settlement to the public. The owners rightfully believed they could count on the average fan not being too overwrought about the rights of star veterans making upwards of $75,000 a season.

The players, on the other hand, saw the owners' plan as a public relations ploy. MLBPA calculations showed that only five current players would qualify for free agency under the owners' proposal. Letters in Miller's papers demonstrate the players' high level of frustration with owner attempts to dodge the real issues relating to free agency.[54] Bowie Kuhn's public presentation of the owners' proposals, handled as if they bore the commissioner's personal seal of approval as being in the best interests of the game, further infuriated the players. Miller called a press conference at which he decried Kuhn's actions as those of a "rank amateur" in terms of good-faith bargaining: "Obviously when one side starts negotiating publicly instead of with the other party it has the effect of hardening positions on both sides and makes the reaching of an agreement far more difficult. . . . The damage comes from forcing people to stick to positions, once they are made public, that they may have been more flexible about in private."[55]

Miller was trying to keep the owners in line with the players' agenda, but fans and the media did not necessarily appreciate his efforts. Letters in the *Sporting News* called Miller "the worst thing that ever happened to baseball" and argued that Miller did not like Kuhn's public revelation of the owner's offer because he feared it would make the players look bad in the public eye.[56] The press saw lines being drawn in the sand, and public discussion of a possible strike intensified in December. *Boston Globe* columnist Ray Fitzgerald believed Miller's continued influence could only harm the game. He predicted that the MLBPA's current negotiating stance would only lead to yet another strike. Fitzgerald suggested that the Opening Day scene at Fenway Park would include players reading the "Worker's Manifesto, while in the corner batboys were boning up for a quiz on the history of the child labor dispute in America."[57] Fitzgerald's comments were typical of traditionalists in the baseball press, who saw labor activism in baseball as one more sign of what they felt was a deteriorating American national character.

Others, such as the *New York Times'* lead baseball writer, Leonard Koppett, tried to create a level bargaining field by encouraging both sides to take a more rational approach. Koppett claimed the 1972 strike was primarily a result of an emotionally charged situation in which the owners had questioned the players' collective manhood. The financial differences, according to Koppett, were not so great as to necessitate a players' strike. Koppett argued that the same was true of the situation heading into the 1973 negotiations, and he called on the owners to treat the players as equals at the bargaining table, especially by carrying out negotiations in good faith.[58]

Into January, Miller and the players continued to press the idea of free agency for all players after a set number of years in service. In reality, Miller and the player representatives were likely more interested in winning the right to salary arbitration. Kuhn restated the owners' position on free agency, reinforcing the idea that the magnates' offer of late November was as good as it was going to get. The players decided at this point to make a show of giving in on the issue of free agency. They agreed to another three-year study of the reserve system and what became known as the ten and five rule, the idea that a ten-year veteran with at least five years of continuous service to the same club could veto a proposed trade.

Having taken a pass on free agency, the MLBPA turned much of its attention to salary arbitration, much to the owners' dismay. The magnates feared salary arbitration would inevitably result in decisions being made by arbitrators from outside the game, who would simply split the difference between the player's proposed salary and that proposed by the club. This practice, the magnates argued, would encourage players to inflate their salary demands well beyond reasonable levels. Miller anticipated this position and pushed for "either-or" arbitration. Such a system forbade the arbitrator to split the difference and required him or her to choose either the player's proposal or the club's. This type of system required both parties to be much more reasonable in their demands, for fear that an unreasonable position would be rejected out of hand. Miller understood it would do a great deal to smooth things over in the court of public opinion if the players demonstrated a willingness to submit themselves to self-regulation.

The PRC was not fully prepared for the MLBPA's rapid response and instructed the clubs to refuse players access to club training facilities until a deal had been reached. This lockout increased anxiety about the fate of the 1973 season but lost its effectiveness early on when a few clubs allowed their players access to the facilities. The owners then offered salary arbitration for three-year veterans every other year. The MLBPA rejected this proposal out of fear that their salaries would be slashed every other year, when they were not eligible for arbitration. Supporters of the owners among the baseball public believed the ongoing lockout was simply further evidence that Marvin Miller was the primary party to blame and was doing a disservice to the players with his failure to accept the owners' proposals. The *New York Daily News*' Joe Trimble claimed, "The rank and file is incensed at the lockout by the owners. . . . The magnates threw a curveball at Marvelous Marvin Thursday when they offered an unprecedented arbitration setup to settle salary disputes between clubs and players." Trimble interviewed players such as Pete Rose who were upset that the 1972 strike cost them the opportunity to reach statistical milestones attached to incentives in their 1972 contracts. Rose said, "If there's another strike the Players Association won't get my support."[59] Despite Trimble's depictions of dissent, things were relatively calm in the players' camp. Most players understood that the owners were far from unified in their views on salary arbitration and that the motivations of hard-liners, such as Charlie Finley, came primarily from the fact that their players were among the lowest paid in the league.

Walter O'Malley and other large-market magnates refused to see the month of February come to an end without a peace deal in place. O'Malley publicly split with the hard-liners, leaving Busch and Finley out on a limb. Kuhn, not surprisingly, threw his weight behind O'Malley, and the two sides restarted talks on February 17. A new agreement was reached by the end of the month. The players and owners agreed to salary arbitration for every player with at least two years' experience who requested arbitration after his contract expired. The magnates agreed to provide salary data to the players so that they might be able to better prepare their arbitration cases, no small thing given the fact that the players often had difficulty gathering reliable salary information. The arbitrator for each case would be chosen from a preselected pool of arbitrators, who would hear arguments from both sides in mid-February and make a final decision within seventy-two hours. The agreement also included the ten and five rule, as well as an increase in the minimum salary to $15,000 for the 1973 season and $16,000 by 1975. The players, in turn, dropped their demand for a return to the 154-game season and agreed to an extra year of study on the reserve system. In its early years, salary arbitration proved not quite as sinister as the owners feared. The first round of hearings involved twenty-nine cases, sixteen of which were decided in favor of the owners.

The economic impact for most clubs amounted to a $20,000–$30,000 increase in total payroll.[60]

The 1972 strike and 1973 lockout posed the greatest threats yet to MLBPA solidarity. Earlier gains came back to haunt the union, as much of the baseball public seemed to think the players had won enough concessions from the owners. After all, the pension was now secure and player salary negotiations were now eligible for a new, more impartial, arbitration process. Fans and the media seemed to believe that the time had come for the MLBPA to sit back and take a more moderate stance in the best interests of the game. Despite the challenges of this era, from the Supreme Court's decision in the *Flood* case to the shifting tides of public opinion, there was little doubt the players understood what was necessary in order to accomplish their final remaining goal: the elimination of the reserve clause. The players were confident that, by following Marvin Miller's lead, they could reach the promised land of free agency and the chance to pursue the full value of their services in the free market. The players' goals were clear, but it was equally clear that the baseball public still needed some convincing. As Doc Young put it in the *Chicago Defender*, "The players, especially in light of modern thinking, are right to demand such as a loosening of the now-all-binding reserve clause. But, let's face it: Baseball players are very well paid for playing their game, they have a fantastic pension plan, and while it is true that some inequalities still exist in the area of pay—they can lose more than they can gain by constantly, or too-often repeatedly, bitching about money."[61]

8

Freedom at Last?

Following their successful 1972 strike, only a few of the players' primary goals remained unrealized. They won the right to salary arbitration in the 1973 Basic Agreement, leaving the removal of the reserve clause as the only remaining barrier to player freedom from the old restraints of the monopsonistic baseball labor market. The *Flood* decision, which the players hoped would bring relief from the courts, left the reserve system intact. The *Flood* proceedings, however, were not without their benefits. Throughout the original trial and later appeals, the owners insisted that the reserve clause was an issue that could be resolved only through collective bargaining. This tactic committed the owners to dealing with the clause through bargaining and arbitration, two areas that played to the strengths of Marvin Miller and the MLBPA leadership.

The players got their first chance to challenge the reserve clause courtesy of a small-market owner well known for his cost-conscious ways, Charlie Finley of the Oakland A's. Two star Oakland pitchers wanted to free themselves from the constraints of the reserve system, knowing they could earn a great deal more with another club. The first of these pitchers was Vida Blue, who attempted to hold out at the start of the 1972 season in an effort to cash in on an amazing 1971 season, when he won both the American League MVP and Cy Young Awards. Blue hired an agent and demanded his $14,750 salary be raised to $115,000; although the new salary would be a significant raise for Blue, it was a mere two-thirds of the salary commanded by the Major League's highest paid player, Carl Yastrzemski. In a relatively new bargaining strategy, Blue insisted he deserved such a large increase because more than twice as many fans came out to the park on the nights he pitched, a fact that clearly delineated his contribution to the A's bottom line. Blue's holdout lasted nearly two months. He finally signed a contract on May 2, ultimately agreeing to a $63,000 salary for the 1972 season.[1]

The second pitcher was Jim "Catfish" Hunter. Hunter and Blue were the cornerstones of a dominant pitching staff that made Oakland one of the best teams in baseball during the early 1970s. Hunter, a man with more business savvy than many of his peers, was already planning for life after baseball. He took part of his salary in an annuity funded by the Athletics. This annuity quickly became a source of tension between Hunter and Finley, as they clashed several times over Finley's inability to keep up with the required annuity payments. Hunter went to Miller in 1973 to see if the MLBPA could help him make a case for breach of contract against Finley for his failure to make payments. He hoped such a case would help him break free from the Athletics in order to negotiate freely with other clubs.

Hunter's situation was unprecedented. He was at the top of his game in 1973. Teams throughout the Majors knew that, in Hunter, they would be signing a proven winner, the kind of player who could turn a third- or fourth-place team into an immediate pennant contender. Team owners all understood that a club in contention generated a great deal more ticket revenue through the last two months of the season than teams that were out of the running. It was easy for many magnates to see the immediate financial impact of signing a player like Hunter.

The MLBPA helped Hunter bring his grievance before the arbitration panel at the conclusion of the 1974 season. On December 13, 1974, arbitrator Peter Seitz ruled that Finley and the Athletics were, indeed, in breach of contract. Hunter was free to sign a contract with the club of his choosing. The baseball public anxiously awaited the bidding war for Hunter's services. Hard-line and small-market owners, who desperately wanted to hold the line on player salaries, watched in dismay, as many of their "new-breed" brethren jumped at the chance to bid for Hunter's services. The results were even more startling than originally anticipated. Hunter signed with the New York Yankees for an annual salary of $600,000, or seven times the amount he had been paid the previous season by the Athletics. His new contract included a $1 million signing bonus from the brash new Yankees owner George Steinbrenner and amounted to total compensation of $3.5 million over five years.

Although many public voices decried this type of open bidding as harmful to the interests of the game, there was a great deal of interest in the sort of free agency experiment that was Catfish Hunter. Finley was a well-known spendthrift, and Hunter's cause resonated with those players, and their fans, who felt the financial constraints of playing for small-market clubs with limited resources. Fans of the teams actively seeking Hunter's services anxiously awaited the outcome of the bidding war. The pitcher's arrival in their city could mean an instant change in the fortunes of their hometown team. Baseball fans were used to waiting years for their favorite club to turn its fortunes around. Traditionally, it took time to build a quality roster by bringing in new talent through the farm system. Free agency, which meant any player with an expired contract could sign with the club of his choosing, offered the promise of overnight change in a team's fortunes. Even traditionalist fans, long fearful of the negative impacts of free agency, found themselves drawn to the promise of such a dramatic change in fortune for the home team.

Hunter's case was made all the more compelling by Steinbrenner, whose free-agent signings did not stop with Hunter. In the next few seasons, he signed a number of other notable stars, including the brash slugger Reggie Jackson, and quickly returned the Yankees to the dominance they had enjoyed during the 1950s. Reaction to Hunter's signing was telling. Many of the same magnates who were heavily involved in the bidding war were quick to condemn Hunter's new contract. According to Braves vice president Eddie Robinson, "This points up what would happen in baseball with no reserve clause. . . . All this tells me that, without it, baseball would be torn down." Robinson believed the perceived greed of stars like Hunter could only mean that "the average guys would have to play for a lot less money."[2] Chicago Cubs owner Phil Wrigley was not so concerned about the reserve clause as he was about the impact of such salaries on ticket prices, and on the fans who bought the tickets. "From our point of view, things now seem to be out of hand. The offers [to Hunter] mentioned in the media represent, in our opinion, more money than the average fan will pay to see a whole team. Much less one player."[3] The players were excited about Catfish's new contract, despite the magnates' claims that Hunter's contract would only hurt the average player and keep fans from coming through the turnstiles. When asked about resentment toward Hunter, Yankees manager Bill Virdon said, "All of our players will realize having him increases our opportunity to win a pennant and I know that's what they want more than anything."[4] Virdon's thoughts reflect the shift in clubhouse thinking teams needed as free agency moved closer to reality.

Hunter's case demonstrated the explosive potential of free agency, in terms of both the actual free-market value of a star player and the huge amount of public interest in the signing of such a proven talent. Star players badly wanted the opportunity to provide their services to the club willing to make the most attractive offer. Fans throughout the country were fascinated by the idea that their favorite team could change its fortunes overnight by signing just the right player. Teams with enough foresight to grasp the long-term ramifications of free agency came to realize how their pursuit of established stars demonstrated a commitment to winning. Ultimately, though, Hunter's experience was not much more than a trial balloon for free agency. It lacked several of the key elements of true free agency. Hunter had not earned free agency through length of service, the criteria the MLBPA wanted badly to establish; he had won the right to negotiate freely only because an arbitration panel found the owner of his team to be in breach of contract. He entered a market in which he was the only available free agent. His value undoubtedly would have been lower in a market where clubs seeking a new starting pitcher had a variety of players to choose from. Hunter was baseball's first free agent, but the reserve system remained very much intact.

McNally and Messersmith: Much More than Trial Balloons

Marvin Miller and the MLBPA leadership knew they needed more than a breach-of-contract grievance in order to formally challenge the reserve clause before baseball's arbitration panel. Miller's hopes rested with finding a player willing to play for an entire season without signing a new contract. Such a player could then go before the arbitration panel to challenge the reserve system's automatic renewal feature. During the 1975 season, a pair of players in very different circumstances presented themselves as the ideal challengers. The first of these men was Andy Messersmith, who, like Catfish Hunter, was a pitcher at the peak of a very strong career. When the time came to negotiate his contract for the 1975 season, Messersmith held out for a $175,000 salary and demanded a "no trade," or at least a trade approval clause, from the Dodgers. The Dodgers' initial response was to renew Messersmith's contract automatically, a decision that would, the MLBPA hoped, make Messersmith eligible for free agency in the event he remained unsigned at the end of the 1975 season.[5] The club offered Messersmith a lucrative contract but, on the specific instructions of National League president Chub Feeney, refused to budge on the issue of the "no trade" clause.[6]

The negotiations continued throughout the 1975 season. By August, Messersmith was having one of the best seasons of his career and was talking frequently with Miller about challenging the reserve clause. In order to make his challenge viable, Messersmith needed to play the entire 1975 season under the terms of his 1974 contract. As the 1975 season drew to a close with the pitcher still unsigned, it was readily apparent that Messersmith intended to challenge the reserve clause. After winning his last start of the season, to finish a very strong year in which he won nineteen games and posted a 2.29 ERA, Messersmith told the *Los Angeles Times*, "I like it here and I want to stay. I've talked to Al [Campanis—the Dodgers' GM] and to Peter [O'Malley—the Dodgers' team president] and I believe them when they say there's little chance I'll be traded. But I don't like the idea that there's even the slightest chance I'll be shoveled off to Cleveland or Detroit or anything like that."[7] Messersmith's desire to cash in his star status for a guarantee that he could play the rest of his days in Southern California, aligned with the MLBPA's goals. Limiting the magnates' ability to trade players like any other commodity had been a dream of every player since the days of the Brotherhood nearly a century before.

The 1975 season ended without Messersmith having a new contract in place, and he requested free-agent status. The Major League clubs refused. Miller argued, "By not declaring Messersmith a free agent, the 24 clubs have acted in combination to deprive him of his rights in violation of the Standard Players Contract." The owners charged that Messersmith never intended to sign a contract. They argued, correctly, that Miller and the MLBPA leadership specifically set Messersmith up to be their test case.[8] Legally, though, Messersmith's intentions mattered little. He had played a full season under the terms of his old contract and believed he was entitled to pursue free agency. The arbitration panel scheduled Messersmith's hearing for November 21. The Dodgers were desperate to sign the pitcher, especially to avoid playing a part in the creation of baseball's first legitimate free agent, but they were also unwilling to cave in to his demands. Even though negotiations continued into the postseason months of October and November, it was no surprise that the two parties failed to reach agreement on a contract.

Miller and the player representatives felt good about Messersmith's chances but still wanted one more player to join the grievance. Miller wanted a backup on hand in case the Dodgers and National League president Feeney came to their senses and signed Messersmith before the arbitration panel could grant him free agency. They found their man in the veteran pitcher Dave McNally, who was still unsigned by the Montreal Expos.[9] McNally, a longtime player representative and MLBPA supporter, was traded from the Baltimore Orioles to the Expos with the promise that the Expos would sign him to a two-year contract worth $125,000 per season. When he arrived in Montreal, he instead received a one-year contract for $115,000. McNally struggled with arm trouble throughout the 1974 campaign, and thought about leaving the game. When the pitcher proved reluctant to negotiate, the Expos unilaterally renewed his contract for 1975. After starting the season with only three wins against six losses, he left the Expos on June 8 and returned to his car dealership in Billings, Montana. McNally sat out the remainder of the 1975 season while evaluating his options. Since the Expos had unilaterally renewed his contract for 1975, he met the requirements for joining Messersmith's grievance, but unlike the younger Dodger pitcher, McNally had little to lose in the event his grievance ended in owner retaliation.

In contrast to the public criticism that surrounded the 1972 strike and 1973 lockout, the two pitchers enjoyed support from several reliable voices in the media. Red Smith accused the owners of deferring issues they did not want to deal with, such as blacklists and boycotts, to collective bargaining. Once at the bargaining table, Smith argued, the owners refused to bargain. He believed the same pattern was developing in Messersmith and McNally's case. "So he [Messersmith] didn't sign. He now has fulfilled the all the terms of the last contract he did sign. In any business in the world outside of professional team sports he would be free to work where he pleased. Does a contract he never signed renew itself annually as long as he lives? That wouldn't be a contract. It would be a set of leg irons."[10] Many writers echoed Smith's argument that the terms of the contract essentially set Messersmith free. This was critical support the players needed. In order for the post–reserve clause era to get off on the right foot, the MLBPA needed Messersmith to be seen in a favorable public light as he entered the free agent market.

There was serious concern, especially among moderate magnates, regarding the possible outcomes of Messersmith and McNally's grievance. As the owners' chief negotiator, John Gaherin, cautioned, "Miller can afford to lose a hundred times as long as he wins once." He encouraged the owners to begin talks with the players about revisions to the system that would allow for free agency in certain circumstances. In the immediate lead-up to the hearing the Dodgers and Expos did their part by trying to buy the two pitchers off with increasingly large sums of money. On November 19, Messersmith rejected a last-second effort by the Dodgers to lure him in with a larger salary, standing firm on his demand for a trade approval clause.[11] Expos management continued to travel out to Billings in an effort to woo McNally with salary offers much higher than one would expect for an aging starter who had lost twice as many games as he won the previous season.[12] The teams were much too late. Messersmith's agent, Herb Osmond, maintained a public posture that was open to continued negotiation, but in truth, neither pitcher would accept any contract short of complete capitulation by the magnates on the reserve clause. Even when the Dodgers made substantial concessions, offering Messersmith a three-year contract worth $540,000 that included the no-trade clause he wanted, it was evident that the club had waited too long. Messersmith had pitched a full season under the pressure of playing without a contract. He was now determined to see things through to the end.

The grievance went before the three-member arbitration panel on November 21. Messersmith and his agent, Osmond, had good reason to eagerly await the results. Messersmith was a pitcher close to the quality of Catfish Hunter, and even if he received only half as much as Hunter in free agency, he stood to easily triple his $115,000 salary. The panel consisted of Marvin Miller, representing the players; John Gaherin, representing the owners; and the independent arbitrator Peter Seitz. Seitz was the same man who set Catfish Hunter free just one year earlier, and he strongly encouraged both sides to solve the issue through collective bargaining before coming to him with the grievance.[13]

Seitz was a man already out of favor with the magnates. Management seriously discussed firing Seitz, a move well within the PRC's powers. National League attorney Lou Hoynes and Baseball Commissioner Bowie Kuhn advised the PRC to fire Seitz rather than give him the opportunity to rule on Messersmith's grievance. Their reasoning was sound. Seitz's earlier rulings, especially the Catfish Hunter decision, indicated he was uncomfortable with the restrictions of the reserve system. Try as they might to convince the PRC that firing Seitz was the right move, Kuhn and Hoynes faced resistance from magnates who feared doing so would be a public relations disaster. Kuhn conceded that the "grandfatherly Seitz" was quite popular with the public and well regarded in arbitration circles.[14] The commissioner further understood that Seitz's popularity, in part, stemmed from the Hunter decision. It is more than a little ironic that the magnates understood the Hunter decision was popular but failed to understand how a move toward free agency might, in turn, increase baseball's popularity. This was yet another instance in which many conservative magnates failed to recognize that a more progressive path could better serve the interests of a traditionalist institution such as baseball. Ultimately, owners feared the ill will that firing Seitz would generate and rejected Kuhn's suggestion that Seitz be removed. The players' case for free agency had swung the tide of public opinion in their favor, and the owners feared the public backlash that firing Seitz might bring.

These challenging circumstances presented a real crisis for Bowie Kuhn, who even considered invoking Article 10, Item A.1 of the Basic Agreement, which allowed the commissioner to reject any grievance that involved an "action taken with respect to a Player or Players by the Commissioner involving the preservation of the integrity of, or the maintenance of public confidence in, the game of baseball."[15] Kuhn later wrote, "There was no doubt in my mind that the game's integrity and public confidence were at stake in the potential destruction of the reserve system."[16] The commissioner was closely tied to the old ways of baseball and had difficulty seeing the potential for good in free agency. Kuhn could not envision the game without the contractual controls kept in place by the 1922 antitrust exemption—so much so that he was unable to see that public support for the magnates was eroding under his feet.

Baseball's Emancipation Proclamation: Or Not?

When Seitz handed down the panel's decision on December 23, the owners' worst fears were realized. Seitz sustained the pitchers' grievance, paving the way for them to negotiate freely with any club of their choosing for the 1976 season. The players understood that management would challenge the arbitrator's ruling but knew their victory was the critical first step toward real free agency. Seitz encouraged players and owners, once again, to find a permanent, systematic solution for the free agency problem through collective bargaining. The magnates quickly made it clear they no longer had an interest in listening to Seitz. He was dismissed within hours of the ruling's announcement with the statement that "professional baseball no longer has confidence in the arbitrator's ability to understand the basic structure of organized baseball."[17]

In dismissing the man whose ruling ushered in the free agent era, the owners demonstrated the difficulty many of them were having envisioning the game without the reserve system. As Red Smith wrote, "The owners wanted an impartial arbitrator who was more impartial on their side." Smith predicted the owners would once again say, "'These are matters best left to collective bargaining,' Then they refuse to bargain."[18] Seitz downplayed the decision: "I am not Abraham Lincoln signing the Emancipation Proclamation. Involuntary Servitude has nothing to do with this case. I decided it as a lawyer and an arbitrator. This decision does not destroy baseball. But if the club owners think it will ruin baseball they have it in their power to prevent the damage."[19] Seitz's comments demonstrate his firm belief that baseball's popularity could once again boom in the modern era if the game freed itself from the restrictions of nineteenth-century management practices.

Reaction in the press was mixed in the days following the ruling. Many writers, such as Charles Maher of the *Los Angeles Times*, warned readers not to overestimate the power of Seitz's ruling. As Maher argued, the primary outcome was "that the players will have more leverage when they sit down with owners next month to work out a new basic agreement. It is that agreement, and not the Seitz decision, that will really spell out the rights of the players."[20] Red Smith agreed with Maher's interpretation of the ruling's significance but also made sure to criticize the owners for the foolishness and hypocrisy of their ways: "Feeney and MacPhail and Kuhn are trotting out that old bugbear, the mildewed myth that if the clubs didn't own the players for life, all the stars would wind up in New York or Los Angeles. Even if there are owners with the selfish stupidity to destroy their own business, it would be easy to protect them against themselves. The players have suggested a way. . . . At last report the owners had refused to discuss it. . . . Baseball fans have been fed a double ration of hogwash, misinformation and plain untruths since Christmas Eve." Smith believed Seitz had done his job in interpreting and applying the "agreements and understandings of the parties" when he decided that a year meant a year, and not "20 or 200," as the magnates interpreted the language of Section 10A of the Basic Agreement.[21] It was time for the owners to accept the realities of the modern age of professional sports.

It did not take long for other players to begin their efforts to leverage Seitz's decision. Star Minnesota Twins pitcher Bert Blyleven, who was in the early stages of a very promising career, started telling reporters he would be more than happy to play out his option year with the Twins and then head west to his native California to play for the Angels or Dodgers. It was Blyleven's way of turning up the heat on the cost-conscious Twins owner Calvin Griffith. "He says he doesn't have the money," Blyleven said, "but he's got his whole family on the payroll in the front office. Maybe he should cut back on them and pay more to the ballplayers."[22] Blyleven's message was simple: pay me more, trade me to a West Coast club, or I'll take matters into my own

hands and play out my option year. The additional leverage provided by the Seitz decision surely struck fear in the hearts of
owners, especially small-market family owners like the Griffiths,
who found themselves in competition with the likes of George
Steinbrenner, a man who had amassed a fortune in other industries and was willing to spend extravagantly to win immediately.

The magnates' next move was to turn to the courts, much to
the players' consternation. The players expressed frustration that
the owners had agreed to binding arbitration and then, when
they were unhappy with the result, went to court. The owners'
suit, officially brought by Royals owner Ewing Kauffman, was
heard in a Kansas City federal court, which the owners believed
provided a friendlier venue. On February 4, Judge John Oliver
rejected the magnates' request for an injunction setting aside
Seitz's decision. The magnates, who were in the midst of negotiations with the players on the new 1976 Basic Agreement,
attempted to delay by pretending they still had plenty of legal
options to pursue. It seemed clear that Major League management was willing to take whatever steps necessary to prevent the
Seitz ruling from becoming the law of the land.

Miller expressed his disbelief, saying, "We are dealing with an
irrational approach, an Alice in Wonderland outlook." Judge Oliver left little doubt in his ruling that it was time for the owners
to wake up and realize they were operating in a new era: "There
can be no doubt that the club owners' apparent preoccupation
with how baseball clubs were operated in the 19th century and
before the year 1968 . . . may have affected the willingness of
some club owners to recognize the quite fundamental differences between these two periods of baseball."[23] Oliver's reference
to 1968 was pointed; that was the year the players and owners
reached their first Basic Agreement, ushering in the era of collective bargaining. The judge wanted the owners to understand
that the sooner they embraced the terms of the new era, the better off they would be. The owners asked for a stay of Oliver's
decision, knowing that if they allowed Seitz's ruling to stand
unchallenged it would serve as a final blow to the reserve clause.

Messersmith soon learned how the owners would respond to baseball's first-ever free agent. Not surprisingly, the owners began with a variety of stall tactics. They told MLBPA officials that they could not negotiate a new agreement involving the reserve system while the Messersmith ruling was tied up on appeal. The clubs also refused to discuss possible contract terms with the pitcher, telling Messersmith's agent they needed approval from Commissioner Kuhn before bidding for Messersmith's services. The pitcher admitted to his fears regarding the process: "I am somewhat frightened by the owners' attitude. It's as if they don't know how this could have happened, as if almost it didn't happen. . . . What it says to me is that the sport is heading to chaos, a real mess if cooler heads don't prevail. These are good business people. They've got to recognize the need for compromise. I don't see how they could have been surprised by the decision . . . since there have been similar decisions in other sports."[24] Most importantly to Messersmith, the owners' response meant that the final resolution of his situation was still far from complete.

Owner resistance to Seitz's decision complicated negotiations on the new Basic Agreement well into late February. As *New York Times* baseball writer Murray Chass pointed out, the Seitz ruling effectively turned the tables. The players were content with the reserve system, as defined by the Seitz ruling. Now it was the owners who went to the bargaining table to demand change in the reserve rules. Marvin Miller told Chass, "Any dispute that exists arises because of the owners' demands for change. To those who ask what the players want now, the answer is nothing. . . . We're willing to sign a four-year agreement. That's a four year, no-strike pledge."[25] The owners had no interest in such a pledge if it included de facto free agency, and negotiations dragged on into early March. The magnates received bad news on March 9, when a panel of three judges in St. Louis denied their final legal appeal on the Seitz ruling. The judges upheld Oliver's ruling, which affirmed Seitz's jurisdiction in the Messersmith-McNally grievance. The court order cleared the way for Messersmith to start contract talks with interested clubs on March 16.[26]

Negotiations continued to founder on what became known as the "one and one" problem presented by the Seitz ruling. Management feared that if the ruling was maintained in its current form, it would allow any player to play for only two years, one year under contract plus the "option year," even as the club invested heavily in the player's development. After just two years in the Major Leagues any player would be able to enjoy complete freedom of contract. Two years of service was not nearly enough for the owners, who understandably wanted a larger payoff on their initial investment in player skill development. The owners demanded a "six and one" formula, in which a player could play out his option after six years with his original club. The players countered with a proposal for "five and one." When this situation remained unresolved on March 1, the owners locked the players out of their spring training camps. At first, players organized their own camps and trained on their own, but as negotiations dragged on, many players, such as Reds pitcher Tom Seaver, concluded that by staying in shape they were only playing into the owners' hands. The players disbanded their informal camps and awaited an agreement.[27]

Messersmith and his agent, Herb Osmond, geared up to start accepting bids for the pitcher's services on March 16. Dodgers president Peter O'Malley made it clear that the Dodgers were done bidding for the pitcher's services. Anticipating a bidding war like the one for Catfish Hunter, O'Malley said, "I don't think it's good common sense to pay any man two or three times what he's worth. In the interest of the longevity of the franchise, you just can't start playing with monopoly money. The profit line in professional sports is too thin. I realize that trying to determine a player's worth is a gray area and some franchises might be willing to offer considerable money. But I doubt this one will."[28] O'Malley, very much the son of his longtime magnate father, Walter O'Malley, did his best to trot out the tried-and-true arguments about why free-market economics played little or no role in the management of a Major League Baseball team. Once again, O'Malley, president of one of the wealthiest teams in all of professional sports, chose to respond to a player's position with pleas of poverty and veiled threats of exclusion or black-listing. In doing so, the Dodger owner failed to recognize that the baseball public was not so easily swayed by the arguments and tactics the magnates had repeatedly used in earlier times.

Baseball fans and the media paid close attention once the bidding for Messersmith's services got underway. More experienced voices knew Messersmith was unlikely to experience the outpouring of interest shown in Hunter. The simple reason was that Messersmith's grievance cleared the way for many more free agents to follow. One year earlier, Hunter was seen as a one and only type of opportunity. As Ted Turner, the new owner of the Atlanta Braves and prototype of the modern-era baseball owner, told the *New York Times*, he was interested in Messersmith, but "this situation is different than with Catfish because the supply of superstars available as free agents probably will be a lot higher than in the past."[29]

March 16 also brought news of an owner compromise in the Basic Agreement negotiations. The owners offered a "one and one" compromise for existing players. Such a deal made it possible for almost any current big leaguer to become a free agent, simply by playing the 1976 season without signing a new contract. In exchange, the owners wanted an "eight and one" rule for all new big leaguers. This would keep the existing reserve system essentially in force for the first eight years of a player's career. Any player who pursued free agency after that period would be able to negotiate only with the bottom eight clubs in the league standings. It is significant that, in offering this proposal, the owners openly accepted Seitz's ruling on the Messersmith grievance for the first time. The magnates talked as if they were finally relinquishing the keys to the kingdom. Of the decision to offer "one and one" to current players, the American League president, Lee MacPhail, said, "We bit the bullet. We are also reluctantly willing to face whatever consequences may come of this. Now it's up to the players to accept it. This is our final offer." MacPhail and the magnates vowed that training camps would not be opened until the players accepted. Miller promised to take the proposal to the players for a vote but, of course, offered no guarantees.[30]

There was a fair amount of surprise the next day when Miller made it clear he expected the players not to accept the owners' "final offer" and instead to ask for continued bargaining. The players took exception with several aspects of the owners' proposal, but the primary complaint was with the strictly limited free agency provided by the PRC's proposal. The players saw the opportunity to negotiate with only a limited number of teams, and not all interested clubs, as something well short of free agency. They did not want a piece of the free market; they wanted the freedom to operate in the whole market. Miller wanted all future players to be "free agents in the Messersmith sense: Free to deal with all 24 clubs."[31]

The players' response left many magnates livid. John Gaherin commented, "We offered the olive branch and now we may have to go to the shillelagh. I don't know if it's stupidity or arrogance or what. But he's [Miller] got this thing in some fine position now." While the owners blustered, many players took a low-key approach, one that reflected the rights consciousness Miller began nourishing back in 1966. Star Pittsburgh first baseman Willie Stargell told the press, "The owners have taken some guys out of prison and some out of the ghettos. I don't know what I'd be doing if I wasn't playing ball. But this has been our lives. To destruct yourself doesn't make sense. The courts have granted us certain rights, and we're willing to see now what we can live with."[32] Baseball players fought, off and on, for nearly a century for freedom from the reserve clause. They were not going to give away freely what arbitration, and then the courts, had granted them.

It was no surprise, by now, that Red Smith seethed at what he saw as owner duplicity. "As a pressure tactic, they [the owners] padlocked the training camps and threatened to call off the season. Many players went to Florida or Arizona and trained at their own expense until they realized this was just playing into the owners' hands." Smith again criticized the owners for their hypocrisy in clinging to the reserve system, claiming it was necessary for establishing community allegiance and maintaining competitive balance.

> They say community identity is vital to their business, that the fans identify with players on the home team over a period of years. This winter 89 players were traded away by the owners, including favorites of the fans like Rusty Staub, Bobby Bonds, Jim Kaat. . . . They suggest ballplayers are not decent human beings but creeps who enjoy dragging their families from town to town. . . . The other day John McHale said that the reserve system was necessary "to preserve competitive balance." John is president of the Montreal Expos, who have . . . always lost most of their games and never finished higher than fourth in a six-club division. John wants to preserve this balance.[33]

Smith no longer wrote as the voice of outside opposition. His views now represented a much more mainstream take on owner disingenuousness. The excitement of the chase to sign Hunter, the rational freedom of contract sentiment expressed in the Seitz decision, and the players' calm insistence that change must come had effectively swung the tide. Free agency was a newly accepted reality in professional baseball, and while there would always be opposition to it, especially from sentimental traditionalists, the baseball public was excited to see how free agency might shape the future of the game.

In the meantime, Messersmith's search for a new contract dragged into its second week amid talk of owner collusion and the inevitable claims that bidding wars would only bring about the end of the game. The remarks of Reds vice president Bob Howsam were typical. After rejecting Messersmith's request for $1.5 million over four years with a "no-cut" guarantee, Howsam said, "We have admiration for Messersmith's pitching ability, but we have to operate our club on a sound basis. To sign him under those terms is poor business. No club in our industry can truly afford this and survive."[34] The MLBPA was convinced the owners were colluding to lowball Messersmith, and MLBPA counsel Dick Moss prepared to file charges against the owners for failing to follow the letter of Messersmith's arbitration ruling. Moss claimed Dodger owner Walter O'Malley was pressuring other clubs to steer clear of the pitcher. Herb Osmond, Messersmith's agent, expressed disbelief: "We are talking about one of baseball's best pitchers and the fact that we have received only three firm offers for him and the fact that these offers are not of the type we had anticipated for him just doesn't add up." Osmond also criticized Howsam for claiming the pitcher wanted $1.5 million over four years, when the two parties had not, according to Osmond, even discussed the financial aspects of the contract.[35]

More clubs showed interest as the bidding headed into its second week, although it was now obvious Messersmith was not going to command "Catfish money." On March 29, the Yankees announced they had agreed to a four-year, $1 million contract with the pitcher. Things quickly fell apart with the Yankees, however, when the club claimed it owned Messersmith before he had signed an official contract. Messersmith recoiled against the Yankees' high-pressure tactics and backed out of the deal. This back-and-forth resulted in a media firestorm in New York, and speculation began as to whether Messersmith would pitch at all in 1976. Finally, on April 10, the pitcher came to terms with the Atlanta Braves. The two parties agreed on a no-cut, no-trade, three-year contract at $200,000 per season. Messersmith received a $400,000 signing bonus.[36]

This resolved Messersmith's situation, but the inability of the players and owners to reach a final agreement on the 1976 Basic Agreement pushed collective bargaining negotiations well into the regular season. Commissioner Kuhn, using his "best interests of the game" powers, forced the owners to open the camps on March 17. Negotiations sputtered on and off until mid-July, when a deal was finally reached at the All-Star break. The agreement included the "one and one" free agency formula for existing players and a "six and one" formula for all new players. It also restricted a player to filing for free agency only once every five years. Free agents could negotiate with up to twelve teams, which would be selected through a draft process. Gussie Busch believed the agreement amounted to "surrender terms." Many others on the management side, including Commissioner Kuhn and American League president Lee MacPhail, believed this was a reasonable settlement, one that left baseball with "the best reserve system in professional sports." The impact of this agreement lay in how the owners handled the terms, and as Kuhn put it, "What we had not counted on was how ridiculously the owners would behave once the whistle blew." The era of free spending was on, and in the decade to come the average player salary would increase by almost 800 percent.[37] Perhaps even more significantly, the MLBPA had finally achieved its primary goal, and at a time when unions across the country found their power limited at every turn.

1980: Free Agency, Round Two

Free agency and salary arbitration ushered in a new era in baseball labor relations. Salary arbitration continued to be of the either/or variety: the arbitrator was expected to choose either the amount suggested by the player or the amount suggested by management but could not split the difference to reach what would be considered a fair figure by most. The bidding for free agents drove salaries higher, and as a result the salary figures proposed in arbitration cases rose as well. The results were staggering. The average player salary more than doubled during the first three years of the free agent era, from $51,500 in 1976 to $113,558 in 1979. Additionally, the owners, so long opposed to the multiyear contract, began using three- and four-year pacts in order to keep players from abandoning their club in favor of free agency. These contracts drove up salaries as well, because players knew they should demand more in exchange for giving up the right to pursue their full free-market value.

The owners were outraged, largely with each other, over the spectacular new salaries resulting from the bidding wars. During negotiations for the new Basic Agreement in 1980, they proposed a new compensation system designed specifically to rein in free agency. Under the existing free agent system, any team that lost a player to free agency was compensated by the signing club with a pick in the upcoming amateur draft. These picks could be of great value, but, since players chosen in the amateur draft often took years to become Major Leaguers, the draft picks did little to make up for the immediate loss of an accomplished Major League player. Under the owners' new proposal, a team that signed a free agent would be expected to "compensate" the free agent's original club with a player of the original club's choosing. The only restriction was that the "compensation player" could not be one of fifteen players the signing team was allowed to protect. With twenty-five players on the average Major League roster, 40 percent of every team's roster was left "unprotected."[38]

The PRC's new negotiator, Ray Grebey, made this system the centerpiece of the owners' negotiating strategy from the outset. Grebey floated a couple of other proposals to the players, including immediate eligibility for the pension and a set salary schedule for younger players in the first four years of their big league service. These ideas were primarily intended only for distraction or later concession. The owners' main push was the new free agent compensation plan, a proposal in which they were essentially asking the union to help protect the owners from themselves.[39]

The players opposed free agent compensation for obvious reasons. The plan dramatically reduced club incentives to sign free agent talent. This, in turn, falsely suppressed the free agent market, driving down player salaries and constricting player movement. Accustomed by now to the owners' tactics of claiming substantial financial losses and delaying the bargaining process, the MLBPA got an early start on its public relations campaign. In January 1979 Miller released a statement to the press in which he and the MLBPA executive committee sought to counter "the public statements of Bowie Kuhn and other baseball management representatives who have been peddling two basic distortions: (1) that the reserve system changes have resulted in worsening baseball's 'competitive balance' [not defined], and (2) [that the changes] have brought Major League Baseball to the brink of financial ruin."

Miller argued that the 1977 and 1978 seasons had seen improved competitive balance. He acknowledged, "Players' salaries, reflecting the change from the air-tight monopoly control . . . to a somewhat free market, have increased considerably. However the Club owners' revenue has increased even more in the same period." Miller bristled at Kuhn's allegations that the MLBPA would refuse to negotiate on certain key issues, stating, "The MLBPA will be prepared to negotiate on all bargainable matters. As in prior years the Players Association intends to negotiate on a firm, factual basis, and not on the basis of fantasy, conjecture or factual distortion."[40] The players prepared for the usual owner campaign pleading poverty and helplessness, as the magnates once again positioned themselves as the protectors of the national pastime, sparring with their self-interested employees.

When negotiations officially began the following December, the players found themselves once again facing an adversary unwilling to respond to their proposals. The magnates made it widely known that they were building a $3.5 million war chest for the sole purpose of helping clubs recoup losses in the event of a players' strike.[41] These owner preparations added fuel to the players' fire, especially as several of the more hard-line magnates described the fund as a their "line in the sand." Otherwise, the owners did their best to silence public comment from the management side, establishing a structure of penalties that made it a $500,000 offense for a high-ranking club executive to speak publicly about the ongoing negotiations. They assured traditionalists in the baseball press that this would be the moment they refused to give in to the players' demands. Commissioner Bowie Kuhn opened baseball's annual winter meetings with dire depictions of the game's future. The only hope, Kuhn believed, lay in taking immediate steps to restrict free agency and limit player salaries. "The game is enjoying great success," he claimed, "but the bottom eight clubs lost more than $2 million each last year, and one half of the clubs are in a loss position. . . . Today they [player salaries] average $121,000 and heading up. That's a remarkable, and disturbing, increase. Also, clubs are losing players in the free agent draft and cannot replace them from the minor leagues."[42]

The war chest and fine system were not the only signs of divisions within the management ranks. December's free agent signing period showed there were plenty of magnates still thrilled to embrace the free market. These men negotiated a number of sizable new contracts, eliciting protests from many of their peers. *Washington Post* columnist Thomas Boswell called it "capitalism in full laissez faire frolic: supply and demand run amuck." Milwaukee general manager Harry Dalton had another name for it: "We are seeing the auction syndrome. You go to the auction and see an old moose head that you never thought about until you got there. The auctioneer says, 'Available today only and never again. Here's your once-in-a-lifetime chance.' So you get the auction fever. Then when you get the damn moose home . . . it looks hideous . . . and you want to throw up. I don't want to denigrate the players in this year's draft, but I think a lot of teams have bought a lot of ugly moose heads." Baltimore general manager Hank Peters was much more direct: "I don't blame the players or their agents. They must not be able to believe what is happening themselves. Management is totally at fault. We're dragging each other down in this mad grabbing for free agents."[43] In early January the *New York Times* reported that the 1979 free agent class signed for a guaranteed total of $32 million, not counting the twenty-two free agents still unsigned.[44] Even as they prepared to enjoin the MLBPA in a battle to restructure free agency, many magnates still could not resist the opportunity to stockpile talent, however questionable its quality. Booming salaries in a popular industry that openly discussed its financial troubles remained one of the great contradictory story lines of the 1980 negotiations.

At this point, the owners' attempts to limit salaries for younger players emerged as another one of the players' primary concerns.

Miller and MLBPA counsel Donald Fehr wrote to the membership, "What if [the salary scale proposal] turns out to be, simply, a blatant attempt to have the Players Association agree to a severe reduction in salary and other benefits to players with less than six years service?"[45] If Grebey intended to use the salary schedule as a distraction, it was certainly working at this early stage of the negotiations. The salary structure went right to the heart of the association's most cherished accomplishment, the right to pursue maximum compensation in the free market. Miller told the press, "It's an affront and an insult to come to the Players Assn. and ask it to help police the amount of money its players can make. Here's an industry coming off four years of record prosperity and yet is trying to cut salaries by about a third."[46] Miller tried to rattle the PRC's cage by issuing a statement in mid-January that hinted at a possible strike: "The players see that [continued PRC foot dragging] as an attempt to strangle their bargaining power. What can a player do to protect himself once the season starts?"[47]

Miller repeated his warning to *Los Angeles Times* reporter Ross Newhan one week later, but to the surprise of no one close to the game, Miller's attempts to bring forth more fruitful negotiations were thwarted by more PRC delays. *Washington Post* columnist Thomas Boswell wrote, "The owners have realized that since laissez faire capitalism is killing them in the wallet, maybe they'd better opt for a sort of gaudy baseball socialism. . . . Management has carefully built a negotiating atmosphere in which almost every factor is designed to weaken the resolve of the players' union."[48] Many of the magnates were happy to see the negotiating climate take on a more adversarial tone. Ray Grebey had been hired, in part, as a move toward a more confrontational negotiating relationship. If that meant greater public vexation for the players and the press, then so be it. In the years since the adoption of free agency many owners had realized that they were falling behind in the court of public opinion. This realization on the part of the owners gave Grebey free rein to try anything he could to break down player unity.

Many public observers saw the salary scale as an owner attempt to divide and conquer using the time-tested tactic of turning the highest-paid, established stars against their younger brethren. Red Smith wrote, "When a club offers a player three to four times what the wage scale would permit, it is obvious that the owner recognizes the proposal as a farce. . . . Accustomed to a feudal relationship with the helots, owners have always believed that that the players would break ranks under economic pressure."[49] When members of the baseball press questioned player unity and militancy in the wake of all the big free agent contracts, Yankee pitcher Tommy John responded, "We as players have to be united to keep the association strong, whether you're making the minimum or you're making $900,000 a year."[50] Reggie Jackson also took exception, telling the owners, "You assume the high salaried players don't know how they got those high salaries. By sticking together."[51]

Miller did his part to maintain unity by responding to the one issue the PRC was trying to use as leverage with the younger players, immediate eligibility for the pension. "It is a blatant attempt to curry favor with the younger players, whom they might want to use as strikebreakers."[52] One thing was clear, especially when nothing had been resolved by late February: strike fears were growing. The calendar turned to March, and players continued to insist they were willing to strike if necessary rather than give back their hard-earned gains. Typical were the remarks of future Hall of Fame shortstop Ozzie Smith: "The Players Association has worked hard to get where we are. There's no way we're going to give up something we've fought years for."[53] Many players also responded to owner protestations of poverty by demanding to see their books, just one of the many ways Major League Baseball players, now under the leadership of Marvin Miller for fourteen years, were demonstrating a better understanding of the inner workings of the collective bargaining process.

The player reps made this all the more clear on March 4, when they authorized a strike if necessary. The players offered a glimpse of their solidarity the next day. The first club surveyed by Miller, the Philadelphia Phillies, voted 40–0 in favor of a strike in the event a new Basic Agreement was not reached by Opening Day on April 9. Minnesota pitcher Mike Marshall described player militancy and activism: "I used to picture Marvin Miller in a rowboat tied to a freighter, pulling the players along. Now he's on a surfboard on top of a tidal wave trying to stay on top."[54] Marshall's depiction certainly seemed accurate when, one week later, player support for a strike tallied 276–1.[55] Only one thing had changed: public discussion had moved away from the salary structure, which the MLBPA now called a joke, to the owners' free agent compensation plan, which was now the focal point of the negotiations. The owners continued to insist on a compensation plan that allowed any team losing a free agent to choose any player from the signing team's Major League roster who was not on the fifteen-man protected list.

March came to a close with no new progress. Grebey and the PRC maintained their unified, no compromise approach to the negotiations. Grebey's primary public relations strategy was to try and make Miller out to be the bad guy, in exchange for making the magnates look like the bad guys. "Miller's basic strategy is to make us look like the bad guys. Well, I've got no intention of stooping to name calling in return. We don't regard the players as the bad guys . . . the owners *do not* want a strike."[56] As the players agreed to strike the last eight days of the exhibition season, a federal mediator, Ken Moffett, joined the process in an effort to avoid baseball's second major work stoppage.

Marvin Miller sent a memo to the MLBPA membership on April 9, laying out the key issues in negotiations. Miller warned the players that the owners were trying to provoke a strike early in the season, a time when attendance was typically low, team revenue losses would be minimal, and player losses in unpaid salary would be substantial. He indicated that the executive committee wanted the regular, or "championship," season to get under way as planned, so as to not alienate baseball's fan base. The MLBPA would continue negotiations in the hope of reaching an agreement by May 22. In the event no agreement had been reached at that time, a players' strike would commence on May 23. Miller concluded the memo by saying, "It is to be expected that the owners and club and league officials will increase their efforts to pressure the players to surrender. . . . They include efforts to portray the players in the worst possible light. . . . None of it will work. The only thing that will produce a settlement is good faith negotiations. And that will be brought about by the unity of the Players—either before *May 23rd*, or after a strike."[57] Miller once again sought to build a positive relationship with the baseball public in order to maintain as much leverage as possible for the players.

Little immediate progress was made under Moffett's guidance, and in mid-April the mediator decided to put the talks in recess. His primary hope was that, by restarting the negotiations closer to the union's strike deadline, both sides would return in a more cooperative mood, and with a greater sense of urgency. The crucial issue in negotiations continued to be free agent compensation, especially for the top-flight players considered "premier free agents." Miller remained publicly confident about MLBPA solidarity, although privately he worried about the willingness of younger players to risk their careers to maintain free agent rights for more senior players.[58]

A settlement did not appear to be immediately in the offing in the days leading up to the strike deadline. Finally, a group of owners desperate to avoid a season-ending strike, like the Astros' John McMullen and the Orioles' Ed Williams, pressured Kuhn to get involved. The commissioner agreed to step in, and Grebey and Miller stayed up all night hammering out a new Basic Agreement. The two men emerged from a hotel room at 5:00 a.m. on May 23 to announce the details of the new contract. In many ways, their solution was not a solution at all. Minimum salaries were scheduled to gradually increase from $30,000 in 1980 to $35,000 in 1984. The owners agreed to increase their pension contribution to $15.5 million, almost doubling the $8.3 million agreed to in 1976.

These measures did nothing to clear up the major issue of

the 1980 negotiations, free agent compensation. The two parties agreed to turn that issue over to a four-member committee for study. The committee's findings would then be taken into account in new negotiations on the issue. If the two sides failed to reach agreement, the owners retained the right to unilaterally impose the terms of their last compensation proposal. If the owners took this route, the players reserved the right to strike in protest of the owners' compensation plan. If the players decided not to strike, they essentially forfeited their right to strike for the remaining three years of the four-year agreement.[59] Those who desperately wanted the 1980 season to go on got their wish, but only by putting the boiling compensation pot on the back burner for seven months. The owners immediately began preparations for implementing their compensation plans, and for the protracted work stoppage their plan would surely incite. Whatever happened in 1981, it would happen in front of a baseball public more than ready for final resolution of the issues that still plagued Major League Baseball after more than a decade of almost continuous labor strife.[60] As it approached, 1981 was shaping up to be the most significant year yet in nearly a century of conflict between baseball owners and players.

The 1981 Strike: Baseball's Painful Entry into the Modern Age

Tensions between players and owners ran high as the 1981 season got underway. Many team owners still wanted desperately to modify the 1980 Basic Agreement to include their free agent compensation plan. Rather than head into the 1981 season without terms for free agent compensation in place, the owners tried to impose the same plan for compensation that the MLBPA had rejected during the 1980 negotiations. The players, who had been working since the mid-1960s to reduce absolute owner control, saw this as an unacceptable step backward. It was no secret that this would be the biggest showdown yet between baseball's players and owners.

The 1981 season began on schedule, but strike rumors grew as the owners insisted they would unilaterally implement their free agent compensation plan over the course of that season. The MLBPA tried a two-pronged approach. The association went to the National Labor Relations Board seeking relief and also sought an injunction from the federal courts preventing the owners from putting their compensation plan into place. In mid-June, Federal District Judge Harry Werker denied the players' injunction, and the MLBPA set a strike deadline. When the owners failed to budge, a strike ensued. Public response to this strike marked a dramatic shift from 1972. The media, and the public, now held a far more sophisticated view of the business of baseball, a view made apparent time and again throughout the 1981 strike.

The confrontation took place amid a major shift in American attitudes toward labor. Many working-class Americans left the Democratic Party during the 1980 election and cast their votes for Ronald Reagan, who as California's governor had intervened in the 1974 Los Angeles Rapid Transit District strike and, during the 1981 Professional Air Traffic Controllers (PATCO) strike, would soon author one of the largest government crackdowns on a union in the nation's history. Larger numbers of Americans now thought of unions as a threat, not an aid, to their personal economic growth and security. Winning over public support in an atmosphere such as this would be one of the most difficult challenges yet for the MLBPA.

Many columns written in the months before the strike foretold a changing tide in media opinion. The *Kansas City Times'* Mike McKenzie understood what was going on and was well aware of the public relations battle. "Truth is, you should have no sympathies," he wrote in February 1981. "Not only is it inane that grown men can't find middle ground over a game that has made most of them wealthy, it is inexcusable how they played charades in their attempts to settle since last May."[61] Red Smith was tired as well, writing in April, "It is not easy to believe that businessmen who own the clubs would invite a strike over an issue that effects only 3 out of 650 players. And, in spite of strike insurance, a strike would be ruinously expensive."[62]

One month later, Smith continued his assault on the owners

in a column entitled "Baseball's Star Chamber." Smith's title was not a tongue-in-cheek jab at the star players of the game; rather, the venerated columnist took the owners, and their chief negotiator, Ray Grebey, to task for their approach to the negotiations. Smith's specific topic was the large fine imposed on Milwaukee Brewers general manager Harry Dalton, who committed the sin of speaking his mind to the press regarding the ongoing negotiations. In early May, with a strike more than a month away, Smith challenged the owners to prove that their tactics were anything more than an attempt to reassert their authority over the players' union and to test the will of the MLBPA to carry out a strike in midsummer, the time of year when baseball had the nation's almost undivided attention in regard to sports: "Some owners, at least, cannot believe that players would sacrifice million-dollar salaries to fight for a principle. If you saw nothing but dollar signs when you looked at baseball, you wouldn't believe it either."[63] By blasting the owners for their economics-first approach, Smith's parting shot placed him firmly in the players' camp. His understanding of the dynamics of the free agent market and the disciplined nature of the MLBPA was much more sophisticated than the owners'. Smith's tone and approach changed dramatically between the two strikes. In 1972 he had used his sharp wit to mock both sides, with Marvin Miller and the MLBPA receiving the harshest treatment. Nine years later Smith took baseball's labor crisis much more seriously, picking out the owners as his sole target.

Smith was not the only member of the *Times'* sports staff whose perspective on baseball's labor problems had changed. On June 11, the day before the strike began, Dave Anderson also took a shot at the owners: "The labor negotiations have shown that what the owners do best is nothing."[64] Anderson believed that by revisiting the issue of free agent compensation after it had been settled the previous year, the owners wanted to change the rules of a marketplace they themselves had established when they threw millions of dollars at free agents during the late 1970s. Anderson portrayed the players' union more sympathetically.

He asserted faith in the players' ability to stick together in the face of owners who believed they could break the union's back by waiting out a strike. Dave Kindred, a syndicated columnist for the *Washington Post*, echoed many of the same sentiments. With the strike looming, Kindred urged fans to reject the arguments of owners who wanted people to believe their primary motivation was to continue to operate Major League Baseball in the best interest of the public.[65] Anderson and Kindred joined Smith in their pessimistic view of the financially fanatical owners, a view not limited to media on the East Coast.

Jim Murray's column of June 13 was yet another example of the new type of regard the press held for the MLBPA. Murray had always looked for a way to spread the blame to everyone who deserved it, and the first part of his column on the thirteenth, the second full day of the 1981 work stoppage, followed this pattern. In his opening paragraphs Murray criticized the players and the owners equally for preparing to execute the "golden goose." Toward the end of his piece, however, Murray, the same man who nine years earlier had described Marvin Miller as "a guy who would order salad," offered praise, albeit backhanded, for the union. Murray believed the owners wanted to place limits on their own greed, but they wanted those limits set by the very group that would suffer most if limits were put in place. "They [the owners] are not so much giving the players the rope to hang themselves as giving the players the rope so that they, the owners, won't hang themselves."[66]

Murray's support for the players was further apparent in his description of free agency as something guaranteed not by the collective bargaining agreement but by "George Washington and Thomas Jefferson." Murray's connection of free agency to the ideological origins of the nation is especially intriguing, because he was a staunch member of the "old school" of sportswriting, a group of reporters so caught up in the beauty of the game that they were in virtual denial of the business side of professional sports. Murray's shift in attitude between 1972 and 1981, similar to that of his counterpart Red Smith, a man who once testified to a congressional committee in favor of the reserve clause, exemplified the way that media coverage shifted in favor of the players during the 1981 strike.

While Murray represented the august voice of wisdom, his younger colleague Mark Heisler reflected the new approach of more business-minded sportswriters. The headline on one of Heisler's columns made his position clear: "No Good Reasons for This Strike: The Players Don't Want It and the Owners Don't Need It." Unlike Murray and Smith, Heisler recast the 1972 strike as "necessary," arguing that the first strike solved many critical unresolved issues. Comparatively, he felt the current work stoppage was completely unnecessary, arguing, "It is a basic tenet of labor negotiations that a union never gives back anything that it has won, even though the MLBPA was willing to." Heisler pointed to the fact that, since the 1972 work stoppage, MLB franchises had risen consistently in value, attendance had risen, and the emergence of cable TV promised even brighter TV revenues in the future. Here Heisler epitomizes the new breed of sportswriter, looking past nostalgic reminiscence and toward the "economic present" of baseball, a present Heisler believed would be marked by continued economic growth, even though many parts of the nation's economy struggled through the late 1970s.

The strength of Heisler's critique lay in his analysis of the game in the new age of free agency. One example is his criticism of California Angels management for failing to sign Nolan Ryan, a move that Heisler estimated cost the club much more than the $1 million Ryan eventually received from the Houston Astros. Heisler also shot down the argument that a new wave of maverick owners, flush with TV millions, were solely responsible for the free agency craze. The sportswriter pointed out that none other than Peter O'Malley, the scion of one of baseball's great families, had waded hip deep into the free agent market after suffering through an awful 1979 season with a bullpen decimated by free agency. In the end, Heisler argued, the only thing the owners did not like about free agency was the idea that they no longer held on to players through the reserve clause.[67]

This new breed of sportswriters had come to grips with the notion that professional baseball was indeed a business. Fans, these sportswriters argued, should turn their attention not only to the on-field exploits of their hometown heroes but also to the team's owner and general manager for their successes and failures in building the most competitive roster.

The pages of another national newspaper, the *Wall Street Journal*, also criticized the owners' attempts to turn back the clock. In mid-June, as the inevitability of a strike grew, *Journal* columnist Frederick C. Klein observed, "It's axiomatic in labor-management negotiations that no union worth its salt gives up something for nothing, but that's what the owners have been asking the players to do." Klein argued that the owners were determined to provoke a strike, as evidenced by their myriad preparations for a work stoppage. He criticized the owners for not realizing that any free agency, even with a compensation plan in place, would continue to drive player salaries higher. "It is doubtful, for instance, that the threat of losing his 16th-best player would have kept New York Yankees owner George Steinbrenner from shelling out the $20 million or so it took to sign Dave Winfield last winter."

Klein contended that the salary arbitration process would inevitably foil any owner attempts to suppress salaries for younger players. Thanks to the salary arbitration process and "the big-buck, long-term pacts that owners have tossed at players of modest achievement," younger players would have no trouble, according to Klein, winning higher salaries through arbitration. Finally, Klein argued that "owners' attempts to force the players to amend their freedom to wander is counter-historical," pointing out that professional basketball, football, and hockey had all given up the ghost of free agent compensation. Klein concluded, "The baseball players' union is the deepest entrenched and best-led in sports, and it won't give way easily on the issue."[68] Klein's discussion, in one of the world's most well-known financial news outlets, demonstrates precisely how far the baseball media had come in its understanding and acceptance of the new business of the game.

Owner efforts to "break the union" during the 1981 strike also played poorly with the baseball media and fans. This discussion of "union busting" was one that Marvin Miller was happy to see play out in the court of public opinion. Murray Chass, the *New York Times* writer assigned to follow the negotiations, spent a great deal of time exploring Miller's charges of union busting. Glenn Dickey of the *San Francisco Chronicle* made this same charge much more directly in a column titled "What Most Baseball Owners Really Want." "No matter how much they deny it, the majority of the baseball owners want to break the union [the MLBPA]. In this issue, as in so many others, baseball is about 50 years behind the times. To get a comparable labor management relationship in other industries you have to go back to the 1930's."[69] In the 1981 strike, the media perception was that the owners were too far behind in their ways, not that the players were too progressive. Recognition of the MLBPA for its strength as a union was an important step in redeveloping the relationship between player and fan. The media's increased recognition of the legitimacy of the MLBPA proved helpful in shifting the fans' perspective on both the union and the importance of the individual player's economic rights. This shift played out over the course of the strike, and when the dust settled the players enjoyed significant support from media and fans alike.

As the 1981 strike wore on, negative fan reaction became an increasingly large part of the strike picture. The shrinking number of fans, usually traditionalists, who did side with the owners often did so out of a general sense that the players were greedy and out of touch with the lives of regular Americans. Fans who wrote to the *Sporting News* referred to the players as "overpaid punks" and "overpaid crybabies" who "need to go out in the job world and find themselves a minimum wage job where they have to work year round." Many echoed the sentiment that unions and strikes belonged to those who labored, not played, for a living: "Whenever a labor strike occurs in the real world, I support the workers. Now that the ballplayers have chosen to strike in their fantasy world, I say let them find real jobs." Other fans focused on the players' insensitivity in depriving the "hospital-ized people, the handicapped veterans, the elderly shut ins, the fans who have supported and followed the game for years and the kids who look up to the players as role models and heroes." These fans agreed, "A strike against baseball is un-American."[70]

Fans who sided with the players saw the owners' attempts to forcibly instate their free agent compensation plan as reactionary. These fans backed the players largely because they believed the MLBPA was simply trying to hold on to what the players had right-fully gained in the 1975 Messersmith and McNally ruling: "The owners have had five years to stabilize their business, and for their lack of imagination, they now expect the players to give more." Other fans called the owners "robber barons" and accused them of being "avaricious and megalomaniacal." One fan, after noting that player salaries totaled $110 million while total revenues were in the neighborhood of $300 million, wrote, "If the owners can honestly claim that a majority of clubs are losing money, then the owners must include some of the most inept business men in America."[71]

A large number of fans blamed both sides equally. Sixty-two fans, all employees of a Sears store in Kansas City, drafted a petition, declaring, "We are fed up with both management and players. We can do without baseball." Many fans, fed up with baseball's inability to reach labor peace, called for a boycott. Sev-eral grassroots fans' organizations sprung up across the country, including Fans Against Strike Talk (FAST) and a group that tried to organize a national "Boycott Baseball" week. Reports of fan pro-tests, ranging from mass baseball card burnings to letter-writing campaigns, were common throughout the five-week strike.[72]

The 1981 strike was so lengthy and involved that the average fan had no choice but to become more knowledgeable about the game's inner business workings. This educational process slowly but surely paid off for the players, especially for its effects on fan outrage, as compared to fan responses during the 1972 strike. A telephone poll conducted by NBC on June 15, two days into the strike, showed the fans still slightly in favor of the owners, though in much smaller numbers than in 1972. Some fans still clung to older notions of the "purity of the game," not wanting to cheapen their relationship with baseball by thinking of the game in business terms. A poll conducted a month later showed the owners losing ground to the players in the eyes of the public. This AP-NBC poll showed the owners with a slim 31 to 30 percent advantage over the players, also a shift from polls taken in 1972. The poll also indicated that many fans felt that the strike had "lowered their opinion of the game and the people involved in it." Fans decried their "loss of innocence" and stated that they felt forced to see the game as a business.[73]

Two weeks later, little had changed. A *New York Times*/CBS News poll showed that fans remained evenly split as to who deserved the blame for the strike. More specific results from this poll were less than surprising. People with higher incomes tended to favor the owners, while lower-income subjects favored the players. Younger fans sided with the players, older fans with the owners. Republicans favored the owners, Democrats the players.[74] Ultimately this changed view of the game served to further the interests of the players and to work against the interests of the owners, as fans became savvier to the ins and outs of the business of baseball.[75]

One way many high-profile fans demonstrated their displeasure was by pressuring President Reagan to intervene and give the two sides no choice but to reach a solution. Jocko Conlon, a member of Baseball's Hall of Fame, wrote Reagan, "When I shoke [sic] your hand at your luncheon for baseball Hall of Famers I told you you would be the greatest President in the last 100 years. . . . The greatest of all umpires can order 'Play Ball.' That umpire is you."[76] Senator Ted Kennedy pushed through the Senate a resolution that held, "Whereas baseball is loved by millions of fans as America's national sport . . . The parties to the major league baseball strike have a responsibility to the baseball fans of America to settle the issues in the strike as soon as possible."[77] Kennedy wrote Reagan "to urge you to take whatever steps you feel are appropriate to facilitate an immediate settlement of the major league baseball strike."[78] Records from White House senior staff meetings show that the president decided early on to personally stay out of the dispute.[79] He eventually sent mediator Roy Donovan in an effort to settle the strike, although Donovan did not play a major role in its settlement.

Players felt the burden of this public uproar, and MLBPA solidarity began to appear vulnerable in the face of this pressure. The mounting financial losses players faced also took their toll as the strike dragged on. One particularly divisive issue among the players was that some of them had a provision in their contract that paid their salary in the event of a strike, while others did not. As a result, the number of disgruntled players grew steadily. In late July, Miller responded to criticism from star players like the Dodgers' Davy Lopes and the Red Sox's Dennis Eckersley by holding a series of regional "information sessions" to help shore up player solidarity. Several players later admitted that, as the strike entered its second month, the MLBPA was on the brink of fracturing.[80] Ultimately, Marvin Miller's ability to hold the players together throughout the final weeks of the strike proved essential to the strike's successful resolution.

Settlement: The Players Hold the Line

The potential loss of the significant amount of television revenue tied to postseason play finally brought the owners back to the table in a more cooperative mood. The magnates knew that a settlement needed to be reached by August 1 in order to salvage a legitimate regular season. The regular season had to be seen as valid in order for baseball to stage league playoffs and the World Series, the postseason contests that generated the vast majority of television revenue. Additional stress came from the depleted state of the owners' strike insurance fund. Under these circumstances, hard-line owners, and their PRC front man, Ray Grebey, came under serious pressure from many of their more moderate management peers to reach a settlement. Push had come to shove, and American League president Lee MacPhail went directly to Marvin Miller with a proposed "pool compensation" solution.

MacPhail's peace efforts set the wheels in motion, and the

strike was officially settled on July 31. Under the terms of the new agreement each club could protect twenty-four players throughout its entire organization. Clubs that pledged not to sign any free agents could protect an expanded, forty-man roster of players. The remaining players in a club's system, whether proven veterans or unheralded rookie Minor Leaguers, were then considered unprotected. All unprotected players automatically became part of the free agent compensation pool. Any club that lost a premier player—one ranked in the top 20 percent of all players—to free agency could draft a player of it choosing from this pool. Clubs that lost a lesser, or nonpremier, player to free agency were to be compensated with a pick in the upcoming amateur draft.[81]

The owners essentially agreed to this system because, in the end, it was better than nothing. After forcing a strike over the issue of free agent compensation, they desperately needed to walk away with something tangible. The players agreed to this system because pool compensation did not automatically punish a team for signing a free agent, a condition that would surely suppress demand for free agents. Marvin Miller believed this settlement represented an outright victory for the players:

> Owners in the so called moderate group have been quoted . . . to the effect that the owners' insistence on forcing a strike for free agent compensation was an error and that the owners got nothing. . . . These are interesting perceptions. I believe they signify that the players' impressive display of unity and understanding throughout a long, difficult period has had the desired effect. The players' determination forced the owners to settle and change both their short term and long term goals: to weaken or destroy the Players Association and to diminish the players' rights and other terms of employment.[82]

The magnates had made one last effort to break the MLBPA, only to fall short. Not only was the union firmly entrenched, but the baseball public now understood the business of the game in a much more sophisticated way. Through their ongoing solidarity, consistently sound strategic moves, and pursuit of economic freedom in the marketplace, the players played a significant role in bringing baseball into the modern age and ushering in the era of the modern sports fan.

A full shift toward acceptance of the players' union was clearly underway but far from complete in 1981. Fans continued to express their dissatisfaction throughout the remainder of the 1981 season. Attendance fell sharply for all but seven clubs, even though all clubs started play on August 10 with an equal chance at a "second-half championship" and a postseason berth. Television ratings fell sharply as well. Longtime observers of the game took notice. Bob Feller, the Hall of Fame pitcher from the Cleveland Indians, moaned, "The sad part is, for some reason, the fans have set the players apart from the entertainment field, which is what they are basically in. Stage and screen stars and rock bands can make thousands of dollars for a week's engagement or just one show. But a baseball player is supposed to be above all that, no matter how talented."[83]

Feller enjoyed a twenty-year career in the big leagues, spanning from 1936 to 1956, and served many years as a player representative. His analysis, delivered a full quarter century after his final game, is remarkable for the way in which it captures the traditionalist nature of baseball fans, who were so caught up in the "beautiful purity" of the game that they failed to recognize that the talented individuals they loved were entitled to the same kind of high compensation as other talented individuals in our free-market society. Fans still needed their heroes to play for the love of the game, the purity of purpose of competing for the hometown squad, even if that hometown squad had started in Philadelphia, moved to Kansas City, and then finally wound up in Oakland, as in the case of the Athletics, or had traveled from Boston to Milwaukee to Atlanta, as was the case for Feller's own team, the Braves. In the end Feller foretold the future. In 1981 fans began to see players as belonging to that special class of entertainers and accepted the idea that owners needed to compensate players at rates determined by the free market.

This shift in fan response is even more fascinating given that the strike of 1981 was over a somewhat abstract issue, free agent compensation, while the strike of 1972 was focused on pension contributions and salaries, the kind of "bread-and-butter" issues that most working-class Americans were more likely to connect with. Despite the abstract nature of the issue, the American public was much savvier in 1981 to the methods and motivations of the owners and their negotiators. One reason for this growing distrust was that free agency was in full swing by 1981, but it had not destroyed the game in the way that many owners had claimed it would. With the growth of free agency in the late 1970s, the public saw many clubs gleefully pursue the players they coveted, instead of letting them wither and die on the vine. Free agency was especially popular in major media centers such as New York, where George Steinbrenner built the Yankees into a championship team once more with the acquisition of free agents like pitcher Catfish Hunter and slugger Reggie Jackson. Fans, especially those in the larger markets, decided that free agency was not so evil after all. This new awareness of the importance of player personnel decisions continued to move fans toward a stronger interest in the business side of the game and gave them a more sophisticated understanding of the dynamics of player-management negotiations. Professional sports culture in the United States had clearly entered the modern age.

Finally, it is noteworthy that the MLBPA held on to its hard-won gains, and actually built public support, during a time of crisis for organized labor. President Reagan's response to the PATCO strike marked the beginning of an era in which large employers ground concession after concession out of the unions. As the Reagan era went on and unions continued their decline, the MLBPA continued to thrive. Labor was no longer the conscious force it had long been in the lives of many, but professional baseball players enjoyed great prosperity. Their ability to form a successful craft guild, built on the solidarity of its members, their highly specialized skill sets, and pursuit of personal liberty in the free market, continued to serve both the players and the game of baseball well in the years to come.

NOTES

I. The Birth of a Pastime

1. Burk, *Never Just a Game*, 29.

2. Goldstein, *Playing for Keeps*.

3. Seymour, *Baseball: The Early Years*, 171.

4. A. G. Spalding, "Base-Ball," *Cosmopolitan*, February 1890, 603–12.

5. Abraham Mills's revised draft of Spalding's address to the magnates, November 12, 1889, Mills correspondence files, Giamatti Research Center, National Baseball Hall of Fame, Cooperstown NY.

6. Burk, *Never Just a Game*, 243.

7. Burk, *Never Just a Game*, 3.

8. Burk, *Never Just a Game*, 82.

9. "The Baseball Convention," *New York Times*, October 18, 1885, 2.

10. Seymour, *Baseball: The Early Years*, 116.

11. John M. Ward, "Are Players Chattels? Abstracts from a Ball Player's Letter," *New York Times*, July 17, 1887, 9.

12. "The Baseball Brotherhood," *New York Times*, September 19, 1887, 1.

13. "Ball Players' Brotherhood," *New York Times*, October 2, 1887, 3.

14. "Ball Players' Ultimatum," *New York Times*, November 6, 1887, 10.

15. "The Men Make Their Point," *New York Times*, November 18, 1887, 2.

16. Burk, *Never Just a Game*, 97.

17. "The Men Make Their Point," 2.

18. Abraham G. Mills to A. G. Spalding, July 30, 1889, Mills correspondence files, Giamatti Research Center.

19. Seymour, *Baseball: The Early Years*, 122.

20. "The Ball Players' Revolt: Cast off the Yoke of League Bosses," *New York Times*, September 23, 1889, 2.

21. "Backed by League Men," *New York Times*, October 12, 1889, 4.

22. "From the Players Side," *Chicago Daily Tribune*, November 23, 1889, 7.

23. Lowenfish, *Imperfect Diamond*, 41. One such case that upheld the contractual rights of the player was *Alleghany Baseball Club v. Bennett*. See Jarvis and Coleman, "Early Baseball Law," 125.

24. "League Men Will Fight," *Chicago Daily Tribune*, September 23, 1889, 3.

25. "The Brotherhood Suddenly Adjourn for Two Months," *Sporting News*, November 9, 1899, 1.

26. Seymour, *Baseball: The Early Years*, 230–32.

27. "They Are Two to One," *Chicago Daily Tribune*, October 24, 1889, 1.

28. "Against the Players," *New York Times*, October 26, 1889, 2.

29. "Against the Players," 2.

30. Baseball War Declared," *New York Times*, November 5, 1889, 8.

31. "The Brotherhood Plans," *New York Times*, October 29, 1889, 3.

32. This marks the first major struggle between players and owners over a salary cap. The issue still haunts Major League Baseball today. One hundred years later the salary cap issue was the primary cause of the 1994 strike, and Major League Baseball remains the only major professional sport without some sort of salary cap.

33. "Danny' Richardson's Views," *New York Times*, December 8, 1889, 6.

34. "The League and the Brotherhood," *New York Times*, December 13, 1889, 4.

35. "Ball Players Expelled: The Brotherhood Does Not Want Deserters," *New York Times*, December 19, 1889, 3.

36. "The Latest News: Details of the Desertion of Jack O'Connor," *Sporting News*, January 11, 1890, 1.

37. A.G. Mills to Francis Richter, editor, *Sporting Life*, December 6, 1889, Mills correspondence files, Giamatti Research Center.

38. "Baseball News: Connor Will Join the Giants if the Reserve Rule Is Legal," *New York Times*, January 4, 1890, 8.

39. "Short Stop Ward in Court," *New York Times*, January 10, 1890, 8.

40. "Ward Wins His Fight," *New York Times*, January 29, 1890, 2.

41. "That Bomb Shell: Ward Wins His Case in the New York Courts," *Sporting News*, February 1, 1890, 1. Also see "Ward Wins His Fight," 2.

42. "Arbitration in Baseball," *New York Times*, January 30, 1890, 2.

43. "John Day's Latest Bluff," *Sporting News*, March 1, 1890, 1; "A Tempting Offer," *New York Times*, February 13, 1890, 3.

44. "The Players' League: Secretary Brunell to the Men Who Have Joined It," *New York Times*, February 26, 1890, 3.

45. "No Fear of the League," *New York Times*, March 23, 1890, 5.

46. John Ward as quoted in the *Players National League Baseball Guide for 1890*.

47. Burk, *Never Just a Game*, 111. Also see Lowenfish, *Imperfect Diamond*, 46.

48. "The Baseball Season," *New York Times*, July 17, 1890, 4.

49. "The Cruel War Ends," *Sporting News*, October 11, 1890, 1. Also see "All in Favor of Peace," *New York Times*, October 10, 1890, 3.

50. "The Great Baseball War," *New York Times*, October 6, 1890, 2.

51. "Another Baseball Row: Players Fearful Their Salaries Will Be Cut," *New York Times*, October 19, 1890, 10.

52. Burk, *Never Just a Game*, 112.

53. "A.L. Johnson Is Mad," *New York Times*, December 1, 1890, 5.

54. "The Consolidation Is Perfected," *New York Times*, December 20, 1890, 8.

55. "Baseball for 1891," *New York Times*, January 22, 1891, 4.

2. Monopoly and Trade War

1. "End of the Baseball War," *New York Times*, January 17, 1891, 2.

2. Burk, *Never Just a Game*, 117.

3. "American Baseball Association," *New York Times*, October 19, 1894, 3. "Barnie Is Reinstated: Pfeffer Blacklisted," *New York Times*, December 21, 1894, 7. Also see Seymour, *Baseball: The Early Years*, 270.

4. Burk, *Never Just a Game*, 128–29.

5. Burk, *Never Just a Game*, 138–40.

6. *Sporting Life*, December 28, 1899, as quoted in Burk, *Never Just a Game*, 141.

7. See "Ban Johnson," BaseballLibrary.com, http://www.baseballlibrary .com/ballplayers/player.php?name=ban_johnson.

8. "Hart and Johnson in a Quarrel: Desire for an American League Club in Chicago Causes Trouble," *Chicago Daily Tribune*, November 18, 1899, 6.

9. "American Baseball League: Plans for the New Organization in Opposition to the National Body," *New York Times*, November 20, 1900, 7.

10. S. Fullerton, "Will Branch Out: American to Annex Baltimore and Washington," *Sporting News*, October 13, 1900, 1.

11. William Cauldwell, "Decline of Baseball: Interest in the National Game Has Steadily Decreased," *New York Times*, September 23, 1900, 22.

12. Lowenfish, *Imperfect Diamond*, 63.

13. Seymour, *Baseball: The Early Years*, 310.

14. Lowenfish, *Imperfect Diamond*, 61.

15. "Radical Baseball Changes: Proposed by the Players Association to the National League," *New York Times*, October 14, 1900, 9.

16. "Ball Players Defied: National League Rejects All Their Claims and Demands," *New York Times*, December 15, 1900, 11.

17. SY, "May Mean War to the Death: Decision of the National League to Fight the American," *Chicago Daily Tribune*, December 16, 1900, 18.

18. "Baseball Badly Mixed: Players Determined That League Managers Will Abdicate," *New York Times*, December 16, 1900, 9.

19. "They Side Stepped: Magnates Did Not Treat the Players Fairly," *Sporting News*, December 22, 1900, 1.

20. Burk, *Never Just a Game*, 144.

21. "Ball Players Are in Revolt," *Chicago Daily Tribune*, December 17, 1900, 8.

22. "Baseball Players Aroused," *New York Times*, December 21, 1900, 10.

23. "Poorly Prepared: National League Ill Fixed for a Fight," *Sporting News*, December 29, 1900, 1. Also see "Is Not Bluffing: Johnson Has Nothing to Fear from a Fight," *Sporting News*, January 12, 1901, 1.

24. "Will Hear Ball Players," *New York Times*, February 26, 1901, 10.

25. "New Baseball Agreement: American Association to Be Revived to Fight Johnson," *New York Times*, January 6, 1901, 8.

26. "Concessions with Conditions: Zimmer Promises That Players Will Stay Loyal to the League," *Sporting News*, March 2m 1901, 1.

27. "Zimmer Will Stand by Agreement," *New York Times*, March 7, 1901, 7.

28. "Players Issue a Statement," *New York Times*, March 10, 1901, 8.

29. Seymour, *Baseball: The Early Years*, 314. Also see "Stars Stampede," *Sporting News*, March 9, 1901, 1.

30. Burk, *Never Just a Game*, 153.

31. As a result of these rule changes the mean batting average in the National League fell from .279 in 1900 to .257 in 1902. The average number of runs per game fell even more precipitously. In 1900 the average National League team scored 5.21 runs per game; by 1902 that number was 3.98. "1900 National League Team Statistics and Standings," Baseball-Reference.com, http://www.baseball-reference.com/leagues/NL_1900.shtml; and"1902 National League Team Statistics and Standings," Baseball-Reference.com, http://www.baseball-reference.com/leagues/NL_1902.shtml.

32. Burk, *Never Just a Game*, 151.

33. Burk, *Never Just a Game*, 155–57.

34. "McGraw Accuses Johnson," *New York Times*, July 3, 1902, 6.

35. Seymour, *Baseball: The Early Years*, 322–23.

36. Burk, *Never Just a Game*, 157.

37. Burk, *Never Just a Game*, 178–80.

38. Barnstorming usually meant that star players would organize their own, informal, all-star teams and then tour the country during the off-season, putting on exhibition games to the delight of fans in areas without Major League teams. Barnstorming was quite lucrative for these players, especially for the most well-known among them.

39. I. E. Sanborn, "Players Combine to Uplift Sport," *Chicago Daily Tribune*, August 12, 1912, 8. Also see Burk, *Never Just a Game*, 186–88.

40. "Should Benefit the Players: President Johnson and Comiskey Have No Objection to the Fraternity," *New York Times*, September 8, 1912.

41. "What the Baseball Fraternity Really Is," *New York Times*, September 8, 1912, sec. s, 2.

42. Lowenfish, *Imperfect Diamond*, 81.

43. "Ball Players Organize: Elect Officers and Discuss Aims at Meeting Held Here," *New York Times*, October 21, 1912, 9.

44. "Would Stop Rowdyism," *New York Times*, December 15, 1912.

45. "Did Commission Make a Break? Recognition of Fraternity Might Cause Contract Troubles," *Sporting News*, January 15, 1914, 1. Also see Lowenfish, *Imperfect Diamond*, 87.

46. "Baseball Leaders to Hear Players," *New York Times*, January 5, 1914, 14. Also see "Ball Players Pleased," *New York Times*, January 9, 1914, 12.

47. Lowenfish, *Imperfect Diamond*, 83.

48. "Jumping Players to Be Blacklisted," *New York Times*, February 13, 1914, 10.

49. Sam Weller, "Baseball Strife a Boon to Players," *Chicago Daily Tribune*, January 11, 1914, 6.

50. "Sinners Wanted to Dictate What the Terms Would Be for Their Salvation," *Sporting News*, November 26, 1914, 5.

51. Lowenfish, *Imperfect Diamond*, 90. Also see Burk, *Never Just a Game*, 208.

52. "Base Ball Writers Defend O.B., Federals Show Their True Colors: Unanimous Trend in Opinions," *Sporting News*, January 14, 1915, 3.

53. Lowenfish, *Imperfect Diamond*, 91.

54. "Big Leagues Are Attacked in Suit," *New York Times*, April 20, 1922, 23.

55. Staudohar, *Diamond Mines*, 84.

56. *Federal Baseball Club of Baltimore, Inc. v. National League of Professional Baseball Clubs et al.*, 259 U.S. 200 (1922), Oyez Project at 11T Chicago–Kent College of Law, http://www.oyez.org/cases/1901-1939/1921/1921_204; also see "Baseball Is Victor in Trust Law Fight," *New York Times*, May 30, 1922, 12.

57. M. L. C., "Baseball and the Law."

3. 1946, a Year of Postwar Tumult

1. Attendance figures are from "Ballparks, Baseball Stadiums, and Fields of Dreams," Baseball-Almanac.com, http://baseball-almanac.com/stadium.shtml.

2. Art Flynn, "Major Salaries Head for $5,000,000 High," *Sporting News*, February 21, 1946, 1, 2.

3. There were more than forty-six hundred strikes in the United States in the first year after the end of the war. Many of them focused on the same issues that baseball players were concerned with, especially that of pay keeping up with inflation.

4. Marshall, *Baseball's Pivotal Era*, 45–47.

5. John Drebinger, "Gardella Reveals Jump from Giants," *New York Times*, February 19, 1946, 29.

6. Roscoe McGowen, "Dodgers Continue Efforts to Lure Olmo Back through Young Rickey," *New York Times*, February 22, 1946, 28.

7. UP, "Seeks to Organize Baseball Players," *New York Times*, April 18, 1946, 32.

8. "Baseball Guild Will Investigate Reports of Players Intimidation," *New York Times*, April 19, 1946, 22. Also see "Players Fearful, Says Guild Boss," *Los Angeles Times*, April 19, 1946, 7.

9. Vincent Flaherty "Union Won't Cure Ills of Ball Players," *Los Angeles Examiner*, April 23, 1946; reprinted in *Sporting News*, April 25, 1946, 3.

10. H. G. Salsinger, "Contrasts in Skill Snag Players' Union," *Detroit Free Press*, April 23, 1946; reprinted in *Sporting News*, April 25, 1946, 3.

11. Jack Malaney, "Guild Charges Washington Club with 'Unfair Labor Practices,'" *Sporting News*, May 2, 1946, 4. Also see "Baseball Guild Reveals Charges against Griffith and the Senators," *New York Times*, April 30, 1946, 25.

12. "Guild Head Quizzed on Objectives," *Sporting News*, April 25, 1946, 1.

13. Lowenfish, *Imperfect Diamond*, 143.

14. A minimum salary of $7,500 would have been higher than the mean 1946 player salary of $6,500. See House Judiciary Committee, *Organized Baseball*.

15. AP, "Majority Claimed on 6 Clubs by Guild," *New York Times*, June 5, 1946, 35.

16. Lowenfish, *Imperfect Diamond*, 145.

17. "Aims of Pirate Players in Bargaining Request," *Sporting News*, May 23, 1946, 7.

18. "Pirates to Confer with Guild June 5," *New York Times*, May 28, 1946, 35.

19. "Bucs Threaten Game Strike Tomorrow," *Los Angeles Times*, June 6, 1946, A7. Also see AP, "Guild Threatens Strike by Pirates," *New York Times*, June 6, 1946, 33.

20. "Unions Back Bucs Strike Threat," *Los Angeles Times*, June 7, 1946, A8.

21. Louis Effrat, "No Split among Pirates after Vote to Strike," *New York Times*, June 9, 1946, 72.

22. All quotes from Sewell are from Rip Sewell, interview (unrehearsed) by William Marshall, Plant City, FL, April 23, 1980, A. B. Chandler Oral History Project, University of Kentucky Library, 800H54.

23. Oscar Ruhl, "Regard for Benswanger Shaped Course—Handley," *Sporting News*, June 19, 1946, 3.

24. Louis Effrat, "'No Strike' Is Voted by Pirates Players," *New York Times*, June 8, 1946, 3.

25. Al Wolf, "Sportraits," *Los Angeles Times*, June 7, 1946, A9.

26. Tom Swope, "Players May Lose More Than They Can Gain," *Sporting News*, June 19, 1946, 4.

27. Fitzgerald and Salsinger's columns as reprinted in *Sporting News*, June 19, 1946, 5.

28. AP, "Murphy Gives His Views," *New York Times*, June 10, 1946, 30.

29. AP, "Guild's Charges against Pirates Must Be Withdrawn or Dismissed," *New York Times*, June 12, 1946, 19.

30. UPI, "'Unfair' Charges Dropped by Guild," *New York Times*, June 18, 1946, 21.

31. Les Biederman, "24 Pittsburgh Players in Guild, Organizer Says," *Sporting News*, July 24, 1946, 11. Also see AP, "Pennsylvania Labor Board to Hear Guild's Petition to Act for Pirates," *New York Times*, July 17, 1946, 16.

32. UPI, "Pirates' Brief to Labor Board Calls Baseball Guild a 'Threat,'" *New York Times*, July 30, 1946, 27.

33. AP, "Pennsylvania Labor Board Orders Pirates' Election on Guild Aug. 20th," *New York Times*, August 8, 1946, 32.

34. AP, "Pennsylvania Labor Board Orders Pirates' Election," 32.

35. "Players Granted Voice in Majors," *Los Angeles Times*, July 19, 1946, 8. Also see Dan Daniel "Early Agreement Seen on Removal of Squawks," *Sporting News*, July 31, 1946, 3.

36. "New Uniform Player Contract to Be Drafted by Major Leagues," *New York Times*, July 19, 1946, 14.

37. Hugo Autz, "Players Asked to Help Draw New Contract Form," *Sporting News*, July 24, 1946, 2. Also see John Drebinger, "New Player-Owner Advisory Body Is Envisioned by Major Leagues," *New York Times*, July 20, 1946.

38. William Fay, "Majors Give Players Voice in Contracts," *Chicago Tribune*, July 20, 1946, 18.

39. "Ten Majors Clubs Name Players for Meeting," *Los Angeles Times*, July 21, 1946, A6. Also see "Players Cautious on Contract Plan," *New York Times*, July 20, 1946, 6.

40. "Veteran Players to Talk for Mates," *New York Times*, July 23, 1946, 36.

41. At this time teams from the National and American Leagues did not play each other during the regular season. Interleague play as we now know it started in 1997.

42. "Marion Outlines Player Pension Plan to Cost Club Owners Only $2,500 Year," *Sporting News*, July 31, 1946, 10.

43. Sewell, interview.

44. "$4,000,000 Pension Plan Drafted by Marion for Players in Majors," *New York Times*, July 25, 1946, 25.

45. "League Owners Get Player Demands at History-Making Talks Today," *New York Times*, July 29, 1946, 27.

46. Dan Daniel, "Full Acceptance of Players' Demands Seen: All Points Viewed as Reasonable," *Sporting News*, August 7, 1946, 1.

47. John Drebinger, "Sports of the Times: And Now the Players Shall Be Heard," *New York Times*, July 21, 1946, s2. Drebinger was a longtime baseball writer and is enshrined in the Baseball Hall of Fame. A brief biography can be found at "1973 J. G. Taylor Spink Award Winner John Drebinger," National Baseball Hall of Fame, http://baseballhall.org/discover/awards/j-g-taylor-spink /john-drebinger.

48. "Chandler Sympathizes with Quest of Ball Players for Improved Lot," *New York Times*, August 3, 1946, 20.

49. "Agreement on Baseball Reforms Is Indicated at Meeting Today," *New York Times*, August 5, 1946, 25.

50. "American Baseball Guild Dies," *Sporting News*, August 28, 1946, 10.

51. "Majors Meet All Player Demands and Set Up New Executive Council," *New York Times*, August 29, 1946, 31.

52. Marshall, *Baseball's Pivotal Era*, 205.

53. Marshall, *Baseball's Pivotal Era*, 209.

4. The Birth of the MLBPA

1. In the early 1950s alone there was "The Catch" by Willie Mays, Bobby Thompson's "shot heard round the world," The Brooklyn "Boys of Summer" in 1955, and Don Larsen's World Series perfect game in 1956.

2. George Toolson was a first baseman in the Yankee system who believed he would have the chance to play at the Major League level with another club if the Yankees would just release him from his contract. His case reached the Supreme Court, where the court upheld the *Federal Baseball v. National League* decision. See *Toolson v. New York Yankees, Inc.*, 346 U.S. 356 (1953), http://supreme.justia.com/us/346/356/case.html.

3. Roughly the equivalent of $9.5 million in 2012 dollars; inflation calculator at http://www.westegg.com/inflation/

4. Burk, *Much More Than a Game*, 110.

5. Staudohar and Dworkin, "Impact of Baseball's New Television Contracts."

6. Statement of Commissioner Ford Frick, August 28, 1961, before the Antitrust Subcommittee of the House Judiciary Committee, hearing on H.R. 8757, 87th Cong., 1st sess.

7. Burk, *Much More Than a Game*, 111.

8. House Judiciary Committee, *Organized Baseball*. The total increase in the CPI over this period was 20 percent.

9. Helyar, *Lords of the Realm*, 13–14.

10. The act of pitching a baseball overhand is not a natural motion for the human body, and pitching a baseball at a velocity of upwards of eighty-five miles an hour puts a great deal of strain on a pitcher's body. Starting pitchers usually throw between 90 and 120 pitches per start.

11. Like Roberts, Bunning would ultimately be inducted into the Baseball Hall of Fame in recognition of a consistently outstanding playing career. Little did Bunning know it at the time, but he was just starting out on a career in public life. After his career in baseball he moved on to a seat in the Kentucky legislature. In 1987 he was elected to the U.S. House of Representatives, and he has served in the Senate since 1999.

12. Sid Ziff, "O'Malley Unruffled," *Los Angeles Times*, February 24, 1966, B3.

13. Sid Ziff, "Bavasi Digs In," *Los Angeles Times*, February 28, 1966, B1.

14. Frank Finch, "Sandy, Drysdale Must Sign," *Los Angeles Times*, February 28, 1966, B1.

15. Melvin Durslag, "The O'Malley Admires 'Entry'—Dressen Ran Alone," *Sporting News*, March 12, 1966, 12.

16. Paul Zimmerman, ". . . K&D Are Making Other Plans," *Los Angeles Times*, March 17, 1966, C1.

17. Murray Robinson, "Fans Getting Fed Up with Players' Greed," reprinted in *Sporting News*, April 2, 1966, 14.

18. Frank Finch, "Club Jubilant, Alston Expects Aces to Pitch during Season's First Week," *Los Angeles Times*, March 31, 1966, B1.

19. Charles Maher, "L'Affaire Drysdale-Koufax: Villains or Heroes?," *Los Angeles Times*, March 27, 1966, G1.

20. "Voice of the Fan," *Sporting News*, April 16, 1966, 2.

21. Hoffa used this opportunity for a great deal of self-promotion, claiming that he had the necessary muscle to organize all professional athletes into one big union, the Wobblies of the sports world.

22. Miller, *Whole Different Ballgame*, 39.

23. Miller, *Whole Different Ballgame*, 52.

24. Dick Kaegle, "Miller Confident Despite Players' Noisy Opposition," *Sporting News*, March 26, 1966, 27.

25. John Hall, "Angels Fight Choice of Ex-Union Leader," *Los Angeles Times*, March 11, 1966, B7.

26. "Dodgers, Braves May Buck Miller," *Los Angeles Times*, March 14, 1966, B4.

27. Miller, *Whole Different Ballgame*, 61.

28. Miller, *Whole Different Ballgame*, 68.

29. "Story Inaccurate, Miller Asserts," *Sporting News*, August 6, 1966, 4.

30. Leonard Koppett, "Baseball Labor Dispute Still a Battle of Words," *New York Times*, June 7, 1966, 58.

31. Miller, *Whole Different Ballgame*, 176.

32. "Profits & Return on Radio & Television Revenues," Marvin Miller's handwritten notes, Marvin Miller Papers, Wagner Archives, Tamiment Library, New York University, box 4 folder 1.

33. Jerome Holtzman, "'Owner Alibis on Pension Issues Are Childish,' Miller Declares," *Sporting News*, September 10, 1966, 3.

34. New York State Department of Insurance to the MLBPA, Miller Papers, box 2, folder 1.

35. "Major League Baseball Players' Association Statement of Policy," July 8 1968, Miller Papers, box 2, folder 1. Also see Leonard Koppett, "Baseball Pension Fund Is Increased," *New York Times*, December 2, 1966, 66.

36. AP, "Players Lawyer: Greed of Owners Breeds Militancy," August 26, 1966.

37. Miller, *Whole Different Ballgame*, 142.

38. Bob Addie, "Miller Denies He Was Players' Third Choice," *Sporting News*, August 27, 1966, 14.

39. Burk, *Much More Than a Game*, 152.

40. House Judiciary Committee, *Organized Baseball*.

41. Miller, *Whole Different Ballgame*, 157.

42. Burk, *Much More Than a Game*, 155.

43. Burk, *Much More Than a Game*, 154.

44. Bouton, *Ball Four Plus Ball Five*, 3.

45. Inflation data from "Historical Consumer Price Index (CPI-U) Data," http://inflationdata.com/inflation/Consumer_Price_Index/HistoricalCPI.aspx.

46. Miller, *Whole Different Ballgame*, 158.

47. Miller, *Whole Different Ballgame*, 161.

48. The warning track is the strip of dirt between the outfield grass and the outfield fence. The size and condition of these tracks are critical to the safety of outfielders, who run at high speed toward the fences in their efforts to field the ball and count on the warning track being well maintained in order to allow them to safely field the ball.

49. Joe King, "Cronin Answers Miller's Bad Faith Charge," *Sporting News*, June 24, 1967, 15.

50. Bob Addie, "Digging for Gold," *Washington Post*, August 4, 1967, D1.

51. Joe King, "New Contract Form and Reserve Clause Sought by Players," *Sporting News*, August 12, 1967, 4.

52. The simple fact that the public failed to grasp was that the reserve system allowed wealthy teams to stockpile established talent at the expense of teams with tighter margins. This pattern played out in a way that made major-

market teams like the Yankees and Dodgers the preeminent franchises in Major League Baseball during the "Golden Age"

53. Leonard Koppett, "Labor Negotiator Gets Special Job," *New York Times,* August 11, 1967, S22.

54. Helyar, *Lords of the Realm,* 33.

55. Harry Bernstein, "Miller Makes Organized Baseball a Reality," *Los Angeles Times,* August 13, 1967, D3.

56. "Miller's Blast 'Shocks, Angers' Moguls, but They Cool Off Fast," *Sporting News,* December 16, 1967, 31.

57. Helyar, *Lords of the Realm,* 39.

58. "1968 Basic Agreement," Miller Papers, box 2, folder 1. Also see "Agreement Signed for Minimum Pay," *Sporting News,* March 9, 1968, 23.

5. The Players Grow a Backbone

1. Major League Baseball Players Association, Statement of Policy, July 8, 1968, Miller Papers, box 2, folder 3.

2. The new clubs in the National League were the Montreal Expos and San Diego Padres. The new clubs in the American League were the Kansas City Royals and Seattle Pilots.

3. Major League Baseball Players Association, Statement of Policy, July 8, 1968, Miller Papers, box 2, folder 3.

4. Burk, *Much More Than a Game,* 160.

5. Marvin Miller to the MLBPA Executive Board, memorandum, October 31, 1968 Miller Papers, box 2, folder 4.

6. "What's the Rush, Marvin?," *Sporting News,* August 17, 1968, 2.

7. Marvin Miller to all MLBPA Members, memorandum, January 15, 1969, Miller Papers, box 2, folder 4 (emphasis in original). Also see Jack Lang, "Players Reaffirm Holdout Stance, Urge Drills Boycott," *Sporting News,* February 15, 1969, 33.

8. Charles Maher, "Top Stars Back Threatened Baseball Strike," *Los Angeles Times,* December 5, 1968, C1.

9. Maher, "Top Stars Back Threatened Baseball Strike," C1.

10. Marvin Miller to all MLBPA Members, memorandum, December 31, 1968, Miller Papers, box 2, folder 4. Also see MLBPA press release, February 3, 1969, Miller Papers, box 2, folder 4.

11. Marvin Miller to all MLBPA Members, memorandum, December 31, 1968, and MLBPA press release, February 3, 1969, both in Miller Papers, box 2, folder 4.

12. Joseph Durso, "Ballplayers Threaten Holdout Unless Owners Revamp Pensions," *New York Times,* December 5, 1968, 63.

13. Durso, "Ballplayers Threaten Holdout," 63.

14. Joseph Durso, "Baseball Owners Deny They Are Using Delaying Tactics in Pension Negotiations," *New York Times*, December 6, 1968, 63.

15. Richard Dozer, "Ball Players Demand Pension Increases," *Chicago Tribune*, December 5, 1968, C1.

16. Charles Maher, "A Baseball Argument," *Los Angeles Times*, December 6, 1968, F2. Also see Stan Isle, "Threat of Umpire and Player Strikes Hanging over Majors," *Sporting News*, December 14, 1968, 24.

17. Leonard Koppett, "Victim of Circumstance: Eckert, Chosen as Compromise, Leaves Post Made Powerless by the Owners," *New York Times*, December 7, 1968, 66.

18. Joseph Durso, "Burke Tops List as Hunt Begins for New Leader," *New York Times*, December 8, 1968, 255.

19. Leonard Koppett, "Bowie Kuhn, Wall Street Lawyer, Named Commissioner Pro Tem of Baseball," *New York Times*, February 5, 1969, 27.

20. Official Statement of the Player Relations Committee (PRC), December 17, 1968, Miller Papers, box 4, folder 1. Also see "Urge Baseball Owners to Increase Pension Pay," *Chicago Tribune*, December 18, 1968, C1.

21. Marvin Miller to all MLBPA Members, memorandum, December 31, 1968, Miller Papers, box 2, folder 4; Leonard Koppett, "Baseball Club Owners $5.1-Million Offer Is Assailed as Inadequate," *New York Times*, December 18, 1968, 58. Also see "Fraudulent, Outrageous," *Sporting News*, December 28, 1968, 29.

22. Kuhn, *Hardball*, 79.

23. John Hall, "One Strike Too Many," *Los Angeles Times*, January 22, 1969, G3; emphasis in original.

24. Hall, "One Strike Too Many," G3.

25. "A Starting Point," *Sporting News*, December 28, 1968, 14.

26. Edward Prell, "Owners Ready to Act to Prevent Baseball Strike," *Chicago Tribune*, January 15, 1969, C1.

27. Bob Oates, "Baseball: Would a Strike Put It Out of Business?," *Los Angeles Times*, February 5, 1969, A1.

28. Oates, "Baseball: Would a Strike Put It Out of Business?," A1.

29. Dick Young, "Joe Fan Has No Sympathy for Baseball's Labor Pains," *New York Daily News*, February 23, 1969, 105.

30. Edward Prell, "Knowledgeable Baseball Men Wondering If Game Placed in Jeopardy," *Chicago Tribune*, February 2, 1969, B1.

31. "Major League Player Group Rejects Offer," *Chicago Tribune*, January 18, 1969, C3. The vote was actually 432–5, according to a memorandum from Marvin Miller to all MLBPA Members, January 15, 1969, Miller Papers, box 2, folder 4.

32. MLBPA press release, January 22, 1969, Miller Papers, box 2, folder 4.

33. Leonard Koppett, "Players Call Owners Offer 'Deceptive,'" *New York Times*, February 21, 1969, 55.

34. The New York Mets, including a number of young stars like Jerry Grote and Tom Seaver, had some of the biggest problems with solidarity. See Joseph Durso, "Mets Give Seaver $35,000 Pact, Highest on Club: Koosman Accepts $25,000," *New York Times*, February 27, 1969, 51.

35. "Richards Calls Marvin Miller 'a Four-Flusher,'" *Los Angeles Times*, February 11, 1969, C1. Also see A. S. "Doc" Young, "Baseball's New Year," *Chicago Defender*, February 24, 1969, 36.

36. Stan Fischler, "Relentless, Resolute—That's Miller," *Sporting News*, February 15, 1969, 33.

37. John Gaherin and the PRC to Marvin Miller and the MLBPA, memorandum, February 17, 1969, Miller Papers, box 2, folder 4.

38. Phil Pepe, "Players' Side: We're Just Trying to Help Little Guys" *New York Daily News*, February 23, 1969, 105.

39. Leonard Koppett, "Players, Owners OK New Pension Package," *Sporting News*, March 8, 1969, 26.

40. "Agreement re Major League Baseball Players Benefit Plan," February 25, 1969, Miller Papers, box 2, folder 4.

41. "Baseball Players Win Pension Hike," *Los Angeles Times*, February 26, 1969, C1.

42. Leonard Koppett, "Stormy Future Ahead for the Reserve Clause" *New York Times*, March 19, 1969, 53. Also see Burk, *Much More Than a Game*, 162.

43. Leonard Koppett, "Baseball Pension Dispute Is Settled," *New York Times*, February 26, 1969, 50.

44. Burk, *Much More Than a Game*, 163.

45. Many teams moved out of historic old ballparks and into new, modern stadiums in the mid- to late 1960s. The new stadiums included Three Rivers Stadium in Pittsburgh, Busch Stadium in St. Louis, Veterans Stadium in Philadelphia, Jack Murphy Stadium in San Diego, Shea Stadium in New York, and the Big "A" in Anaheim.

46. Burk, *Much More Than a Game*, 165–67.

6. Magnates' Worst Fears Confirmed

1. John Gaherin to All Major League Clubs, "personal and confidential" memorandum, April 1, 1969, Miller Papers, box 4, folder 5.

2. George Vecsey, "The $90,000-a-Year Rebel," *New York Times*, January 17, 1970, 36.

3. Leonard Koppett, "Flood, Backed by Players, Plans Suit to Challenge Baseball Reserve Clause," *New York Times*, December 30, 1969, 42. See also "Flood, Goldberg to Meet on Suit," *New York Times*, January 3, 1970, 31.

4. Sandy Grady, "Miller Pointed Out Pitfalls, but Flood Refused to Back Off," *Sporting News*, January 24, 1970, 38. See also Miller, *Whole Different Ballgame*, 186.

5. Flood, *The Way It Is*.

6. Miller, *Whole Different Ballgame*, 185–86.

7. Miller, *Whole Different Ballgame*, 189.

8. "Sound Off, Sports Fans!," *Chicago Tribune*, January 31, 1970, A3. Gilhooley later went on to become a powerful player agent in his own right during the era of free agency.

9. "Structure of Baseball Threatened," *Los Angeles Times*, January 17, 1970, B1.

10. "Baseball Is Sued under Anti-Trust Law," *New York Times*, January 17, 1970, 1.

11. "Baseball Could Cease: Cronin, Feeney," *Chicago Tribune*, January 18, 1970, B2. Also see Leonard Koppett, "Baseball Chiefs Attack Flood Suit," *New York Times*, January 18, 1970, 175.

12. "Miller Hurls 'Libel' Blast in Flood Case," *Chicago Tribune*, January 20, 1970, B5.

13. Ross Newhan, "O'Malley: The Dodgers Are His Legacy," *Los Angeles Times*, February 15, 1970, C5.

14. Jim Murray, "The Curt Flood Case: Lift That Bat, Chop That Ball," *Los Angeles Times*, January 21, 1970, C1.

15. Richard Dozer, "Players Want Change, Not Death of Reserve Clause," *Chicago Tribune*, January 22, 1970, D2.

16. Leonard Koppett, "Flood Asks for an Injunction to Make Him a Free Agent," *New York Times*, February 4, 1970, 50.

17. Cooper was referring to *Radovich v. National Football League*, in which the Supreme Court held that professional football leagues were subject to antitrust laws.

18. "Flood Bid to Be Free Agent Denied," *Los Angeles Times*, March 5, 1970, D1.

19. Leonard Koppett, "Judge Says Hearing Must Solve Issue," *New York Times*, March 5, 1970, 49.

20. Joseph Durso, "Allen Agrees to Play after Cardinals Issue an Ultimatum," *New York Times*, March 12, 1970, 67.

21. Carlton's salary in 2006 dollars would be roughly $164,000, or less than half of the current Major League minimum.

22. "Koufax Attacks Kuhn's Logic in McLain Case," *Los Angeles Times*, March 22, 1970, C3.

23. Mike Rathet, "Reserve Clause Robs Players of Dignity, Argues Attorney," *Los Angeles Times*, March 15, 1970, C5. Many of these arguments are also found in Miller's personal notes from 1970, Miller Papers, box 4, folder 2.

24. Kuhn, *Hardball*, 77.

25. Kuhn felt so drawn to the opportunity to be the "Next Landis" that he titled the chapter of his autobiography dealing with his rise to the commissionership "Commissioner Landis Beckons."

26. Leonard Koppett, "Ex-Stars Back Reserve Clause Changes," *New York Times*, May 22, 1970, 20.

27. Leonard Koppett, "Flood's Side Finishes Its Inning, Baseball Gets Up to Bat Today," *New York Times*, May 27, 1970, 56.

28. Leonard Koppett, "Football's Integrity Not Harmed by Option Clause, Kuhn Agrees," *New York Times*, May 28, 1970, 45.

29. Leonard Koppett, "Feeney Says Baseball Clubs and Players Need Each Other," *New York Times*, June 2, 1970, 46.

30. "Owners Say Reserve Clause Reason They Invested in Baseball," *Chicago Tribune*, June 4, 1970, G2.

31. Leonard Koppett, "Bargaining Gains Cited in Flood Case," *New York Times*, June 6, 1970, 34.

32. Leonard Koppett, "Baseball Finance Base Seen as Imperiled," *New York Times*, June 9, 1970, 48.

33. "Veeck Offers Court Laughter, Alternatives," *Los Angeles Times*, June 11, 1970, D1.

34. Leonard Koppett, "Baseball Will Survive Law Suit," *New York Times*, June 14, 1970, 179.

35. "Judge Dismisses Flood Suit against Baseball," *Los Angeles Times*, August 13, 1970, F3. See also Thomas Rogers, "Lawyers to Make Speedy Appeal," *New York Times*, August 13, 1970, 53.

36. Charles Maher, "Fair and Equitable," *Los Angeles Times*, August 15, 1970, D2.

37. Jim Murray, "A Flood Warning," *Los Angeles Times*, February 23, 1971, G1.

38. Fred P. Graham, "High Court Gets Suit on Baseball," *New York Times*, October 20 ,1971, 1. Also see Ronald J. Ostrow "High Court to Hear Baseball Trust Suit," *Los Angeles Times*, October 20, 1971, A1.

39. "Lament by Griffith: Rich Teams to Rule If Flood's Suit Wins," *New York Times*, October 20, 1970, 57.

40. Shirley Povich, "Alarmists View Congress' Attempt to Get DC a Team as Blackmail," *Washington Post*, December 9, 1971, C1.

41. Red Smith, "Booming Times in the Flesh Market," *New York Times*, December 8, 1970, 73.

42. "High Court to Hear Arguments This Week on Baseball Suit," *New York Times*, February 27, 1972, S2.

43. Kuhn, *Hardball*, 90.

44. *Flood v. Kuhn*, 407 U.S. 258 (1972) at 406–7, http://supreme.justia
.com/us/407/258/case.html.

45. Jim Murray, "High and Flighty," *Los Angeles Times*, June 22, 1972,
F1.

46. *Flood v. Kuhn*, 407 U.S. 258 (1972), http://supreme.justia.com/us
/407/258/case.html.

47. "Court's Decision Praised by Kuhn," *New York Times*, June 20, 1972,
45.

48. Morris, "In the Wake of the Flood." See also Leonard Koppett, "Players to Make Next Pitch to Congress," *New York Times*, June 23, 1972, 33.

49. "Court's Decision Praised by Kuhn," 45. See also Robert Barkdoll,
"Justice Blackmun: Opinion Leaves No Doubt He's a Fan," *Los Angeles Times*,
June 20, 1972, E1; Glenn Elsasser, "Reserve Clause Upheld by Court," *Chicago Tribune*, June 20, 1972, C1.

50. Arthur Daley, "The Sad Story of the Leaky Umbrella," *New York Times*,
June 22, 1972, 31.

51. Charles Maher, "Pro Athletes Have a Point on Restricted Movement,"
Los Angeles Times, June 30, 1972, E1.

52. At this time the National Football League had a modified form of free
agency that made it more straightforward for a player to play out his option
year and then sign with a different club. The NFL had tried to implement a
compensation plan, known as the "Rozelle Rule," so that the team losing the
free agent would be compensated for its loss, but the courts ruled against the
rule's legality.

53. Red Smith, "The Buck Passes," *New York Times*, June 21, 1972, 33. See
also Murray, "High and Flighty," F1.

7. "Strike" Gets a Whole New Meaning

1. Having high offensive statistics, such as batting average, runs batted in,
and slugging percentage, allows a player to negotiate a higher salary because
he appears to be more productive than many of his historical counterparts.
In other words, once a player breaks certain benchmarks in offensive performance, he knows he can demand a higher salary.

2. Burk, *Much More Than a Game*, 165–67.

3. Helyar, *Lords of the Realm*, 117.

4. Burk, *Much More Than a Game*, 172.

5. Marvin Miller to All Players, Managers, Coaches and Trainers, memorandum, September 14, 1971, Miller Papers, box 2, folder 3.

6. "Baseball Players Reject Owners' Offer," *New York Times*, February 26,
1972, 21.

7. "White Sox Vote by 31–0 to Strike over Pension Aid," *New York Times*,
March 10, 1972, 27.

8. "Baseball on the Brink of a Player Strike," *New York Times*, March 31, 1972, 19.

9. "Busch Stands Up to Strike Threat," *New York Times*, March 16, 1972, 66.

10. "Angel Boss Awaits Poll," *Los Angeles Times*, March 21, 1972, E3.

11. Leonard Koppett, "Ball Clubs Bar Rise in Pensions," *New York Times*, March 23, 1972, 57. See also "Baseball Owners' Stand: Not Another Cent for the Players," *Los Angeles Times*, March 23, 1972, G1.

12. Marvin Miller to Wes Parker, April 24, 1972, Miller Papers, box 1, folder 5. Miller's letter to Parker demonstrates Miller's ability to allow open dissent in the ranks and eventually bring dissenters back into the MLBPA fold. Also see "Dodgers Vote to Authorize Strike Action," *Los Angeles Times*, March 18, 1972, C6.

13. Arthur Daley, "It Even Includes Maternity Benefits," *New York Times*, March 30, 1972, 49.

14. Red Smith, "Department of Fun, Games, and Finance," *New York Times*, March 31, 1972, 19.

15. "No Agreement, Baseball Players Strike Today!," *Los Angeles Times*, April 1, 1972, B1.

16. Dick Young "Miller the Foe, Is Owners View" *New York Daily News*, April 2, 1972, 37C.

17. Jerome Holtzman, "Gaherin Unimpressed by Players' Strike Vote," *Sporting News*, April 1, 1972, 25.

18. Kuhn, *Hardball*, 106.

19. C. C. Johnson Spink, "We Believe," *Sporting News*, April 15, 1972, 14.

20. Miller, *Whole Different Ball Game*, 210.

21. C. C. Johnson Spink, "We Believe," *Sporting News*, April 15, 1972, 14.

22. Cincinnati Reds, news release, April 6, 1972, Giamatti Research Center.

23. "Insiders Say," *Sporting News*, April 29, 1972, 4.

24. Melvin Durslag, "How the Grievances Grow," *Sporting News*, April 1, 1972, 26.

25. Dick Young, "Ballplayers Mesmerized By an Old Smoothie," *New York Daily News*, March 23, 1972, C27.

26. Ed Rummill, "Players Striking Out with the Fans on Strike Threat," *Christian Science Monitor News Service*, March 28, 1972.

27. C. C. Johnson Spink, "We Believe," *Sporting News*, April 1, 1972, 15.

28. Rick Sage, "Players All Wet, Fans Declare in Sizing Up Strike Issues," *Sporting News*, April 22, 1972, 15.

29. Shirley Povich, "Baseball Fans Offer Little Support for Players," *Washington Post*, April 6, 1972, G1.

30. Dave Anderson, "Another Chip in the Diamond," *New York Times*, April 2, 1972, S3.

31. Arthur Daley, "The Players Vote to Strike," *New York Times*, April 2, 1972, S2.

32. Ray Sons, "Strike Hard to Rationalize," *Chicago Daily News Service*, April 2, 1972, reprinted in *Philadelphia Enquirer*, April 2, 1972, C1.

33. "Baseball Strike, Both Sides Talk a Good Game," *Los Angeles Times*, April 1, 1972, B1.

34. "No Settlement; Players Will Strike Today," *Los Angeles Times*, April 1, 1972, B1.

35. Oscar Kahan, "Players Walk Out!," *Sporting News*, April 15, 1972 (dateline April 1, 1972), 1.

36. Jermoe Holtzman, "'Owners Trying to Break Association'–Miller," *Sporting News*, April 15, 1972, 8.

37. Bob Sudyk, "The Villain? A Father Figure Leads the Ballplayers," *Cleveland Press*, April 4, 1972, 27.

38. Murray Chass, "Negotiators in Baseball Strike at Odds over Key Issue," *New York Times*, April 3, 1972, 51.

39. Actuarial report from Retirement Plans of Cleveland Ohio, Miller Papers, box 2, folder 4.

40. Murray Chass, "Players' Offer Is Rejected; Long Strike Seems Likely," *New York Times*, April 4, 1972, 49.

41. Red Smith, "Game Called on Account of Hard Heads," *New York Times*, April 5, 1972, 53.

42. Murray Chass, "Miller Charges Baltimore Executive with Falsifying Issues," *New York Times*, April 5, 1972, 57.

43. Murray Chass, "Players' Return Depends on Pact," *New York Times*, April 6, 1972, 57.

44. Frank Lane, general manager of the Milwaukee Brewers, interview by Frank McGhee, *Today Show*, April 5, 1972 (transcript), Miller Papers, box 2, folder 7.

45. Marvin Miller, notes on Frank Lane's *Today Show* interview, Miller Papers, box 2, folder 7.

46. Murray Chass, "Miller Opposes Owner Pay Offer," *New York Times*, April 11, 1972, 49.

47. Miller, *Whole Different Ballgame*, 222.

48. C. C. Johnson Spink, "We Believe," *Sporting News*, April 29, 1972, 2.

49. Jim Murray, "De Judge Am Gone," *Los Angeles Times*, April 19, 1972, E1.

50. R. O. Gau, "A Buyer's Strike," *Los Angeles Times*, April 29, 1972, D3.

51. "Dodgers Hoping L.A. Reception Will Be Friendly," *Los Angeles Times*, April 21, 1972, F1.

52. Marvin Miller, meeting notes October 30, 1972, Miller Papers, box 4, folder 2.

53. Burk, *Much More Than a Game*, 185.

54. Joe Cronin to the American League Players, n.d., Miller Papers, box 4, folder 2.

55. Leonard Koppett, "'Act of Most Rank Amateur' Says Miller of Kuhn's Report," *Sporting News*, December 23, 1972, 38.

56. "Voice of the Fan: Letter from Tom Maguire," The Sports Network (TSN), January 6, 1973.

57. Ray Fitzgerald, "Next Strike's the Third One . . . ," *Boston Globe*, December 13, 1972.

58. Leonard Koppett, "Emotional Climate All Important," *Sporting News*, December 30, 1972.

59. Joe Trimble, "Rebellion Brews over Stoppage," *New York Daily News*, February 10, 1973, C6.

60. Burk, *Much More Than a Game*, 184–87. Also see Lowenfish, *Imperfect Diamond*, 217–18.

61. Doc Young, "Good Morning Sports!," *Chicago Defender*, February 20, 1973, 24.

8. Freedom at Last?

1. Kuhn, *Hardball*, 133.

2. Wayne Minshew, "Robinson Doubts Ill Effects of Catfish Case," *Sporting News*, January 25, 1975, 40.

3. Jerome Holtzman, "P.K. Sounds Economic Storm Warning," *Sporting News*, January 18, 1975, 48.

4. Phil Pepe, "Yankees' $2.85 Million Land Catfish," *Sporting News*, January 18, 1975, 45.

5. Jeff Prugh, "Dodgers Put the Pressure on Messersmith and John," *Los Angeles Times*, March 5, 1975, sec. 5, 1.

6. "Marshall Plan Costs Dodgers $270,000," *Los Angeles Times*, August 8, 1975, E1.

7. Ross Newhan, "Messersmith Signs Off on No. 19," *Los Angeles Times*, September 28, 1975, C2.

8. "Messersmith," *Los Angeles Times*, October 16, 1975, D4.

9. Lowenfish, *Imperfect Diamond*, 220.

10. Red Smith, "The Men Who Run Baseball," *New York Times*, October 26, 1975, 221.

11. Ross Newhan, "Messersmith Rejects Latest Dodger Offer," *Los Angeles Times*, November 20, 1975, F3.

12. Red Smith, "Where One Year Is Forever," *New York Times*, December 5, 1975, 31.

13. Ross Newhan, "Messersmith Wins Still Another Round," *Los Angeles Times*, February 5, 1976, D1.

14. Kuhn, *Hardball*, 157.

15. 1973 Basic Agreement, Miller Papers, box 5, folder 3.

16. Kuhn, *Hardball*, 157.

17. Joseph Durso, "Arbitrator Frees 2 Baseball Stars," *New York Times*, December 24, 1975, 45.

18. Red Smith, "Christmas Spirit," *New York Times*, December 24, 1975, 15.

19. Durso, "Arbitrator Frees 2 Baseball Stars," 45.

20. Charles Maher, "Ruling Gives Players More Leverage," *Los Angeles Times*, December 25, 1975, D1.

21. Red Smith, "Wanted: New Ghostwriters," *New York Times*, December 28, 1975, 139.

22. Dave Distel, "Blyleven Looks to the West," *Los Angeles Times*, January 3, 1976, B9.

23. Newhan, "Messersmith Wins Still Another Round," D1.

24. Ross Newhan, "Messersmith Feels Dodger Career Over," *Los Angeles Times*, February 10, 1976, B1.

25. Murray Chass, "Ballplayers Shun Hasty Agreement," *New York Times*, February 13, 1976, 55.

26. Murray Chass, "Baseball Owners Lose Again: Free Agent Status of 2 Upheld," *New York Times*, March 10, 1976, 63.

27. "New Lockout: Players Do It to Themselves," *Los Angeles Times*, March 13, 1976, D1.

28. "Dodgers to Skip Messersmith Auction," *Los Angeles Times*, March 10, 1976, E1.

29. Murray Chass, "Messersmith Open to Bidding Today," *New York Times*, March 16, 1976, 42.

30. "Baseball Club Owners Give In—Sort Of," *Los Angeles Times*, March 16, 1976, D1.

31. Joseph Durso, "Players Reject 'Final' Offer; Talks Collapse," *New York Times*, March 17, 1976, 27.

32. Durso, "Players Reject 'Final' Offer," 27.

33. Red Smith, "In the Spring an Owner's Fancy," *New York Times*, March 19, 1976, 55.

34. "Messersmith Takes Strike One," *New York Times*, March 24, 1976, 34.

35. Ross Newhan, "Messersmith Conspiracy Charge Aimed at Owners," *Los Angeles Times*, March 24, 1976, D1.

36. "Messersmith Finds a Home, in Atlanta," *Los Angeles Times*, April 11, 1976, D1.

37. Kuhn, *Hardball*, 167–69.

38. Miller, *Whole Different Ballgame*, 286.

39. Burk, *Much More Than a Game*, 223.

40. "Statement of Marvin J. Miller," January 11, 1979, Miller Papers, box 3, folder 4.

41. Joseph Durso, "New Labor Contract Tops Baseball Talks," *New York Times*, December 2, 1979, s4.

42. Joseph Durso, "Kuhn Sees Free Agent Time Bomb," *New York Times*, December 4, 1979, c5.

43. Thomas Boswell, "Free Agentry: Ceiling Unlimited," *Washington Post*, reprinted in *Los Angeles Times*, December 18, 1979, D3.

44. Murray Chass, "Free Agents Prosper in '79 Baseball Pacts," *New York Times*, January 6, 1980, s1.

45. Miller and Fehr to All Players, memorandum, January 7, 1980, Miller Papers, box 5, folder 1.

46. Ross Newhan, "Nobody Ready to Play Ball Yet," *Los Angeles Times*, January 22, 1980, D4.

47. Murray Chass, "Miller Advises Owners to Negotiate in Earnest," *New York Times*, January 15, 1980, c12.

48. Thomas Boswell, "Owners Pitch a Salary Curve at the Players," *Washington Post*, reprinted in *Los Angeles Times*, February 27, 1980, E1.

49. Red Smith, "Players vs. Owners: Fun in Baseball's Counting House," *New York Times*, February 27, 1980, A25.

50. Chass, "Miller Advises Owners to Negotiate in Earnest," c12.

51. Smith, "Players vs. Owners," A25.

52. Smith, "Players vs. Owners," A25.

53. Steve Dolan, "There's One Strike in Baseball Nobody Wants Called," *Los Angeles Times*, March 4, 1980, D1.

54. Murray Chass, "Baseball Strike Threat Looms Stronger; Phillies Vote Support," *New York Times*, March 6, 1980, B7.

55. "Grebey Makes an Appeal," *New York Times*, March 13, 1980, D21.

56. John Hall, "The 3–2 Pitch," *Los Angeles Times*, April 1, 1980, D3.

57. Marvin Miller to All Players, memorandum, April 9, 1980, Miller Papers, box 1, folder 8.

58. Burk, *Much More Than a Game*, 225.

59. 1980 Basic Agreement, Miller Papers, box 1, folder 8. Also see Murray Chass, "Accord Averts Baseball Strike: Free Agent Issue to Be Studied," *New York Times*, May 24, 1980, 1.

60. Letters in the Voice of the Fan section of the *Sporting News* on April 5, 1980, demonstrate a consistently high level of frustration with the state of owner-player relations, almost as if the fans wanted to warn both sides that "enough is enough."

61. Mike McKenzie, "Strike Talk Black Eye to Baseball," *Kansas City Times*, February 21, 1981, E1.

62. Red Smith, "Happy New Year," *New York Times*, April 8, 1981, B11.

63. Red Smith, "Baseball's Star Chamber," *New York Times*, May 8, 1981, A22.

64. Dave Anderson, "The Baseball Strike Situation," *New York Times*, June 11, 1981.

65. Dave Kindred (syndicated from the *Washington Post*), "Shed No Tears for the Poor Owners," *Los Angeles Times*, June 11, 1981, sec. 3, 1.

66. Jim Murray, "There Is no Joy in Mudville, the Golden Goose Has Struck Out," *Los Angeles Times*, June 14, 1981, sec. 3, 1.

67. Mark Heisler, "No Good Reasons for This Strike: The Players Don't Want It and the Owners Don't Need It," *Los Angeles Times*, June 14, 1980, sec.3, 12.

68. Frederick C. Klein, "Baseball Owners Want Something for Nothing," *Wall Street Journal*, June 17, 1981, 28.

69. Glenn Dickey, "What Most Baseball Owners Really Want," *San Francisco Chronicle*, June 16, 1981, 47.

70. Joe Marcin, "*The Sporting News* Readers Speak Out on Strike," *Sporting News*, July 18, 1981, 24.

71. "Voice of the Fan," *Sporting News*, July 4, 1981, 6.

72. R. Scott Rapp, "Fans Torch Baseball Cards," *Syracuse (NY) Herald American*, July 15, 1981, 28.

73. "46% Don't Miss Baseball, Poll Says," *New York Times*, July 18, 1981, 18.

74. "Americans Divided Evenly on Strike, Times Poll Shows," *New York Times*, July 1, 1981, B1.

75. Joseph Durso, "Will Baseball Fans Return?," *New York Times*, July 21, 1981, C11.

76. John "Jocko" Conlon to President Ronald Reagan, June 14, 1981, no. 028556, LA005, WHORM: Subject File, Ronald Reagan Presidential Library, Simi Valley CA.

77. Senate Resolution by Edward Kennedy, June 23, 1981, no. 030067, LA005, WHORM: Subject File, Reagan Library.

78. Senator Edward Kennedy to President Ronald Reagan, June 23, 1981, no. 030066, LA005, WHORM: Subject File, Reagan Library.

79. Agenda for White House Senior Staff Meeting, June 17, 1981, no. 061279, FG006–01, WHORM: Subject File, Reagan Library.

80. Burk, *Much More Than a Game*, 233.

81. Helyar, *Lords of the Realm*, 304.

82. Marvin Miller to All Players, memorandum, August 20, 1981, Miller Papers, box 5, folder 1.

83. "Fan Vote Favors Owners," *San Francisco Chronicle*, June 5, 1981, 46.

ANNOTATED BIBLIOGRAPHY

This project relies heavily on contemporary news accounts, in large part because I attempted to measure public response to the players' efforts at collective action. Public acceptance, I believe, was always critical to any attempt to unionize Major League Baseball. I drew on the news media because it has long enjoyed a symbiotic relationship with baseball, a relationship fostered by the "daily" nature of the game. Even in the off-season there is plenty to report, day in and day out, a fact not lost on a burgeoning twentieth-century sports media hungry for material. Baseball, for its part, certainly enjoys the attention it receives in the press. As the game and the reporters who covered it grew in stature, media coverage both shaped and reflected public opinion. In some ways, then, the fate of the players' union lay in the pens of men like Arthur Daley, Leonard Koppett, Red Smith, Dick Young, Shirley Povich, and Jim Murray.

Archival sources and oral histories were also critical to the completion of this project. The Giamatti Research Center in Cooperstown, New York, operated in conjunction with the Baseball Hall of Fame, contains a wealth of material, especially on the early years of the game. Marvin Miller's papers, in the Tamiment Library at New York University, include everything from correspondence to contracts from his years at the helm of the MLBPA. The missing archival piece is the owners' side of the story. Most Major League teams maintain archives, but they are not open to outside research. Bowie Kuhn's papers are at the Giamatti Center, but they were not opened to researchers until 2012, after I completed the research for this project. The challenge for future researchers, then, is to locate archival materials that will help tell the management side of the story. Until then, most baseball historians will continue to fill in the gaps the best they can with what few sources are open to the public.

Burk, Robert. *Never Just a Game: Players, Owners & American Baseball to 1920.* Chapel Hill: University of North Carolina Press, 1994.

————. *Much More Than a Game: Players, Owners & American Baseball since 1921.* Chapel Hill: University of North Carolina Press, 2001. Burk's work offers a comprehensive narrative of the history of labor relations in professional baseball since the game's inception. He draws on a wide variety of secondary sources, contemporary news accounts, government documents, and statistical data to provide an in-depth, scholarly look at the course of the relationship between players and owners.

Helyar, John. *Lords of the Realm: The Real History of Baseball.* New York: Ballantine Books, 1994. Helyar made his mark when, as a reporter for the *Wall Street Journal*, he coauthored *Barbarians at the Gate*, a book exposing the inner dealings of the leveraged buyout of RJR Nabisco. It is no surprise, then, that he takes a journalistic approach in this work, which exposes the various methods of worker control used by baseball's owners throughout the twentieth century. *Lords of the Realm* was both groundbreaking and timely when it was published in 1994, at the time of the single most devastating work stoppage in baseball history.

Kuhn, Bowie. *Hardball: The Education of a Baseball Commissioner.* New York: Times Books, 1987. Kuhn, who was commissioner through some of the most tumultuous periods in the game's recent history, provides a great deal of insight through this memoir. In it he details both the development of his baseball "world view" and the rationale behind his decision making throughout his fifteen-year tenure as commissioner.

Lowenfish, Lee. *The Imperfect Diamond: A History of Baseball's Labor Wars.* New York: De Capo Press, 1991. *The Imperfect Diamond* was the first book to take a serious look at the history of baseball labor relations. It laid the foundation for the field and inspired a great deal of scholarly activity and interest in the topic.

Marshall, William. *Baseball's Pivotal Era: 1945–1951.* Lexington: University Press of Kentucky, 1999. Marshall is the curator of the papers of the former baseball commissioner and U.S. senator Albert "Happy" Chandler at the University of Kentucky. His work delves into the many challenges Chandler faced as commissioner, including the Mexican League talent raids, the formation of the American Baseball Guild, and the integration of the Major Leagues.

Miller, Marvin. *A Whole Different Ballgame: The Inside Story of the Baseball Revolution.* Chicago: Ivan R. Dee, 2004. Like Kuhn's memoir, Miller's provides invaluable insight regarding his view of the MLBPA's formative years. As Miller and Kuhn were often sparring partners, this book is, in many ways, a response to Kuhn's memoir, *Hardball.*

Seymour, Harold. *Baseball: The Early Years.* New York: Oxford University Press, 1960. Seymour wrote serious baseball history before anybody realized there could be such a thing as serious baseball history. This book, more than fifty years after its first printing, remains an authoritative source on the early years of the game.

Other Published Sources

Bouton, Jim. *Ball Four Plus Ball Five.* New York: Stein and Day, 1981.

Federal Baseball Club of Baltimore, Inc. v. National League of Professional Baseball Clubs et al. 259 U.S. 200 (1922). Oyez Project at IIT Chicago–Kent College of Law, http://www.oyez.org/cases/1901-1939/1921/1921_204.

Flood, Curt. *The Way It Is.* New York: Trident Press, 1971.

Flood v. Kuhn. 407 U.S. 258 (1972). http://supreme.justia.com/us/407/258/case.html.

Goldstein, Warren. *Playing for Keeps: A History of Early Baseball.* Ithaca NY: Cornell University Press, 1989.

Jarvis, Robert, and Phyllis Coleman. "Early Baseball Law." *American Journal of Legal History* 45, no. 2 (April 2001): 117–31.

M. L. C. "Baseball and the Law: Yesterday and Today." *Virginia Law Review* 32, no. 6 (November 1946): 1164–77.

Morris, John P. "In the Wake of the Flood." *Law and Contemporary Problems* 38, no. 1 (Winter–Spring 1973): 85–98.

Players National League Baseball Guide for 1890. Repr., St. Louis: Horton, 1989.

Staudohar, Paul. *Diamond Mines.* Syracuse NY: Syracuse University Press, 2000.

Staudohar, Paul D., and James B. Dworkin. "The Impact of Baseball's New Television Contracts." *NINE: A Journal of Baseball History and Culture* 10, no. 2 (Spring 2002): 102–9.

Toolson v. New York Yankees, Inc. 346 U.S. 356 (1953). http://supreme.justia.com/us/346/356/case.html.

U.S. House. Judiciary Committee. *Organized Baseball: Report of the Subcommittee on Study of Monopoly Power.* 82nd Cong., 1st sess., July 30–October 24, 1951. H. Rep. 2002. Serial no. 6.

INDEX